At thirty you confront yourself—you're no longer an adolescent. You're still a young adult, but you're moving on toward middle age. You really start to assess where your life is going, where it's been, whether you like where it's been. There are all varieties of women, and we all have different dreams and aspirations. But what we confront universally in our thirties is the question of what life is all about.

The thirties bring change: we look back at what we've done since our twenties and decide if we want to continue down that path. If not, now is the time to change course. And all these feelings about our lives are inextricably entwined with how we feel about our bodies. For many of us, this decade is the first time we seriously confront our bodies . . .

—from **THE BODY AT THIRTY**

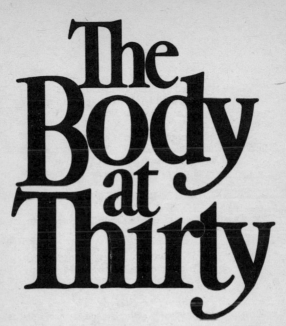

The Body at Thirty

A WOMAN DOCTOR TALKS TO WOMEN

DOREEN GLUCKIN, M.D.

WITH MICHAEL EDELHART

BERKLEY BOOKS, NEW YORK

The fitness tests on pages 45–46 have
been used by kind permission of the
National Board of the Young Men's
Christian Association.

This Berkley book contains the complete text of
the original hardcover edition. It has been completely reset
in a typeface designed for easy reading,
and was printed from new film.

THE BODY AT THIRTY

A Berkley Book / published by arrangement with
M. Evans and Company, Inc.

PRINTING HISTORY
M. Evans edition published 1982
Berkley edition / June 1983

ISBN: 0-425-06070-5

A BERKLEY BOOK® TM 757,375
Berkley Books are published
by Berkley Publishing Corporation,
200 Madison Avenue, New York, New York 10016.
The name "BERKLEY" and the stylized "B" with design
are trademarks belonging to
Berkley Publishing Corporation.

PRINTED IN THE UNITED STATES OF AMERICA

To my mother and father

Contents

Acknowledgments

This book would not have been written without the enthusiastic support of my classmate, friend, and agent, Carol Mann. Special thanks go to my husband for his moral support, patience, and understanding during the long hours of researching this manuscript.

Introduction

BOOKSTORE SHELVES ARE not exactly bereft of books about women's health. Our bodies, in fact, seem to be one of the most written-about topics of recent years. Why then another book about our health as women?

Well, I had four reasons for writing this book. First, many of the women's health books I've seen view us primarily as so much gynecological plumbing. They discuss menstruation and menopause at great length, but skip over any consideration of the normal human aches and pains we may have. I wanted to write a book about the whole of us, from our psyche to our sexual health, from our hands to our bunions.

My second reason was that other books don't focus on a particular time of life—unless it's puberty or menopause. Women vanish from popular medical literature during the prime of their lives. I wanted instead to hone in on these years. Our fourth decade is crucial both to our lives and our bodies. It is the time we confront adulthood.

Third, I am incensed at the number of books that, although enticing, are not factually accurate, that promulgate myths, fads, and nonsense in the guise of genuine medical knowledge and advice. I felt the need to write a scientifically sound, yet personal and enjoyable book, researching every fact thoroughly before including it and balancing information against speculation and uncertainty.

In my book, we take a journey through our bodies and lives during the thirties without hype or any pat schemes. This isn't a "how-to" book, but a "what-is" book and, even more, a "how-do-we-feel-about-ourselves" book. I hope it makes the point that we do not change over time according to any fixed agenda, but rather along a continual curve.

My fourth reason for writing this book is more personal. I am a woman in her thirties myself. The process of examining the body, psyche, and life style of women in this decade is for me a personal review as well as an exercise in authorship. I am educating myself about myself while fulfilling one of my oldest desires, the one that led me into medicine in the first place. That is to teach, to reach out to other women and talk with them through this book as personally as I could sitting in my office. After all, the word "doctor" is derived from the Latin *docēre*, to teach.

So, as a doctor I want to teach, and as a contemporary woman I want to speak intelligently with my friends so we can all understand ourselves better and lead fuller, happier lives.

Doreen Gluckin, M.D.
Savannah, GA

THE BODY AT THIRTY

Thoughts from a Tenth Reunion

I ATTENDED MY tenth-year college reunion last spring. The Smith College campus, which I hadn't seen in a decade, looked incredibly unchanged. The approaches to the leafy quadrangle, with its almost too perfect, ivy-covered brick buildings, still passed through the quaint streets of Northampton, Massachusetts, and up a slight rise to the school.

The sense of *déjà vu*, of permanence and stability, was pervasive. I registered in the building in which I'd once had my French classes. It looked the same. But my sense of unchanging time was shaken when I entered reunion headquarters on the third floor. The place might not have changed, but the women, my classmates, certainly had.

The first person I saw whom I knew was Rhoda. At least, I thought I knew her. What was odd for me initially at the reunion was that I frequently couldn't tell at first glance if I really knew a woman or if she just reminded me of someone I know today. And many of

1

the women, frankly, looked like complete strangers, they had changed so much. Yet, after looking at someone blankly for a few minutes I began to see signs of the person I'd once known. Behind a totally unfamiliar face, an unrecognizable body, I began to see reminiscent movements, familiar mannerisms. Against the changeless backdrop of the school, the effects on us of time and life stood out in sharp relief. If these women all looked so altered to me, how different did I look to them?

Rhoda didn't look at all the same to me, but her mannerisms hadn't changed a bit. The moment she moved I knew who she was, and then it seemed to me as though she hadn't really changed all that much over the decade. Her essence was the same, which I found comforting.

The first night of our reunion there was a huge welcoming dinner in the imposing two-story hall of one of Smith's grand campus buildings. Amid imposing marble artifacts, antiques, and Oriental rugs, before a phalanx of awesome columns and glass doors, stood the class of 1971, ten years later. I arrived during pre-dinner drinks and hors d'oeuvres. People were standing in the library and on the patio, milling about and looking for classmates they knew. I wandered among the crowd and was overtaken by a true bleakness. I didn't recognize anyone in the whole cavernous area. At last, in the main dining hall, I found Rhoda again, and began to pick out vaguely familiar faces from the crowd in the rotunda. Not only were the women different, but they had changed in unexpected ways. Few women resembled my mental images of them.

I was standing in line in a bathroom at one point, and ahead of me was a woman with long brown flyaway hair. She had on wire-rim glasses, a loose T-shirt, and blue jeans with holes in them. She didn't look like anyone I knew, until all of a sudden I heard the voice of one of my classmates, Suzanne. I said, "Suzanne?" She said, "Doreen?" We looked at each other, amazed. In college Suzanne had had short bleached hair, always in a perfectly coiffed pageboy. She wore only the best designer glasses, and usually had on a small amount of makeup. She dressed very carefully, in coordinated outfits. Now she was in baggy jeans and a top that she would never have worn even in the dorm. Her face was devoid of makeup. She is now a Chinese history professor, living in San Francisco, which may explain her altered style. But the same witty and interesting Suzanne was still inside.

Holly was another surprise. I would never have recognized her if we hadn't been introduced. I had remembered her hair as incandescent red; that was the focal point of all my memories. Now she was a pale brunette. I don't know if my memory was off, or if her hair had faded since I'd last seen her.

Susan's hair had obviously changed. She was gray. Susan was still plump, warm, and friendly. She still sat the same way on the floor. But her gray hair startled me. If jolly Susan was getting old, what about me?

It wasn't so much that time had worked its way with us, I decided; we were all still relatively young. The changes I saw in our bodies and attitudes weren't generally derived from vast failings of the flesh. Life was what had altered us. The play of happiness and stress, success and frustration, had molded us into forms far different from the ones we'd had in college, but still young, still forward-looking, and still recognizable in a way.

Take Martha. In school she had been simply gorgeous, a devastating creature who tortured my friends and me with the ease in life her looks and cocky manner guaranteed her. Now she was a corporate lawyer and wife in Virginia. She was still undeniably handsome, but the incredibly long hours and pressures of her law job, coupled with the vicissitudes of being a full-time wife in the South, had begun to etch lines on her face. She seemed stiff, more dowdy, less vivacious and joyful than she had in school. She was a perfect picture of strain. The energy her life was drawing from her body and spirit was greater than the return.

I also discovered that some of my classmates had

grown deeply concerned about their bodies. A woman doctor at the reunion of a women's college hears an abundance of medical stories and complaints. Everyone's foibles, fears, and fantasies pour onto you as a presumably sympathetic, safe receptacle. Not only do women show intense curiosity toward a woman who has become a doctor, but they also express a desire to know if she has somehow found a secret, if her medical knowledge has opened to her vistas of help and sustenance unknown to them.

Unfortunately, at least in my case, it isn't so. I know more than my classmates about bodies and illness, but my personal fears are the same as anyone else's. If anything, my medical knowledge is a detriment, because I can never coast on false hope. When it comes to my body, my mind cannot delude itself.

Still, the myth of the medical woman caused a flood of information to pour down on me. I hadn't gotten a spoon into my fruit cup before the woman next to me (whom I didn't know) informed me that her brother had suffered from melanoma, a skin cancer, and now she had a dark spot at the base of her thumb. It had appeared suddenly, and she was utterly convinced that it was melanoma. I had to examine it then and there and assure her that it was just a benign spot.

Then someone else said that she had had a spot jump up between her toes. She'd had it biopsied because she was so terrified about it, and out came that freckle, which was all it was. But at thirty she had a nagging sense that her body was turning on her, and that spot became the focus for her fears.

Another woman accosted me with technicolor details of her placenta previa pregnancy and birth. She was extremely worried that the problems she'd had with that pregnancy would make it hard for her to have another child. She wanted me to tell her if she would be all right. I was tempted to say, "Take off your clothes, lie down, and we'll take a look."

I don't mean to sound unsympathetic. The concern showed by many of my classmates at the reunion was real, and the conviction with which they bearded me was a sign of how infrequently they'd received detailed medical answers. But even woman to woman, a doctor can tell very little from talking to someone in a crowded dining hall. I found myself wishing there were something more substantial than platitudes to offer these women. That feeling, in part, is behind the existence of this book.

My classmates, I found, had a dizzying range of concerns. Some were concerned about their careers and how to stay on top in a male-dominated business world. Others were focused on husbands and kids. Many more, actually, had chucked the husband and were worried about themselves and the kids. One woman was working part-time at a law firm and trying to raise three kids. She was having a hell of a time; her job hours kept getting longer and longer, and her kids' demands kept getting greater and greater. She felt totally hemmed in.

My classmates and I were constantly checking each other out. We were fascinated by how we each had aged —who had held up well and who hadn't, who had gotten better-looking and who hadn't. Beyond that, we were intensely curious about what we had made of ourselves over the past decade. What were our classmates' positions in the world? What had become important to them? What was satisfying? Who had gotten what slice of life's pie?

Of course, Smith is a pretty limited sample of female life, and circumstances had been relatively kind to most of us. But even in the fairly narrow confines of upper-middle-class life that Smith displays, enormous variations could be seen in what our class had accomplished and how it had affected each individual. We looked at each other and wondered, why her?

Most of us, I think, were looking forward to the decade of the thirties. We still felt that the best was ahead of us; the prevailing attitude was "Let's get on with the work ahead, whatever it turns out to be." There was tremendous optimism among us, yet it was tinged with a vague sense of depression. After all, we were the generation that grew up chanting that you should never trust anyone over thirty, and here we were, over thirty. We couldn't quite assimilate that. Everywhere we looked, our current decade of life was denigrated: when you're over thirty, you're over the hill, untrustworthy—old.

I think most of this feeling is cultural. When I was twelve or thirteen, I thought seventeen was the ideal adult age to be. Now here I am, thirteen years beyond that. It's an odd feeling.

At thirty you confront yourself—you're no longer an adolescent. You're still a young adult, but you're moving on toward middle age, and you tend to look back at the decade of the twenties and what you did with it, and then forward to the decade of the thirties. I had never contemplated the future in large chunks of time before. When I was twenty I never thought of what it would be like to be thirty. It never crossed my mind, and the same is true of a number of my friends. Now that we're thirty, we begin to think, My God, what is it going to be like to be in my forties? We realize that a substantial portion of our life is over.

So around the time you turn thirty, you really start to assess where your life is going, where it's been, whether you like where it's been, whether you want to continue in that direction or change direction altogether. By now, some women have completed their schooling or completed having a family, and must decide what they want to do from here. Women who haven't had children face the specter of the biological clock. They realize that childbearing time is running out. The result may be panic and desperation. Other women decide they never want to have children. There are all varieties of women, and we all have different dreams and aspirations. But I think what we confront universally in our thirties is the question of what life is all about.

In our thirties we face both consolidation and change. It is a time of consolidation because we have had a variety of experiences and can now pick and choose from them and decide what we're comfortable with, what we can make our own. At the same time, the thirties bring change: we look back at what we've done since our twenties and decide if we want to continue down that path. If not, now is the time to change course.

At the reunion I realized that all these feelings about our lives are inextricably entwined with how we women in our thirties feel about our bodies. For many of us, this decade is the first time we seriously confront our bodies. Up until now we've taken them largely for granted. Whatever we've wanted them to do, they've obliged. Now a new realization creeps in: the thirty-year-old body is on the decline. It will never again achieve the peaks of pure youth. The decline is exceedingly gradual, but we can still feel its first inroads even as we turn thirty.

What some of us try to do during the fourth decade is impede this decline by whatever means possible—whether by a fifty-dollar facial or younger clothes or whatever. Maybe it won't arrest our decline, but at least it gives us a lift and the illusion of holding time at bay.

No matter what we do, though, we can still feel the gentle finger of age. We wake up one morning and notice something is different. We become aware of gray hairs and wrinkles that may or may not have been there previously. Still, all the visible signs that bother us are trivial compared to the wear and tear on our organs. Again, we don't feel it, but our organs are aging, changing in small ways that over time result in the alterations we call age.

Part and parcel of this process of reassessing our lives is reassessing our bodies. A woman asks, Am I happy in this body? What do I think about it? Is it operating the way I want it to?

And the thirties are the time when mortality first seems real. Most of us, I think, face the fact that there's a good likelihood that we may be dead at double our current age. Before this decade that's a thought that had never really crossed most of our minds. I also notice, in part because of going to the reunion, that I'm thinking ahead to the next decade, whereas decades were previously too large a time span to contemplate.

My reunion focused many thoughts for me. It coincided with opening my first private practice office, one of the first things I'd done as a doctor that made me feel entirely adult. Like so many others who were at the reunion, I left filled with resolve about the future and questions about myself, particularly about my body. I felt a strong emotional need to explore the world of the thirty-year-old body and mind, to express my feelings about it and assess the pattern of sensations I and my fellow thirty-year-olds are experiencing.

I left my reunion determined to take a tour of the thirty-year-old self.

Our Psyche

YOU WON'T FIND it listed along with the Unification Church, Divine Light Mission, or Scientology, but for its followers, the cult of youth exists every bit as strongly as do the other cults for their followers. Unlike the other cults, though, indoctrination into the cult of youth occurs on a gradual, insidious basis. It begins when we are little children watching morning TV, and continues through Barbie dolls, beach-blanket movies, and college sororities. The creed is simple: young is good; young is the *only* good. Feminine youth is tantamount to feminine worth.

All societies have revered youth and have sought to capture the essence of youth, but in our society it seems that as the average age of the population increases, the average age of role models declines. Brooke Shields, at age sixteen, has been called the epitome of the American woman. Her teenage face smiles at us from billboards, the sides of buses, and magazine covers, suggesting that we buy blue jeans or hair products, all in an attempt to

9

be fashionable, chic, impossibly young. Another high fashion model, Kristine Oulman, is only 13 but is made up to look like an adult woman. The message is clear, the standards set: youth, a flawless face, a slim body with no hips. Kim Chernin, author of *The Tyranny of Slenderness*, feels that the use of such young models promotes an obsession with weight and size, and youth, perhaps leading to the gorge-purge syndrome. There is an unrealistic premium on being thin and young. How does a woman in her thirties feel when she looks at a sixteen-year-old—half her age—and finds that that teenager is being called the essence of American womanhood? Left over, that's how, even though her life may offer far more promise than it ever did when she was younger.

Youth worship is truly a cult. The preoccupation and fascination with youth, facial beauty and slenderness generates millions of dollars for its cult leaders, just as other cults generate huge sums of money for their leaders. It's big business and touches every facet of American life.

Men are vulnerable to the youth cult programming too, but to a much lesser extent than women. Young men are incensed if they are asked for age identification in a bar, but women in their twenties or early thirties are flattered. Men who begin to gray are often considered "distinguished," whereas women with gray hair are "old." We know this but, liberated or not, don't seem to be able to do much about it. I see myriad expressions of the cult of youth in my patients.

There's a ceaseless desire to look younger. I see it at every age; not just women in their thirties, but women in their forties and fifties and sixties are still trying to claw their way back to unrealistic youth. Eighty-year-olds decline to tell you their true age. That's pathetic. If I live to be eighty, I'm going to shout it to the world.

I think the ramifications of the cult of youth are just horrible for women in their thirties. The myopia toward all phases of life except youth cheapens what should be the richest time of a woman's life. It subverts adulthood, and the control and depth that come with it, into a second-best situation: the paltry leavings of our teenage binge of life. It shifts thinking away from enjoying the best of the time we're in, toward trying to recapture a phony youthful adventure. It's a shuck, a merchandising ploy that has wriggled into the national consciousness and bored holes in our self-image.

DEPROGRAMMING

How can we get deprogrammed from this cult of youth? Deprogramming is a difficult process because the inculcation into the cult is so subtle and insidious. Breaking free evolves around our recognizing and accepting that aging is a natural process, a positive process, a growing that cannot be slowed or stopped but that can be affected by our self-concept and mode of life.

We must come to realize that age is definite. Age will come to all of us. Our lost youth is a mirage, desirable only because it's unattainable. I think we always want what we can't have, as long as it remains a dream. But the reality was never so great, and we don't really want it back. We want something we never had, a youth that exists only in media imagination. We forget that recapturing our youth would mean leaving behind our adult personality—the depth and fullness we've acquired. Would we really be willing to give that up?

We get hooked because we're sold a bill of goods by the media. We have it blasted into our heads that young is beautiful, young is desirable, everything else is second to being young. Incredibly enough, we buy it. But the argument doesn't hold up. Is physical stamina the only item of value in life? Isn't a healthy thirty-year-old body as splendid a vision of human creation as a sixteen-year-old one? Sure it is. In fact, it's probably better, because the thirty-year-old body has been tempered by life; it has character, flair, point of view.

Were the teens and early twenties truly so splendid that we can't accept their passing? What about the sweats and stammers, the zits, the embarrassment and putdowns that afflicted virtually all of us? What about the chronic embarrassment with our burgeoning bodies, our shifting lusts, and our feeble romancing?

Most of all, what about the never-ending frustrations that colored every action of those turbulent years? Although exciting, those years of staggering around in search of a personality and an acceptable set of personal values were far from perfect for most of us. We enjoyed them, learned a lot from them. We were carefree about our bodies in a way we can't be now. But our lives were less our own then and our pleasures much less deep. And yet, we allow our subconscious to accept those years as the standard by which our bodies and attitudes should be judged.

I'm not certain why there is such an emphasis on youth today, as opposed to in the past. Perhaps it's because life is easier, because people have more leisure time and so have developed a fascination for a leisure body—mildly athletic, ruddy, slim, and never changing. To be left out of the unending games that life has become—tennis, skiing, rafting trips, convivial softball games, jogging summer after summer—has for many of us become synonymous with being left out of life.

In this view, which I call the California syndrome, our bodies become metaphors for our ability to participate in youth. The be-all and end-all of health is recreation. Since genetics and time conspire to change us from basically thoughtless active creatures to slower but more profound adults, life for the California syndrome sufferer becomes an unending battle against the natural.

The result is topsy-turvy. The perfect fifty-year-old must look like a thirty-year-old; a thirty-year-old should look seventeen. Looking healthy and yet your own age becomes downright sinful, indicative of your failure to stop time. What worries me is that the California syndrome seems to be spreading to all parts of the country.

PERCEPTIONS OF YOUTH

A lot of us perceive youth as more fun now. When we were younger the restrictions on our lives were extreme. We grew up in more conservative times. Many young women today seem to be more mature, and at the same time more giddy. We want to partake of their freedom, to supplement our slowly fading youth with the gilded vision we have of today's youthful experiences. We think it might be fun to dress up in glitter and rags and boogie at Studio 54. We'd like to be able to begin our sexual lives in freer times, to experiment without guilt, to partake of new experiences without coercion.

But, of course, today's young women aren't really any freer or happier than we were. After a year as a medical adviser to Harvard College students, I can attest to that. Life decisions are no easier. There is still conflict between peer pressures and parental values.

Youth does offer more opportunity, in that the fewer choices you have made, the more opportunities you have available to you. As we age we close some of our options. In that sense, our desire to remain young is an attempt to hold off the limitations of adult choices. As long as we are young, we remain unfettered, free to choose among life's plums. As we age we make choices, leaving some paths untraveled, exploring others, limiting our future choices by the paths we take.

DREAMS AND CONTROL

When my patients confront me with concerns about the kind of people they've become, in contrast to what they hoped for, I am reassuring but I also attempt to point out the futility of worrying about past mistakes, about paths not taken in the past. Past choices generally reflect past goals; psychologically healthy women basically determine their own priorities, make their own choices, and get what they want within their realm of possibilities. That is to say, women who haven't married by the time they're thirty-five don't want to be married. They may not have consciously looked at that fact, but generally it's true. Women who are divorced and haven't remarried probably don't want to remarry—at least it's not a high priority. Obviously, people have things happen to them that they don't want to happen—a spouse dies, a child gets sick, they are transferred because of a job. External circumstances influence all of our lives, but we frequently have more control over our lives than we might want to acknowledge. It's easier to blame circumstances than to blame ourselves. Our bodies become symbols of our success or failure at holding back age, signs of our ability to exert control over time and ourselves.

I think there is an overpowering need for control of the world around us in many women our age. There is a terror of things we can't control, so we become compulsive about things we can control—for example, what we put into our mouths. Eating controlled to the extreme becomes anorexia nervosa. Women exert such control and diet so extensively and single-mindedly that they actually lose enough weight to stop menstruating. Some hormonal changes that occur with anorexia feel good and feed the cycle. The women find that they are in a state of increased alertness or awareness so long as they stay hungry. In fact, it has been hypothesized that a kind of a high develops in the early phases of anorexia.

They attempt to get control by excessive denial, but end up making themselves sick. There are many women among us who are unhealthily careful about every item of food that goes into their mouths, who feel tremendous guilt if they eat what they consider to be excessive amounts of food, though these excesses may be really minuscule—a stick of licorice, for example, may be considered grounds for psychological punishment. It's sad.

I had a patient, a very attractive psychiatric social worker, who came to me because of amenorrhea, with no organic cause found. It turned out that she felt very much out of control of her life, battered by life. She was being told what to do by her superiors; she was uncertain whether she wanted to have children. Her sexual desire for her husband had diminished. She wasn't certain whether that was due to the fact that she had lost her periods or whether she really wasn't attracted to the man anymore. All these psychological issues had pressed her to pursue diet and exercise to the point of amenorrhea. At least she could prove she controlled something . . . what she ate.

Many of us are insecure about ourselves, about our attractiveness as people and women, and one of the ways we maintain or establish a superficial security is by achieving a beautiful body. For years that was enough. If a woman paid a lot of attention to exteriors and made a pretty picture of herself, she could feel secure. What a Pyrrhic victory that was.

SHIFT TO THE INTERNAL

Now, I think, there's been a shift from the external to the internal. The inner person is more important to the woman in her thirties than it might have been before, and the external somewhat less important. The reality that people have various talents and different experiences has finally begun to sink in. Today men may be more attracted to women because of their talents than because of their appearance. While we still want to look younger and beautiful, it's not everything anymore.

As we grow older the internal grows, flourishes, and blossoms. When we are young the pressure of the physical is just overpowering. Our bodies are everywhere; our emerging physical needs touch everything we do and virtually everything we think about ourselves. For many of us, adulthood in our thirties is a release from this single-minded pressure.

Our bodies are still there; we are interested in them, even concerned about their appearance and performance. But the power of our personality, our intellect and experience, has begun to overmatch our pure physical being. We are freer to work on our inner selves because perfection of the outside is no longer the imperative it once was.

The growth of the inner self is far more important than any attempt to arrest the decline of our physical self. How we look is determined by our genes far more than how we think or who we are. Our inner selves are much more open to development than our exterior selves. While our exterior attractiveness may rise to a peak early and fade, our inner self can simply keep improving through each decade, much as fine wine improves with age.

One sign in advertising that this idea of inner value is being accepted is what I call the Oil of Olay fantasy. The beach-blanket teenagers are now older, and Madison Avenue is trying to come up with a new fantasy that is not quite as outrageous for a thirty-year-old woman to believe in. It is predicated on more of an inner perspective.

It's very sedate; it's very romantic. The woman need not be gorgeous as much as serene, purringly confident. In the Oil of Olay commercials, the woman isn't overwhelmingly beautiful or young, but she radiates a youthful sense of herself. In these ads there is usually the presence or intimation of a male in the background. He has sent flowers; he's sent candy; he is somehow wooing this woman who appears younger than her stated age. The commercials present a very romantic, idealized picture of what it means to start entering early middle age. And that's what the thirties are—the early middle years of your life.

In their thirties women face a kind of double jeopardy. Those who have what they want are always concerned that they may lose it to a younger woman. And those women who don't have what they want, whether it be to have an intimate relationship with a man, to have children, or to muscle out room at the top, are concerned that they may never achieve these things.

DEPRESSION AND HAPPINESS

Faced with the fear of middle age, of weakness and of no longer being attractive, some of us become victims of a kind of chronic panic. If we don't get it (whatever our particular "it" may be) right now, we never will. And even if we do get it, we will have to twist ourselves into knots to keep from losing it. No wonder depression is so common among women our age. But the fear is chimerical. No one has erected a gate at age forty that says "Abandon hope all ye who enter here." The thirties may be the beginning of middle age, but they aren't the end of everything.

One way of looking at the thirties, which I've already suggested, is as the milestone where we look back and see what we've accomplished, a natural breathing space on our march through life, where we can take stock of our achievements and assess our failures, and decide if we are happy with what we've done.

All through our lives we're told to try to be happy. One goal of life is to achieve happiness. And we try. But until the thirties, I think, many of us are pursuing someone else's view of what happiness means. Now we begin to define happiness on our own terms.

One of the things we haven't touched on is a thirty-year-old woman's relationship with her parents. Happiness fits in with that, in the sense that one frequently develops definitions of happiness and milestones of success—where you're going to school, who you're going to marry—under parental influence. As a woman enters her thirties, she is more apt to define happiness in her own terms according to her inner needs. She sees her parents growing older and sees what has become of their lives, whether they have been happy or unhappy. She reacts to their fate by establishing either similar or radically different goals for herself.

What is my personal definition of happiness since I turned thirty? In all honesty, I'm still in the process of defining happy for myself. Part of that is because in medicine we endure a prolonged period of delayed gratification; we really don't have a chance to think ahead to what we want to do or where we want to be. But I know that happiness for me is a blend of satisfying hard work and intense emotional commitment.

Depression is an all-too-common problem. In fact, it's rampant among women. You can tell when people are depressed because they tend to depress you. You feel down when you are around them. The adage about emotions being contagious is true. When I walk into a room to evaluate a patient, one of the things I consider is the patient's mood. While talking, if I suddenly find myself feeling sad or teary, I know that it's probably coming from that patient. Perhaps there's a certain amount of projection of my feelings involved, but there is a sense of gloom that depressed people carry around with them.

Statistically, women at all ages are much more prone to depression than men are. Why do a lot of women in their thirties get so depressed? A variety of life stresses can depress women these days. One of them is the super-woman complex, the attempt to achieve the unachievable, to do everything—house, kids, man, etc.—fabulously and without strain. And then feel supremely fulfilled by it.

When roles were very clearly defined and separate, things were a lot easier. Women had work in the home that they were supposed to do; men had wage earning work they were supposed to do. The standards of excellence by which you judged and were judged were clearly defined. Now the areas are blurred, it's harder to judge what you should do and how to decide what standards to use in evaluating yourself.

Depression can be described as anger turned inward. Hostility and negative feelings that should be vented at exterior objects or other people are turned inward on oneself. Women are more prone to this, I think, because anger, according to the classical definition of feminine behavior, is unfeminine. Nice girls don't do it. Job disappointments, financial reverses, unmet expectations of any sort can all result in depression for us.

Since the thirties are the time when many of us confront our expectations of life fully for the first time, it is understandable why depression crops up so frequently. Few of us have a totally satisfying life, and when the balance seems too heavily against us, we need to readjust. Depression fills the void between our old expectations of feminine behavior and our new ones.

Turning anger inward occurs more often with women than with men because we are brought up to feel more responsible for our failings—and those of everyone around us—than men are. They can lash out at external forces more easily than we—break furniture, cuss, even batter their mates. We may turn it all upon ourselves and punish ourselves rather than let those around us share our burden.

Depression can be a cruel, isolating taskmaster. When it strikes—really, at all times—we need each other to ward off the pain. Talking, sharing, realizing that others have similar problems, that you aren't unique, is an excellent palliative for depression.

However, when feelings of sadness or hopelessness persist for longer than two to three weeks, consultation with a professional is advisable.

PSYCHE AND OUR BODIES

What is the impact of all these psychological factors on a woman's body in her thirties? She's under more stress, and as a result may feel older, may even age more rapidly. But stress is not, of course, solely responsible for aging. Time goes on and your body ages regardless of what's going on around you in the world. And you can be depressed no matter where you are. You can be sitting in Podunk, a happy town of two hundred, quietly, silently slipping into despair, or you can be in the midst of New York City. The stresses of modern society are going to affect your body in some subtle way whatever kind of life you lead.

For some of us the body's response to stress and depression is hypochondria, in addition to depression.

HYPOCHONDRIA

Approximately 25 percent of cases of severe depression have a hypochondriacal element, according to professor of psychiatry Frederick Lowy of the University of Toronto. In most of those instances, the patient's physical laments overshadow the signs of the psychological disorder, making an accurate diagnosis difficult. One researcher found that out of 234 depressed patients, 50 percent had physical concerns that initially masked their true problem.[1]

Hypochondria commonly accompanies several kinds of depression. In one type, the physical complaints build up slowly over several months. With these patients, a skilled doctor should be able to spot symptoms of depression, such as insomnia or low sex drive. By contrast, in many depressed patients hypochondriacal aches and pains appear suddenly, usually over a few weeks, and telltale sleeplessness or lack of energy is either absent or muted. In more serious disturbances, like schizophrenia, the complaints are usually bizarre. For instance, a person might believe that her bowels are rotting out. The sudden onset of such feelings, particularly in young women, obviously requires immediate attention.

Fear of ill health brought on by aging or by our failure to be superwomen can also trigger the reverse of hypochondria. Witness today's fitness enthusiasts. "Their preoccupation with health reflects the depersonalization of society, diminished expectations about life and threats of nuclear war," says Richard Ehrlich, author of *The Healthy Hypochondriac*. "In general, they worry that life is getting out of control."[2]

For the feel-well zealots, he explains, health becomes

the area they think they can control. They don't develop aches and pains as such. Rather, they stick to a strict regimen of exercise and nutritious diet to fend off trouble. Ehrlich sees them as "Social Hypochondriacs" because they turn health concerns into group activities such as jogging or spa treatments.

In a related category are the "I never get sick" folks. "These people feel threatened by the idea of sickness. To be ill is to be weak," says Ehrlich. "Despite their protests, they're overly concerned with health."

SELF-IMAGE

Your adult self-image coalesces during the thirties. We have a sense of who we are in the world, where we stand, how people look at us, how other people relate to us. And that becomes more definite and clear in our minds during these years. We have an image; we have various roles that we are comfortable fulfilling—wife, mother, professional. These are all more real in our thirties than they were in our twenties.

If someone sat you down and said, "List the ten words that best describe the type of person you are," the ten words chosen by a thirty-five-year-old woman would give a much deeper, more decisive picture than those chosen by a twenty-one-year-old. The younger woman would probably give vague, external words like *helpful, good student, cheerful, friendly, math major*, and so on. The older woman is much more likely to pin the tail on her personality, with words like *brittle, resourceful, fickle, contemplative, tempestuous,* or *sympathetic*.

The years and experiences that accrue between college and the thirties lend perspective to our good and bad points. We understand ourselves much better than when we were younger. This doesn't mean we're much better at changing—our bad habits are persistent and still a nuisance—but at least we know now that they are an intrinsic part of us and not to be despised. They are a quiet challenge for us to meet whenever we're feeling strongest.

LIMITS AND CHOICES

In another sense, a woman in her thirties faces her highest challenge in responding to limitations and choices that arise from her life. It's now that we have to decide what it is that we want to do. Imperatives, whether they are biological or not, are just what the term implies. They can't be denied. We must respond to them. It's like a forced call in bridge—you have to say something, you have to make a decision, or the decision will be made for you.

This squeeze is coming much later in life than ever before, and the social pressures for women in the outside world are much stronger than they've ever been. Our options are wider, so the pressures we face when choosing among them are stronger.

The result of all this is a lot more confused women experiencing intense personal conflict about how to fit the many and varied pieces of life together. While many issues have been settled, many crucial choices already made in terms of career or marriage by our early thirties, a significant percentage of us may decide to change course. In her Columbia University thesis, Dr. Wendy Stewart, studying the life directions of women, found that they were much less predictable than those of men. Women who had committed themselves to the role of wife and mother began to feel suppressed during their thirties, anxious to make their way in the working world; similarly, women who had committed themselves to building a career began to feel a pull toward the more traditional roles of wife and mother. Women have more options and apparently need to exercise them. According to Dr. Stewart, "women's lives don't seem to stand still long enough for one to run a good controlled investigation of what may be happening to them psychologically."

Women want to have a piece of the pie—of every pie. And our eyes are often bigger than our stomachs. We can't eat it all, but we hate to miss a crumb.

There's just too much pie there, and we can't do all of it; we have to make compromises. We simply cannot be at home with our children all day and yet work full-time at a demanding job; cannot pay attention to our husbands *and* be up to date on the international news; cannot wear the latest clothes *and* know the latest books and records, and on and on. We can't do it all. We're going to compromise something, or at least will have to forgo something temporarily. Yes, it's painful, confusing, and depressing, but it is also the source of our growth, a challenge and an opportunity that we can meet and master.

Our Shape

As WE MOVE into our thirties, we grow more conscious of—in some cases downright obsessive about—our shape. In fact, we worry about several different kinds of shape. We want to have a "shapely" shape, and also be "in shape," because if we don't we'll get shipped out to shape up at the fat farm.

But the concept of shape for us thirty-year-olds isn't even that simple. The thought is as subjective as they come. Each of us has several different shapes, and different attitudes toward the shapes we behold.

We have, first of all, our real-world shape. This is what we look like without pretension or artifice. Some of us are stocky, some skinny. Some of us have hips, others don't. Some of us have rear ends that make us feel as if we go around corners with the shimmy of articulated buses. Others have nothing back there. Each of us has a unique shape. It is not the same shape we had at twenty, but it's not radically different, either. We can see our body gradually changing on the continuum from

25

gawky youthfulness to pillowy old age. Our thirty-year-old version is the natural expression of our adult experiences, a form about which we can feel comfortable, if not ecstatic.

For most of us, ecstasy does not reside in real shape, but in perceived shape. And there are several of these, too. We all have a personal ideal shape, an inner notion of the perfect form for a woman of our years and basic body type (the Oil of Olay fantasy again), a dream that is all the more alluring for being just a nudge—well, maybe a few nudges—away from reality. In our mind's eye we see a woman who admits to being in her thirties, who owns up to her faults almost proudly because she has made of them a radiant, ageless package. The perfect us.

But why should we stop with realistic daydreaming? From our personal ideal shape it is a short, slinky course to the dream of ultimate shape. Yes, you too can look like Marilyn, Raquel, and the many other celebrated chunks of unchanging feminine kilowattage. We have all heard stories of the ugly duckling collegian who drops from sight for a decade and turns up for the reunion as a svelte vision, a mink draped over one elegant arm and an Italian count on the other. We all have a tiny thought in the back of our heads that we might willingly take over proprietorship of Dorian Gray's portrait for just a few years.

WHAT IS SHAPE?

The layers of perception we have about our shape are made more complex by our divergent notions about being in shape. What does "in shape" mean? Running a marathon? Bench-pressing four hundred pounds? Matching the male version of the Canadian Air Force exercise plan? Or is shape much more flexible than that—a few rounds of tennis, a little golf, a weekly walk to work? Put ten women in a room and you'll get ten different answers.

It's interesting to note that being in shape and having a dream shape usually don't coincide. Female athletes tend to look healthy, trim, strong, but they don't usually look any more like dream women than you or I. Their shape is dictated by the sweaty reality of their craft, not the easy requirements of dreamland. We, too, should keep in mind that getting into shape has its cosmetic strong points, but it won't lift us out of the real-world skin God gave us.

Still, I think women have definite cultural fantasies of what's ideal and what we're supposed to look like. Perfection starts with a long thin neck, graceful shoulders, mildly muscular and well defined (but not muscularly well defined) arms, long tapering fingers, a nice firm bosom with the nipples standing upright, even shoulders (not too bony, though), nipped-in waist, nice hips, and firm tapering legs that are muscular, but not overtly so.

If you look at that image, who is it? Even Bo Derek, a 10, doesn't have all those features.

The fact is that all of us differ in terms of where we put our weight and how we're shaped. That is genetic, and there's very little we can do about it. Take stubby fingers, for example. There is absolutely nothing that you can do if you have short stubby fingers. You're always going to have short, stubby fingers; you're never going to have long graceful hands. You're never going to model gloves and fake fingernails. That's what you look like.

My aunt has sent away for various remedies for thick legs her entire adult life. She has thick legs; I have thick legs. She has always had thick legs, and has spent a lot of money on them. I will always have them, but I won't spend a lot of money on them, because I recognize that they are part of my genetic background and there's nothing I can do about that.

Often, concerns arise because many of us feel that our bad body features stand out like the Rock of Gibraltar.

Everyone notices them. But people don't focus on our
bad features to the extent that we expect them to. We
struggle to fix something no one else notices is out of
kilter. Even when every part of us is working at absolute
top form, there is minimal correlation between this fantasy of a body and a healthy body. Even a superhealthy
body might look entirely different from what we con-
jure up.

Consider a person who swims five miles a day. She
probably doesn't look as though she swims five miles a
day. We have a fantasy in our minds that swimming five
miles a day will bring us a "perfect" shape. It won't,
because everyone starts with a different mold and then
can go only so far with it.

Some women go awfully far in trying to match fantasies. A famous actress decided there wasn't enough
difference between her chest and waist, so she had her
bottom ribs removed to give herself more taper. For
most of us the reality of achieving our image of perfection carries too high a price.

REALITY AND FANTASY

The crux of the shape question for thirty-year-olds is
that our decade is the time when reality and fantasy
diverge for good. Even among the most athletic and
beautiful of us, the fourth decade frequently brings with
it the realization of faults and shape foibles that time
and our best intentions will never erase. In addition, our
time of life brings significant shifts in our bodies' roles
and appearance. In general, our thirty-year-old selves
grow a bit hippier than we were in our twenties; our
thighs grow a little bit wider no matter how much we
exercise; our skin seems not quite as taut as it once was.

More important for our shape than all these accepted,
universal changes, however, are the experiences of our
thirties. In our age group our shape and appearance say
more about how we live than how old we are. In the

fourth decade our bodies begin to take on the contours of our adult lives. Have you ever noticed that from a distance all twenty-year-olds look alike? Sure there are differences in weight, proportion, a thousand variables, but they all radiate an overpowering sense of youth that washes out the differences.

For us, it's different. We have a lot more shapes to choose from, and they tend to announce our relationship with life more than our age. We look matronly, businesslike, athletic, obese, neurotically thin, radiant, blowzy, taut, and so on. Or perhaps we've just grown into ourselves and look better than we ever have before. In any case, this should be a welcome change, because our life and our looks now come more into line. But it also implies that during our thirties we may have to accept a shape that flies in the teeth of our youthful fantasies; we have to realize that radically changing our shape at this time of our lives implies changing the whole way we live. The heart of the question is whether we want to attempt to remain forever young, whether we want to stay at age twenty-nine for the rest of our lives. In reality, I don't think most of us would.

What would happen if the entire population suddenly stabilized and nothing subsequently happened? I think it would be a crashing bore. There's nothing wrong with aging. There's nothing wrong with looking our best for as long as we can, but the pursuit of eternal youth is destined to fail.

It angers me that there has been so much emphasis on superficials and so much capitalization on our attempts to achieve the ideal body. If you look at texts on plastic surgery, that exploitation is one thing that stands out, at least to my mind. For example, the "saddlebag syndrome" is really just a normal development of fat tissue at the base of the buttocks and hips. It's nothing for a woman to worry about, yet there are a variety of plastic surgery techniques for removing it, and I think that's unfair capitalization on our hopes of looking like ideal, smooth, flawless individuals. We should be so excited about our freedom as adult women, so pleased with the control we have developed over our lives and bodies, that a little extra spread on our hips is of scant importance. But society keeps foisting the unreasonable myopia of shape on us and then making us pay to achieve that restrictive goal.

FEAR OF FAT

Up to now we have been talking about shape without once mentioning that well-worn American bugbear—fat. I think we are far too concerned with fat—more accurately, with the idea of being fat. Our national notion of proper slimness tends to lie in the same neighborhood as the ultimate-shape fantasy. Being slim is dogma. If we don't conform to the skeletal standards of fashion magazines and TV actresses, we are judged, by ourselves and our peers, as too fat.

Hogwash. That standard is neither achievable nor desirable for many women. Furthermore, the concept of shape has a lot more behind it than simply weight. Women athletes often weigh more than average because muscle tissue weighs more than fat. Poundage is only one aspect of shape—how you carry the weight, what percentage of your weight is fat, and how you feel about your size are also important aspects.

However, at the same time we must admit that we live in the most universally overfed country in history, and many of us are too heavy. Scientific studies indicate that between 25 and 35 percent of women beyond age thirty are at least 20 percent above their desirable body weight.[1] This excess baggage isn't healthy, isn't pretty, and isn't sexy, but it's very hard to lose. Losing this excess weight is extremely important for a woman in her thirties. If obesity becomes an established condition, it can bring on numerous health problems in later life. It can even shorten life. Insurance statistics indicate that there is a clear-cut relationship between longevity and weight.[2] For example, the death rate from diabetes mel-

litus is approximately four times higher in those diabetics who are overweight than among those who are at
normal body weight. Being overweight also carries a
higher risk of gallbladder disease, heart disease, and
kidney disease, and increases the risk from anesthesia
and surgery of all types. For some reason the rate of
accidents is also higher in obese people, perhaps because
they are slower, more awkward, or have a limited view
of the ground. And obesity is a risk factor for the development of uterine cancer.

Unfat, however, does not translate into thin. We have
a genetic shape that we're born with, and there's only a
certain amount we can do to alter it. But we persist.
Week after week I see women at my health club who
really want to drastically alter their shape to the perfect,
impossible ideal. These are women who repeatedly fail
in their attempts to diet, because they have an abnormal
fantasy of what they should look like rather than
realistic goals for what they can actually achieve. The
desperation of the quest dictates unending failure.

Women in their thirties who aren't obese should think
in terms of tightening up the shape that they have rather
than trying to shrink into a new one, and this isn't a
cop-out. For example, some women have thick, wide
backs and there's nothing that they can do about it,
aside from starving themselves until they're scarecrows.
What's worse is that our heaviest parts relinquish the
weight last. A dieter who has really broad shoulders will
have the skinniest little toothpicks for arms and legs
before her torso shows any demonstrable change.

At some point—and the thirties mark that point for
most of us—we have to accept what Nature has dealt us,
or what we have dealt ourselves through our eating patterns. We must become comfortable with that and
recognize that we can change certain aspects of our
bodies but can't become someone else altogether. Some
of us are destined to be thin; we will continue to be thin.
Others are destined to be heavier, and will have to fight
that battle every day.

There are two or three critical times during a woman's

life when fat cell number is arrived at: intrauterine life, infancy, and adolescence (around the time of puberty). Some researchers describe two types of obesity: *hyperplastic*, which is due to having more fat cells, and *hypertrophic*, which is due to an enlargement of a smaller number of fat cells.[3] It is felt that the hyperplastic type is associated with childhood obesity and is less responsive to dieting than the hypertrophic type. Once determined, the number of fat cells cannot be decreased. Therefore, women who have too many fat cells have a more difficult problem than those who have the proper number of fat cells but too large fat cells. Thus, many researchers believe that it is more difficult for women who were fat as infants or during adolescence to lose weight because they have a permanent increase in the number of their fat cells.[4] When you go on a diet your fat cells decrease in size but not in number.

In my case, I've always been what I've considered to be heavy. I was a large child, one of the tallest in my class for many years. My weight problem began when I broke my leg at twelve and stayed home all that winter, being stuffed by my mother and my aunt. I gained fifteen pounds, and from that day on it's been difficult to lose those fifteen pounds. I am resigned to the fact that I will continually battle the bulge, that I cannot eat everything I want and maintain my weight. I've become a little more accepting of the fact that it may always be there. I'm still fighting, but perhaps not as seriously as I did in my twenties.

Our metabolism slows a bit during the thirties, which means we tend to come out of the decade somewhat heavier than when we went into it. That's terrible for some of us, splendid for others. The person who enters her thirties thin and wishing she were heavier will, when she leaves her thirties, probably be heavier—and happier. The person who enters her thirties overweight will probably leave her thirties even more overweight.

Often, having children permanently changes women's body chemistry and food needs, also. A patient will tell me that her metabolism was such that she could eat almost anything she wanted; then she had a child, and now has to diet. It happens over and over again. I see thirtyish patients who used to be skinny and now, post-kid, are plump. Part of it is due to a change in eating behavior; a pregnant woman really does eat for two. She eats vast amounts of food and doesn't gain weight. Then the baby's gone and she can't reduce her eating back to prepregnancy levels.

I think it's fair to say in general that during our thirties we face a choice: change our youthful eating habits and keep our shape, or keep our habits and lose our shape.

HEALTHY CORES

There are lots of thirty-year-old-woman shapes that are healthy, but obviously some of us are unhealthily large. It's important to be able to delineate between heavy and obese. I like to explain to my patients that there's a healthy core weight and then a safety zone around that core. The cores vary according to our frame, bone mass, or amount of muscle. Some women who are 5'2" have a core of 100 pounds; others who are 5'2" have a core of 120 pounds and still are perfectly fit. Generally, a healthy core for a woman five feet tall and of average build is about 100 pounds. Add four pounds for each inch taller; subtract four pounds for each inch below five feet.

The true measure of health in relationship to weight, as we judge it now, probably relates to cardiovascular fitness, so that a big chunky person who jogs three miles regularly is probably healthier than the lighter person who can't run a block to catch the bus. The real yard-stick of whether your shape is healthy for you is whether you can perform a certain minimal level of physical activity with ease.

Fat does a variety of things; it is a metabolically active tissue. In polycystic ovarian disease, which is linked with obesity, the ovaries make too much hormone, which begins a cycle that increases the levels of free, active male hormones in the system, and the victims get hairy. They grow mustaches, beards, sideburns, body hair. That is truly paying the price for fat.

Some kinds of fat are actually helpful. So-called brown fat, which occurs in central areas across the breasts and chest (less so in humans than in other mammals, where it serves an important function in hibernation), plays a role in heat regulation. Brown fat may also provide a clue in unraveling the puzzle of abnormal heat regulation that seems to occur in obese people after they eat.

What are danger signs of overweight and overdieting? If you're not pregnant and you can't see your toes, you obviously have trouble. At the other extreme, if you're dieting and lose your period, you've gone too far—your amount of body fat has dropped below the threshold for normal ovulation. The serious problems of weight, those that result in the shortening of life expectancy, do not occur until a woman is more than 20 to 30 percent beyond her ideal weight in either direction.

This brings to mind my experiences in San Francisco, where I saw a lot of Samoan patients. For women and men alike, the accepted cultural standard was to be heavy. Their desires were the opposite of American norms. They didn't like being thin. A 5'5" woman would come in and say, "I'm just dropping the weight. I've gone from 190 to 180; this is terrible. It's falling off me, there's nothing to hold on to." If a Samoan woman could see her toes, she'd get depressed.

Our shape is not static. It changes monthly, daily, sometimes hourly. Some women refuse to accept this fact, to their detriment. A woman who was in college with me modeled for a suntan product. She was absolutely gorgeous by everyone's standards, yet she was a very miserable person, because her "flaws" stood out to her in such tremendous relief. She judged herself entirely by how she looked, and if she didn't feel that she looked her absolute best all the time, she was devastated.

For many women, shape veers back and forth a lot when we're young. Our volatile physical and emotional lives toss us from one set of habits into another, from one shape to another. These fluctuations probably grow more moderate as we grow older. Our life calms down into a more reliable pattern, and so does our shape. In the thirties we are settling into our adult contours.

For most of us, as I've said, the shape we settle into, while different from our youthful form, remains healthy. Our only serious worries are cosmetic.

Some women, though, are chronically, dangerously fat. They don't seem to be able to stop their weight gain by any means. Mild overweight is usually the result of lazy habits, but scientists think these seriously obese women may actually have built-in body systems that make it difficult for them to control their weight.

THE FAT ARE DIFFERENT

Studies of fat people have shown clearly that they respond differently to their environment than do their thin counterparts.[5] Obese people have been shown to respond to external cues and lean people to internal cues of hunger and satiety. Thus, if it's 6:00 P.M. an obese woman is more apt to eat dinner regardless of her lack of appetite than a lean person, who will either eat a smaller meal or delay dinner until she is hungry. More than lean people, fat people tend to accept food offered to them even though they are not hungry. Time-lapse-photography studies have shown that obese people are much less physically active than lean people.[6] For example, in a swimming pool a greater percentage of their time is spent floating than actively swimming.

Studies of dieting that analyzed both lean and obese individuals suggest that there is clearly something different metabolically about obese people.

A recent study in the *New England Journal of Medicine* indicates that perhaps this "something different" is the sodium potassium ATPase enzyme system.[7] This enzyme system is in all cells and is responsible for maintaining the proper concentrations of sodium outside the cell and potassium within the cell. The enzyme system requires energy (calories) in order to perform its work. It probably accounts for some 20 to 30 percent of cellular energy. Dr. Jeffrey Fliers's recent study of obese individuals showed that their enzyme system was more efficient than that of their lean counterparts, so that their cells required less calories to accomplish the same amount of work. According to this idea, in other words, fat bodies work better than thin ones. This capacity to perform more cellular work with less calories might have been advantageous to an individual in an era when food supplies were short, but in today's society it results in obesity.

I think that every physician has encountered the overweight woman who comes in complaining that although she is adhering strictly to a 900 or 1200 calorie diet she is losing weight at a painstakingly slow pace. Is there something different about this woman? Is she merely cheating on her diet or is there really something physiologically different about the obese person who has difficulty losing weight?

An interesting study of obesity, the only one of its kind ever performed, involved 28 male volunteers in a state prison in Vermont who overate in order to gain 20 percent of their basal weight.[8] These volunteers experienced an increase in appetite late in the day and early in the evening, and a decrease in their desire for physical activity. Clear-cut psychological changes occurred as they became obese. But once they had achieved their weight gain, these normal men required almost twice as many calories to maintain their weight as did men who were spontaneously overweight. They also had no difficulty in returning to normal weight. This would suggest that there is clearly something different metabolically about obese people. Another possible cause behind obesity today may be the so-called "smorgasbord syndrome," a leftover environmental compulsion from our prehistoric days. Animal studies have shown that hunger renews at the sight of each new food. An animal faced with a "smorgasbord" will eat more and gain more than one that gets just one food. In past times, that assured that enough nutrients were eaten. Now, it means that we, with our varied diet, may be driven to overeat by this vestigial drive.

DIETS

Dieting is discouraging. Thirty-year-old bodies don't take off the pounds as fast as they did a decade ago. The fading fantasies of youth leave an overwhelming sense of reality in their wake. We can certainly lose weight through patient, sensible diet control, but for some of us, that drawn-out obligation seems too depressing. We become instead prime fodder for fad diets and charlatan thin-makers. The airwaves call us to the mirage oasis of easy slimness. As Beverly Stephens wrote in the New York *Daily News*:

> Now we have foodspeak—a quest for truth walking a thin line between the overabundance of food in America and a national obsession with thinness. Food has become almost a religion, and abusing food has become the only possibility left for sinning. Now that sexual activities are no longer forbidden, the only thing called sinful is chocolate cake. And about the only two things guaranteed to be best-sellers are diet books and cookbooks. The fact that once more another fad diet has captured the imagination of so many bookbuyers has to make us wonder what's going on here.
>
> Maybe if we didn't have this compulsion to be so thin, maybe if we could all stop eating for emo-

tional reasons, maybe if we'd give up the search for magic solutions, people like [diet author] Judy Mazel wouldn't get rich off the fat of the land. None of the above is likely to happen in our lifetime. Probably the best we can hope for is that a new diet messiah will come along before too many people overdose on pineapple.

Everyone is drawn to the dramatic. Reports of kooky diets, starvation in the hospital, and intestinal bypass operations catch the eye of the overweight very readily. When Judy Mazel says eat one kind of fruit every day, people prick up their ears. It sounds so easy. We want dieting to be easy. However, most of us just need to eat less. That's hard and as unglamorous as can be, but not impossible. We simply have to filter out the nonsense, and get to work.

What about diet pills? Studies show that while amphetamines lead to weight loss for the first two to three weeks, most patients fail to lose additional weight and actually return to their original weight rapidly thereafter.[9] Phenylpropanolamine, the effective ingredient in most over-the-counter diet preparations, has been shown to be ineffective in many controlled studies.

Benzocaine, a local anesthetic agent used for sore throats, is the active ingredient in some over-the-counter appetite suppressants, such as Diet Trim tablets and Spantrol capsules. The anesthetic is felt to act by dulling the taste buds and thereby helping the dieter eat less because the food doesn't taste as good. It seems questionable to me whether most women overeat just because food tastes good. The *Medical Letter*, in reviewing the use of phenylpropanolamine and oral benzocaine, concluded that "the only satisfactory treatment for obesity is a lifelong change in patterns of food intake and physical activity" and "there is no good evidence that phenylpropanolamine or benzocaine can help obese patients achieve long term weight reduction."[10]

In fact, diet pills may be dangerous. Phenylpropanolamine can cause palpitations or worsen high blood pressure. It's fine to have a warning on the package, but what about the woman whose high blood pressure has never been diagnosed? Who hasn't seen a doctor for two or three years? For her, that little diet pill may be deadly. Women have suffered hypertensive crises with strokes after taking OTC diet pills. Of course, the manufacturers try to suppress adverse case reports, claiming that they are anecdotal, incidental. But if the pills don't work and have the potential for harm, they should be withdrawn from the market. Some amphetamine-like compounds used in appetite suppressants, such as phenmetrazine in Preludin and phentermine in Fastin, may lead to side effects similar to those of the amphetamines, including bizarre behavior, hallucinations, paranoia and depression.

If pills don't help, what does work? Behavior modification is clearly not the sole answer to obesity, but it does offer some help to the overweight woman by changing the way she eats so that she spontaneously eats less food or foods lower in calories.

Also, dieting is more effective when it is combined with physical exercise. This is particularly true for the woman who is chronically obese, who has a much lower level of activity in all aspects of her life than does her lean counterpart. It is important for her to change her life style, to try to increase her caloric expenditure on an hour-to-hour basis by walking instead of taking the elevator up one flight, taking the parking space a block away rather than circling several times to find one closer, and so on.

Do some foods burn up more calories than they impart? The answer is probably no. Yes, digestion does consume some calories, but there is no particular kind of food, such as celery or grapefruit, which involves such an expenditure of energy to digest it that more calories are consumed in digesting the food than the food contained.

Does the number of meals consumed in one day have any effect on how the calories consumed are proportioned? Epidemiological studies indicate that there probably is some effect. It seems as though the body quickly learns to convert carbohydrate into stored fat if only a single large meal is consumed each day. Therefore, the woman who doesn't eat all day and then devours a large dinner is probably doing herself a disservice. It would be preferable to distribute calories over the entire day; that way you don't become ravenously hungry or nauseated either.

The most important thing is to restrict calories; that is clearly the most important principle of dieting. There are many fads and numerous diet books. Nonetheless, the best diet continues to be the following: a diet restricted to between 900 and 1200 calories per day, with a balanced content of protein, fat and carbohydrate. It may be boring and tedious, but it's healthy and it works, with gradual weight loss that will stay off if you don't return to your previous eating habits.

CELLULITE

Cellulite is nothing more than fat that has clumped together under the surface of the thighs and buttocks. It may appear in the thirties but actually starts at puberty. Women tend to gain weight in different areas at different ages. Weight gained during our teenage years is distributed fairly evenly. Weight gained during our twenties and thirties generally settles on our trunks, particularly our hips and buttocks, under the influence of estrogens, although it may be distributed more evenly. Weight gained after menopause tends to settle around the middle. So, the weight we're putting on now hits the worst areas for cellulite, our thighs and buttocks. Cellulite results from the combination of expanding fat cells, decreased muscle tone, and diminished skin tone. Chemically, cellulite fat is identical to other fat.

The great myth about cellulite is that it's somehow different from other fat and you need to do something special and different for it. I think that arises because women hope that if it is different, there's a magic way it'll go away. There isn't. Sadly, I watch women at my health spa go over the rollers for twenty minutes and then shower and leave. They haven't had any exercise whatsoever, and they haven't gotten rid of cellulite, either, whatever they may have read in the popular press.

Parenthetically, the other thing that drives me crazy at my gym is the current fad for women to wear articles of clothing over the areas of their bodies they consider most obese. Women walk around with rubber belts around their waists or wearing metallic-looking pants. They sweat more in these areas and say, "Look, this is fantastic, my pants are soaking wet. I'm just dripping wet. I've clearly lost weight from my waist or hips."

While I applaud the fact that they're out there exercising, it's a shame that they expend so much money on such useless gimmicks. Sorry, but that's not how our fat is lost. Fat is lost throughout the body, not just from our arms or our legs; when we exercise we're also burning the unseen fat that's stored in the liver and around our hearts and intestines. In fact, fat from our jiggly quarters is metabolized most slowly, unfortunately. Many women know that; they just don't want to believe it.

Well, is there anything you can do for cellulite and other unwanted fat? Certainly there is: exercise with gusto and eat with care. If you reduce your weight, cellulite patches, while they won't go away, will become less obvious. If you exercise, your increased muscle tone can sometimes force cellulite pockets to smooth out. You can't attack cellulite pockets apart from the rest of your body. If you want less cellulite, get all of you in trim.

ELASTICITY AND SHAPE

Skin elasticity declines with age, no doubt about it. You can tell that clearly by feeling an infant's skin and then feeling the skin of someone in her thirties, and finally the skin of an older person. The decrease in elasticity results in a tendency to sag. One of the most peculiar interactions with sagging is dieting. If you lose weight in your thirties, when your skin is no longer as elastic, it gets a little saggy; tissue that was previously filled out with fat no longer has anything to fill it. You have a relative vacuum beneath the skin, so it sags. The tissue won't spring back as it would if the weight had been lost in the teens or early twenties.

That's one reason why skin-tuck operations came into being—for very overweight people who lose weight and then have excess skin. The ultimate in sagging is the person who used to have rolls of fat and now has a lot of extra, loose skin.

The best regimen against sagging is to keep your skin active—make it work, exercise it, eat moderately so there isn't too much fat for it to go around. Some sagging is inevitable but an active woman will see much less of it than her sedentary sister.

I should emphasize that sagging isn't caused by muscle weakness. The problem is in the skin itself. The same is true for sagging of the breasts. Breasts are a combination of glandular tissue and fat. They're supported by various ligaments. With increasing age, if the breasts aren't supported, there's a gradual downward trend. That's going to be exacerbated if you jog or play volleyball without a brassiere. Also, women who breast-feed are going to have more sagging than women who don't breast-feed. It's bound to be.

As for the bra or no-bra controversy, there are two completely opposite views. One is that if you don't wear a bra when you're younger, the muscles and ligaments firm up so that when you're older you have less sag; the other is that gravity does its business regardless, so if you don't wear a bra when you're younger, you'll have more sag. I believe you will probably have a certain amount of sag, according to your genetics. If your mother and your aunt sag, you probably will too. But there's the additional question of what is meant by sag. Just the other week I had a patient come in who was in her early sixties and separated from her husband. Her body was fantastic. While I examined her breasts she apologized twice to me for the fact that they were sagging. There wasn't anything wrong with her, but she felt that because her breasts had moved an eighth of an inch they were sagging.

Most sagging is genetically based, but obviously large breasts are going to tend to sag more than small breasts. There is no doubt that for the large-bosomed woman, going braless will result in more sagging than if she wore some support. For small-breasted women the question is probably up in the air (pardon my pun) because there isn't as much to sag.

In general, I think, society puts too much emphasis on our breasts. The social importance of breasts has caused some women to identify their personalities with their breasts. If their breasts were jaunty they felt high that day, if their breasts were sagging, they felt low that day. Whatever our breasts look like, it seems to me that we should focus on our whole selves; we shouldn't allow our breasts to become a benchmark of beauty or personality. Considering society's incessant harping on breast value, our ambivalent feelings are understandable, but we should struggle to maintain perspective.

BLOATING

Bloating from water retention may become more of a problem in the thirties because we suffer some decrease in skin tone. This is a very gradual process, but we are more likely to retain salt and water. The problem is purely cosmetic, however. The important determinants of salt and water balance, cardiac and kidney function, have not deteriorated to any significant degree in the thirties.

Part of this problem, too, derives from vanity. It's not uncommon to have women come in saying, "God, I'm just so horribly bloated before my period. Look at these designer jeans. They don't fit!" They bought the pants on their fittest day. Without eating breakfast or lunch, they went shopping in the afternoon and bought their skin-tight designer jeans. Then they expect them to fit when they've swelled by a couple of pounds—as we tend to do premenstrually. I've seen women absolutely outraged and distressed by this, and it's their own fault. You can't expect that jeans you buy immediately after your period are going to fit right before your period's due.

PREGNANCY AND SHAPE

Pregnancy produces an alteration in our shape, obviously. That's not a problem. But, when pregnancy's over, women in their thirties may have particular problems getting back to their pre-pregnancy shape. Metabolism is somewhat slower, so getting off the pounds is more difficult. Their skin is less elastic, so even if they tone up their muscles it takes longer for their shape to return to normal.

EXERCISE

I think the importance of regular daily exercise for women of our age cannot be overestimated. Even though daily exercise does not lead to a large enough increase in caloric expenditure to significantly alter the rate of weight reduction, exercise should have a place in any weight-reduction program. What regular exercise does accomplish is to help us keep off the weight we lose by dieting. Studies indicate that weight-reduction programs that include regular exercise improve a woman's chance of maintaining her weight loss.[11] The number of calories consumed by activity is not high, and remains the same for a thirty-year-old as for her younger compatriot: relaxing, roughly 1.3 calories per minute; running, 19.4 calories per minute; swimming, 11.2 calories per minute; walking (at a speed of 3.5 miles per hour), 5.2 calories per minute. In other words, you probably would have to run five minutes in order to utilize the number of calories in an apple, or swim actively for ten minutes in order to compensate for the number of calories in a glass of beer. Drat. But the point of exercise shouldn't be weight loss. Exercise should benefit how you feel, both in your bones and in your brain. Everyone feels good (if not righteous) after exercising. There's enormous satisfaction in feeling a healthy spring to your step, and seeing a firm curve reemerge at your waist. It is the strongest positive reinforcement of our health we can give ourselves.

New light on the "runner's high" came from a fascinating study at Massachusetts General Hospital, which found higher levels of endorphins, naturally occurring opiatelike compounds, in women after physical conditioning.[12] Perhaps these changes explain the change in mood that aerobic-exercise enthusiasts describe as occurring after exercise. Exercise really does provide a high!

FITNESS TEST

Before you become involved in an exercise program, you might want to have some idea of how you measure up to national norms for the bodies of people the YMCA considers in shape. Here are the Y's tests for a well-done body.

1. Check your body shape by taking the deepest breath you can and measuring your chest with a tape measure, just below the armpits. Next, get a measure-

ment for your relaxed waist. Your chest should exceed your waist by ten inches.

2. Test your body balance by standing on tiptoe with your feet together and your arms held straight out in front of you. Close your eyes and try to keep from falling over. If you can manage twenty seconds, you make the grade.

3. Ascertain your agility by kneeling as if you were going to pray. Get your legs tucked under your rear end and stretch your arms straight out in front of you. Swing your arms down, then back up in front, and use the momentum to try to rise to a standing position. It's tougher than it sounds.

4. A good method for determining muscle power is the standing broad jump. Flex your arms, tighten your body, and leap with both feet as far as you can. You should be able to make it about as far as your height.

5. To check endurance, run in place for one minute, lifting your feet at least four inches off the floor. When you're through, your pulse should be under one hundred and you shouldn't be breathing very hard.

6. A woman in good shape should be bendable enough to touch most of her hand to the floor without bending her knees.

7. Upper body strength can be tested with tight pushups. Place your hands just inside your shoulders and lower yourself to within one inch of the floor, with as straight a body as possible. Women should be able to handle about six of these with no problem.

ESTABLISHING A PROGRAM

Every person is different, and every woman should consider her own potential when devising an exercise program. Not everyone can swim the English Channel or run a marathon. Every person is unique, and therefore every exercise program is unique. One thing that frequently discourages women is that they can't do as well as someone else. Usually, that someone has been exercising on a regular basis for years. My advice: concentrate on yourself, and choose an activity you enjoy, at a pace you can maintain comfortably.

Beyond an improved sense of well-being, or an improvement in figure, the most important benefit of exercise for us thirty-year-olds—really, for everyone—is an increase in cardiovascular fitness. Exercise to enhance cardiovascular fitness must elevate the pulse for a prolonged period of time. For a woman in her thirties, the amount of exercise needed to raise the pulse rate varies according to her physical condition. A general rule of thumb is to exercise at approximately 75 percent of maximal pulse rate. A target pulse rate for us, on the average, would be 140 beats per minute. Parameters: exercise at less than 70 percent of the maximal pulse rate is of value but probably does not develop cardiovascular fitness as rapidly, while exercise at 90 percent of maximal pulse rate adds no additional benefit and certainly induces an unnecessary physical stress. It is unclear how much exercise is needed in order to induce improved heart and lung function, but a frequency of at least three to four times per week is probably sufficient if each time you sustain a pulse rate of 75 percent of maximal for at least twenty minutes.

Obviously, if the intent of an exercise program is to stress the heart, then underlying heart disease should be ruled out before the exercise program is embarked upon. For most women in their thirties, this is unnecessary. However, common sense clearly comes into play. The program must be undertaken on a gradual basis, with a buildup over a period of months, particularly for women who have not previously been active physically, and exercise should be stopped and a physician consulted at the first inkling of any problem, including chest pain, dizziness, severe shortness of breath, or cramps in the legs.

An exercise regimen should be preceded by a warm-up period of at least five to ten minutes, and followed by a cool-down stretching period. Warm-ups are important in order to stretch and loosen our older muscles and increase the circulation to the muscles so that cramping does not develop. Likewise, a stretching session at the end of exercising allows the muscles to cool down and continues the active blood flow to the muscles in order to carry away toxic waste products. In addition, for exercises such as running or bicycling, blood will pool in the leg muscles. When the activity is discontinued, the blood continues to be pooled in the legs, but the muscular contractions that normally squeeze the blood back to the heart and the remainder of the body have stopped, leading to a diminished return of blood to the brain and dizziness or even fainting.

It is important to realize that your thirties aren't too late to begin an exercise program, just as it's never too late to begin a diet. There is no value in castigating yourself for what you didn't do when you were younger. It is better to congratulate yourself for having jogged five minutes at thirty or thirty-five than to worry about the ten minutes you didn't jog at twenty.

MASSAGE

Massage feels good, but I don't know that it does a thirty-year-old body any particular good. But who cares? It's relaxing, intimate, warm. Perhaps biochemical changes occur in response to massage. It may be useful. It certainly doesn't do any harm. I believe that anything that feels good and has no specific detriment attached to it is great. Enjoy yourself.

FAD MANIPULATIONS

I take a much less sanguine view of Rolfing, deep cellulite massage, and other fad techniques supposedly designed to unlock hidden potentials or healing powers or release inner tensions. Women get hooked on these schemes and willingly pay for the privilege of being pummeled until they are bruised. When someone is manipulating your body, pain is not a sign of release, it's a warning to stop. Bruises aren't badges of honor, they're signs of abuse.

Massage should never be more than a pleasant, relaxing diversion. It is not a cure for anything. It won't make problem areas disappear (even sagging, if massage is not accompanied by exercise). And it should always be done gently. Hard massage cannot be compared to hard physical effort.

No massage technique I know about will materially improve your shape. That takes work and discipline. There are no substitutes.

Maybe our preoccupation with thinness relates to the amount of leisure time we have. We have a lot of time to think about nonessential things, and being thin is one of them. Or maybe it relates to the fact that there really aren't a lot of crucial things that we need to do. After all, when our forebears were blazing trails, no one worried about becoming thin.

It is my fervent hope that women will develop a sense of health rather than looks. I'd like our knee-jerk response to be "How am I on the inside?" rather than "How do I appear on the outside?" I want to trash the icon of unachievable thinness and raise a new statue to the realistic adult female shape in all its fascinating forms.

Our Superficial Selves

THE ONLY PARTS of you that everybody sees are your skin, eyes, and hair. In this public position they act as your body's emissaries to the rest of the world. Whatever they convey is what everyone else perceives you to be.

It's no wonder that these features have taken on so much importance for all people, but especially for women. One reason why women have traditionally placed greater importance on these visible attributes is that women are supposed to remain constant—which means constantly young—while men are allowed to change. Since a woman is charged with the ridiculous responsibility of remaining exactly as she was when she snared her man or reached her peak of social popularity, the preservation of her visible assets grows very important.

In this context, every wrinkle in a woman is a sign of her failure to arrest change; in a man it becomes a symbol of experience. Every sag around a woman's eyes denotes fatigue and loss of glamour; for a man it etches character. Gray hair on a woman means there's frost on the roof and ashes in the scuttle; for a man it is distinguished, a symbol of achievement.

Today the vast majority of us abhor these stereotypical laminations of old social standards. We rail against them at parties and meetings. We snarl about them to our co-workers. And you know what? Despite it all, we still ask our doctors about our skin, eyes, and hair with an incessant paranoia that confounds us medical types, who expect such concern to be limited to vital problems, not supposedly trivial ones.

What it boils down to is that we women still put great store in the appearance of our visible body parts. We want to look healthy and successful, and a tiny kernel of our minds still wants us to look eternally young. We wouldn't mind being the one at the reunion everyone stares at in awe because she has never changed a whit. She could still wear her cheerleader suit and have it fit perfectly.

It is one of the larger ironies of modern American life that in our unconscious pursuit of perfect skin, unchanging eyes, and the glow of unending health, many of us use chemicals and establish habits (such as suntanning) that in the long run actually speed the process we are trying to slow.

A situation many of us have seen involves two women who were friends in college. Both of them were nice-looking, with smooth skin and nice complexions, both were healthy, both have had similar life styles, both got married, and both exercise a lot. They come back ten years later and one's face is still smooth as a baby's while the other one looks like a worn glove. Why?

GENES VERSUS LIFE

Partly, it's in our genes, but much of the change can be affected by how we live our lives and how well we treat our skin.

As our armor against the outside world, our skin takes a terrible beating if we spend a lot of time in harsh environments. These can include the beach, the woods, dry air-conditioned office buildings, smoggy cities. Truly, every environment carries its own nasty parcel of problems for our skin. What we can do is recognize that the situation exists and keep an eagle eye out for any changes in our skin that result.

Much harder to notice or control are the transformations in our skin that we induce. Stress, which tightens the muscles and jangles the nerves, stretches the skin and encourages wrinkles. Long days and sleepless nights overtire our hides and increase the likelihood of sagging and growing seamed.

Going back to the two college chums, one may have spent much of her life outdoors, drunk hard, smoked a lot. The other had fewer problems and challenges, spent more time working on her skin, did everything in moderation. Now, the first woman's life might have been more interesting and fun than the second woman's. I don't think that the lines on her face are of any importance whatsoever. They don't indicate anything about her health or how long she'll live. But I know that many of us care about the youthful or at least smooth and healthy appearance of our skin, so let's see what we can do to keep it that way without becoming enslaved.

SKIN AND NUTRITION

One of the primary factors in hastening aging of the skin is bad nutrition. Adequate vitamins are a prerequisite of good skin. If you eat a balanced diet you're getting all the vitamins you need. Sadly, many of us won't leave well enough alone and gobble up handfuls of extra vitamins and so-called health supplements. *Bad* idea. Often, adult acne turns out to be caused by excessive amounts of vitamins or health foods. This is because many multivitamins and mineral supplements contain large amounts of iodide and bromide substances that can cause pustular skin eruptions. Startlingly, many health foods, such as kelp and wheat germ, are just as bad. Kelp is full of iodides, and wheat germ stimulates the sebaceous glands to secrete excessive amounts of oil, which can bring on an acne flare-up.

Vitamin therapy can have other negative side effects. The fad of applying vitamin E oil to the skin can cause allergic reactions or acne, and there's no proof that it has any healing effect. Too much vitamin A can yellow the skin (especially the palms) and make it dry.

It is not that vitamins are intrinsically bad for you but that it is not uncommon to unwittingly take an overdose. Vitamins are as easy to get as they are to abuse. For a woman in her thirties, excessive vitamin intake can exacerbate all the natural problems that time inflicts upon her skin. It is literally too much of a good thing.

Information about vitamins and nutrition can be found elsewhere in the book. But one vitamin-like substance that's worth special mention of its own regarding skin is "vitamin F," more correctly called essential fatty acids. Skin grows from the inside out, and as new layers form below, old layers are continually shed off the top; these fatty acids help control skin metabolism and the rate of surface-cell shedding. Vitamin F is essential to regular health maintenance of this basic body system, and diets that eliminate these substances are, by definition, bad for the skin. Major sources are whole milk, cereal grains, and vegetable oils (corn, safflower, and olive).

Vitamin F also comes from lard and the white fat on meat, but these are saturated fats and are not recommended for most thirty-year-old women.

Fast food, such as burgers and fries, is not good for your skin, but not for the reason you might suspect. The food itself is fine; if you cooked it at home you could eat it with impunity. The problem arises from the laudable attempts of fast food restaurants to stay sanitary. Cooking equipment (particularly deep fryers) is often cleaned with high-iodine solutions. The iodine gets into the food (in very small amounts) and increases your chances of developing pimples.

The other drawback of fast food, of interest to us dieters, is the artificial sweetener in soda. Sugar substitutes can sensitize the skin to sunlight. They are strong enough to induce a bad burn in skin that's normally highly resistant to the sun. The increased sun wallop deepens the already vast impact of the sun on skin. So don't sip diet cola when you're tanning—or else.

More important than vitamins for healthy skin are calories. Really radical dieting can wreak havoc with your skin. If starved of calories, skin will literally begin to break down. Even worse, the use of some kinds of diet pills can adversely affect the skin. Water pills can dehydrate skin making it flaky and wrinkled. They may also make you itch like the devil—especially in dry environments.

Amphetamines, another ingredient of diet medications, can affect hormone levels. This can cause hair to fall out, make you miss your menstrual period or even get a bad case of acne. Human gonadotrophic injections can throw your own hormonal levels out of whack and may bring on large acne breakouts and hair loss. Fortunately, the FDA warns against them, so you probably won't have to worry about them.

SKIN TREATMENT

Even the best-fed skin requires decent treatment to stay smooth and even-looking. A problem many of us have in our thirties is that we treat our skin the same way we did at twenty, while what our skin needs from us has changed.

When we're young we tend to have oily skin, but it gradually dries as we grow older. Your skin today is probably much drier than it was when you were twenty. As a result, it can tolerate oil-based products much better. Cosmetics that suited you perfectly a decade ago may no longer suit you now.

In general, skin care practices don't change too much by your thirties. You should cleanse your face first thing every morning. If you change or reapply your makeup during the day, always cleanse your face and start from scratch, and clean all your makeup off before you go to bed.

Some techniques should change. For example, when you wash your face, never use hot water. It causes vasodilation—an expansion of skin capillaries—which, in turn, can lead to redness, blotchiness, and prominent veins. Always wash your face with cool or lukewarm water.

You'd probably blanch if I told you to soak your skin in urine. But in reality, you probably already do. Women have used uric acid, a major component of urine, to keep their skin moist for centuries. Babylonian women kept the skin of their legs soft and supple by wrapping their legs in urine-soaked towels. Today, cosmetics often contain urea, a close chemical relative of uric acid. Urea is a hydrophilic compound, which means it attracts and holds moisture. It helps keep skin from being too dry. So urine derivatives on our face are actually good for our skin.

SKIN PROBLEMS

The biggest skin problem most of us will have in our thirties and beyond is learning to cope with dryness. Our skin will begin to dry out naturally. Personal factors can affect the rate of change and where on the face we get driest first. Much of the course of skin change is a matter of heredity. In many other cases, however, you may cause dry skin yourself by overwashing your face or overtreating an acne problem with extremely drying acne medicines. Contrary to popular notion, the sun isn't good for dry skin. Although sun. exposure does occasionally help some dry-skinned people, its usual effect is to dehydrate the skin, making dryness worse. If you swim in chlorinated pools, take too many saunas, or live in the desert, your skin may become dry. Similarly, water pills or one of the several types of birth control pills can also lead to increased dryness.

My advice for women with dry skin is to bathe less often during the winter. Shower or bathe every other day, if you can, and for less time. Too much bathing dries the skin, especially if you use scented soap. Despite the seemingly logical notion that soaking in water ought to keep skin moist, what really happens is that it removes whatever protective oils are left, making things worse. A shower is less drying than total immersion in a tubful of water. The hotter the water, the more your skin will be dehydrated. I know it feels grand to soak for hours in steaming water, but if your skin is dry you end up feeling pretty uncomfortable. Your best bet is to keep the water a little on the cool side of lukewarm. And always use bath oil. In fact, use twice as much bath oil as the bottle tells you. Don't stay in the bath for longer than five minutes. I'm serious. Keep a clock where you can see it from the tub, or bring in a timer.

Soothing skin masks are a longstanding method for moisturizing drying, aging skin, and a wide selection of commercial masks can be found at any cosmetics counter. Smooth the mixture on, lie back and let the mask harden, then peel it off in one piece if possible. After a quick warm-water wash, your freshly moisturized skin will feel great and look wonderful.

While we tend toward dryness in the thirties, some of us are still coping with residual problems of youthful oiliness. If your skin is still oily you might try washing with freshly squeezed lemon or orange juice from time to time instead of soap. You can degrease your skin this way without affecting the acid mantle, which many doctors claim is important to maintaining healthy skin. You can also use juice to cut through oil on just a part of your skin. Remember, one of the characteristics of thirty-year-old skin is a changing pattern of oiliness and dryness. Sections may be oily even as others are cracking and peeling.

SKIN CHANGES AND COSMETICS

These problems of changing skin and variations in our skin's needs can affect our choice of makeup, too. Happily, the changes our skin undergoes as we move through the thirties make it easier for us to wear more kinds of makeup. The oiliness of our skin when younger made it unwise for most of us to use oil-based preparations; they'd clog our pores and bring on acne. Now, with drier skin, we can use just about any foundation makeup we want. In fact, we may find oil-based preparations better because they help hold moisture on our skin.

Also, since it's been around for more years and has grown a bit less sensitive, our skin today will generally allow us to use more cosmetics than we could a decade ago, without side effects. If a makeup you really liked caused you problems in college, you might want to retry it now. Cautiously.

Hypoallergenic makeups, formulated to reduce allergic reactions, become much less important to women our age. We're pretty unlikely to react to a carefully made cosmetic, so the extra money for hypoallergenic certification is probably wasted.

One makeup worry not to ignore is infection via mascara. It can wreck your eyes. The case of Marigold Padgett of Atlanta shows what can happen. She scratched her eye while applying mascara. Later that day, her eye turned red and began to hurt. Soon, she was hospitalized. Her eye was infected by *Pseudomonas aeruginosa*, a bacteria that can live in mascara. Despite prompt treatment, Padgett lost part of her cornea and nearly 25 percent of the vision in the infected eye.

Historically, health risks have not deterred women from using makeup. In seventeenth-century Italy, women used arsenic to make their cheeks rosy. Only after several women died from arsenic poisoning did Italy pass the first cosmetics regulations.

Today, we women continue to risk our health—sometimes willingly—in quest of youthful looks. Some women continue wearing mascara even after they've suffered bacterial infection.

Serious eye damage from mascara is not common, but the bacteria are. Dr. Louis Wilson of Emory University, who spent six years studying eye cosmetic contamination, found, in a study of several thousand eye cosmetics used by office workers, that half were contaminated with bacteria.[1] A study of demonstrator mascaras at retail cosmetics counters showed that more than half were contaminated.[2] Contaminated mascara may cause not only corneal ulcers but also sties, inflamed eyelids, and loss of eyelashes.

Most cosmetics are free from contamination when first purchased. However, each time you use it and then dip back into the tube, you may plant bacteria inside. Most mascara contains preservatives, but they tend to break down over several months, increasing user risk over time. So, keep your mascara fresh; buying more often is better than waiting too long.

If you use mascara and redness or soreness is bothering your eyes, don't assume it's allergies, nerves, or age. It may be mascara, so see a doctor.

ADULT ACNE

It's extremely frustrating to go into our thirties suffering from a problem of our teens, but we do. Adult acne is a hidden problem. You never hear it mentioned in commercials, and articles about it are rare. But the fact remains that quite a few of us still have some sort of acne flare-up in our thirties. And the embarrassment and frustration we feel is far greater than when we were younger.

Perversely, the hormone changes we are prone to during the fourth decade can increase our chances of getting acne. Some unfortunate thirty-year-olds get pimples for the first time now.

All types of factors can induce acne attacks in thirty-year-old women. Here are a few:

Many women experience some acne when they stop taking birth control pills. Skin eruptions occur because of the resurgence of hormonal activity after a long period of pill-induced repression. It may take six months to a year for the imbalance to subside.

Perversely, staying *on* birth control pills can predispose some women toward acne. If you have facial problems from your pills, see if your doctor can help you by changing to a different type.

Athletic women may have special acne problems because they sweat more. The acne is a side effect of perspiration trapped against the skin. Wearing loose garments when you engage in sports can help.

Other medications, such as danazol for endometriosis, steroids, and certain chemicals like dioxins and PCBs, can spur acne formation. Strong industrial chemicals can cause even more severe skin breakouts, with pits, cysts, and inflamed sores. If you have chronic skin problems, investigate your environment for a toxic chemical that may be adversely affecting you.

Inveterate makeup wearers should be sure they use a makeup that won't hurt their skin. They should test new makeup brands on an inconspicuous patch of skin before using it on the face.

Researchers feel your family history plays an important role in determining whether you will suffer from acne. If adult acne runs in your family take preventive measures early.

Sometimes our diet is an unsuspected cause of acne, but not in the way most of us think. It's not chocolate, french fries, or sugar that causes acne. Acne is caused by hormone changes that stimulate excessive production by sweat glands. None of these substances has any effect on your hormones.

The true cause lies with foods high in iodides, bromides, and androgen-like compounds. These include many health foods, such as wheat germ and kelp, shellfish, peanuts, organ meats such as kidney and liver; and vitamin E, which has a molecular structure similar to androgens. The fewer iodides, bromides, and androgen-like substances in the diet, the fewer attacks of acne. For thirty-year-olds this is particularly important to keep in mind, since so many of us turn to health foods for dieting or fad reasons.

All acne medicines, be they obtained by prescription or over-the-counter, contain varying mixtures of the same chemicals: alcohol (for drying); salicylic acid (for peeling); sulfur (for peeling and mild antibacterial action); and resorcinol (also for peeling). None of the products made from these ingredients affect hormone levels or the rate of oil secretion, so they can't cure acne. But they do promote drying and peeling that can counter the oiliness that is acne's primary catalyst. So for mild attacks they're fine.

By the way, pimples and blackheads can be squeezed.

But beware: while this can relieve pressure and swelling and shorten the time a pimple hangs around, it carries two dangers. One is mundane: if you botch the job, the pimple may get worse. Don't be squeamish—squeeze hard and break the offender open.

Think twice, however, before squeezing a pimple in the "triangle of death." This zone lies on either side of your nose and on the forehead area between your eyes. The reason for this name is that a bad infection here, because of communicating blood channels, can lead to an infection of the brain or meningitis. Still, each of us has squeezed pimples in this area and lived but the fact that we and nearly everyone else are usually lucky at squeezing does not eliminate the possibility that we could some day contract a fatal infection. So be careful.

About the worst kind of acne for us adults is the stress pimple. A zit before a big date was devastating, but a blackhead before a sales presentation can seem catastrophic. Here our mind interferes with normal hormonal activities. Obviously the prescription is to relax, but this is easier said than done. If you're getting married tomorrow afternoon and have a pimple as big as the nose on your face, you'll need more help than soothing words to calm down.

Fortunately, a dermatologist can help in these cases—with an intralesional steroid injection. She takes a little needle and gives you a shot of an antiinflammatory chemical, right into the pimple. Amazingly, it really works. The pimple will disappear within twenty-four hours in almost every case. This is the fastest method; antibiotic pills or drying solutions applied topically won't have any demonstrable effect within the first twenty-four hours.

For severe acne, a typical prescription is oral antibiotics for six to eight weeks, followed by a switch to topical treatment. Vitamin A acid is one topical preparation for such uses. Taking vitamin A orally will not do the trick. In any case, large doses of vitamin A can be dangerous, since it's a fat-soluble vitamin that accumulates in our fat cells, causing problems when the concentrations get high. And it won't help acne. No vitamin pill will help cure acne.

The great trouble with using oral antibiotics as a cure for acne is that they often produce the side effect of Monilia vaginitis, a fungus infection. As a result, topical antibiotic treatments are growing ever more popular. Two you might consider are tetracycline, which has the slight disadvantage that it temporarily stains the skin, and clindamycin, which is more widely used and seems to be at least as good as oral antibiotics.

For truly severe cases of acne, scientists are experimenting with preparations that use retinoids—synthetic cousins of vitamin A. The main drawback is that their effectiveness against acne is usually accompanied by serious skin irritations. However, one of the experimental drugs, 13-cis retinoic acid, has shown great promise in early tests.

SWEAT RETENTION SYNDROME

Without any doubt sweat retention syndrome is the most common sweating problem among young women. It seems to be stress-related and, for unknown reasons, hits hardest in winter. The syndrome is characterized by small, incredibly itchy sweat-filled blisters that erupt on the sides of the fingers and the edges of the feet.

The typical case is that of a woman who finds herself a bumpy, itchy mess just after the birth of a baby, or after a divorce, or other stressful event. She's miserable and the only treatment for her is to calm down. Massage, sauna, even Valium if necessary—anything to relieve the tension. That is the key to this situation. Most important, she must resist the understandable nervous temptation to overwash her hands like Lady Macbeth. This only reirritates the skin, especially when she follows the vigorous soapy washing by applying alcohol-containing skin cream. Shove your hands in your pockets and suffer stoically.

Generally, though, women in their thirties perspire less than twenty-year-olds, because they're less anxious about their lives. They've been exposed to anxiety-provoking stimuli over a longer period of time and therefore they're less apt to get nervous in the next such situation. Also, our sweat glands slow down as we age.

WRINKLES

As we get older, we wrinkle. It's inevitable, and begins in earnest during our thirties. The primary causes are deterioration of elastic skin tissue and dehydration. Neither of these processes can be stopped, but they can be slowed a bit. At the same time, while there are many things we can do to make wrinkles look better, nothing can stop them from appearing altogether. We can't stop the spread of facial lines and creases that steadily engraves our personalities and experiences on our faces.

The kind of life you lead etches itself in your skin. A woman who lived a very outdoor life in her twenties, with a lot of sun exposure, will wrinkle much earlier than her hothouse compatriot. Her situation will probably be exacerbated if she smokes. People who smoke wrinkle more. A lot more. The biggest impact of this doesn't hit in the thirties, but it starts then. Thirty-year-old smoking makes fifty-year-old wrinkles. I can see a fifty-year-old woman from across the room and tell you that she smokes a pack or a pack and a half a day. Fair warning.

What can you do about wrinkles? Here are some current treatments.

ESTROGEN THERAPY

Estrogen, a female hormone, is what makes our skin smooth and soft and helps maintain skin tone. Recently, some women have begun to take it orally as their body's natural levels of estrogen decline. The results of this treatment can be quite dramatic, and might lead you to think that everybody over fifty should be taking estrogen pills.

But nothing in life is that simple. Estrogen therapy is currently the subject of intense medical investigation because many doctors are concerned that it may promote or precipitate cancer. Fortunately, we women in our thirites are still synthesizing estrogen naturally and don't need any extra right now.

INCREASING CELL RENEWAL RATES

Our skin grows from the inside out. Cells are constantly being born way down in the basal layer of the epidermis. Here they are plump and full of moisture. As they migrate up toward the outer, tough layer of skin, they become drier and flatter. Eventually, after serving on the front line at the surface, they die and are shed, to be replaced by a new layer.

This cell journey takes three to four weeks in a younger person, but slows down as we grow older. Makers of cell renewal products claim that they speed up the process again, on the theory that the shorter the journey, the younger the skin cells at the surface will be.

Dermatologist Dr. Jack Cella explained it this way in a 1981 article: "Those cells which stay in the outermost layer a longer time appear to dry out faster. But if the cells stay there a shorter time, they behave—and look —like younger cells. And that means your skin appears softer, more moist and younger-looking."[3] Another specialist, Dr. John Penicnak, agreed, adding, "If the skin cells get to the surface faster, they are separated from the lower layers—their source of nutrients—for a shorter time, so there's less chance for chemical reactions to occur. Therefore, they reach the top in better condition."[4] Many doctors, including myself, remain skeptical about this argument.

ELASTIN TREATMENT

Elastin is a protein found in the lowest level of the skin that works with collagen to give skin its suppleness. Age or sun damage can cause elastin to deteriorate, literally robbing the skin of its ability to bounce back. Some cosmeticians believe that when elastin is added to moisturizers, it can improve skin tone by helping to bind water on the skin's surface. It's probably of some use if you keep in mind that the benefits of elastin are temporary. It works only at the surface and only as long as it's on your skin. Elastin cannot penetrate the connective tissues and revive the original fibers.

ZYDERM

A new medical technique can help diminish acne scars, furrows between the brows, deep expression lines and other flaws that mar our complexions. It involves the injection into the skin of a highly purified collagen protein called Zyderm, which fills up the skin beneath the depressions, making the surface smooth and diminishing the scar or wrinkle.

The implant is a whitish, odorless gel made from a highly purified form of collagen derived from cattle skin. Like natural body collagen, Zyderm is composed of individual fibers that intertwine with each other when warmed to body temperature.

Treatment with Zyderm consists of a series of pinpoint injections directly into the furrow or scar. Because the needle is so fine and the substance contains a local anesthetic, the procedure is not painful and may be done in the doctor's office. The injection is usually followed by the symptoms of slight swelling, mild soreness and redness, which should subside within twenty-four hours. Because it is difficult for a doctor to judge just how much Zyderm is needed to build up the depression, two or three injections, given about two to three weeks apart, are usually required. Each prospective patient, by the way, is pretested with a small injection into the forearm to make sure no preexisting allergy to the Zyderm is present. This test implantation is observed for four weeks before any Zyderm treatment begins.

Initially the injection works by pushing up the skin depression so that it is raised to the level of the surrounding skin. More exciting, once the Zyderm is injected, it provides a framework or matrix for new cells and blood vessels to grow into the new area, making the change more lasting. Unlike silicone, it does not migrate or harden, and within a week or so it feels exactly like your own tissue.

Zyderm works most effectively on shallow acne scars, lines caused by frowning or smiling (including forehead lines and the deep lines that run from nostrils to mouth), postsurgical scars, and indentations caused by injury or accident. It does not work well on tiny superficial skin creases like under-eye lines or on rough scars.

How long does Zyderm correction last? Once the implant is in place the corrected area will change at about the same pace as natural skin tissue. So, if frowning caused the lines originally, the habit will bring them back again. On the average, optimistically, there is a 10 percent loss of correction over a period of fourteen months, but additional Zyderm may be injected at that time. Remember, though, that this bovine cartilage compound is still experimental. The long-range effects, including possible initiation of tumors, delayed allergic reaction and possible subsequent reaction to other cow proteins (such as insulin), are still unknown. And, Zyderm is very expensive; a tiny vial containing roughly one-eighth of a teaspoon costs over $150—wholesale.

FACE LIFTS

Most of us won't have to think about a face lift in our thirties. The typical face-lift patient is over forty. But some of us suffer from accumulated wrinkles and sagging skin severely enough that this operation isn't unheard of in our decade. To begin with, face lifting, contrary to popular misconception, does not tighten up the muscles at all. It is merely a stretching of the skin. The doctor makes easy-to-hide incisions in the skin, then peels the surface back with a scalpel, pulls it tight, and finally snips off any extra skin. Scars are concealed behind the ears or under the hairline. After surgery the face looks less flabby, more youthful, and the sags are diminished. For women with serious skin aging, the results of face lifts can be quite dramatic.

Keep in mind, though, that as time goes by your skin will continue to sag, so that in about five years you may want another lift. The procedure can be repeated, but it gets harder each time—and more expensive.

If you're going to the trouble of a face lift, you might want to have additional cosmetic surgery done at the same time. Having several operations at once costs less than undertaking the work in pieces. In any case, the cost and the trauma of the surgery mean you'd better be as well-to-do as you are healthy.

BLEPHAROPLASTY

This operation tucks up droopy eyelids and baggy circles beneath the eyes. It's a neat, short, very effective procedure. The surgeon cuts along the natural lines around the eye, then snips out the tiny pockets of fat that have accumulated under the skin.

The most serious complication of plastic surgery arises when we expect too much of it. Plastic surgery can bring about improvement, not perfection. But there will always be those among us whose expectations are unrealistic and whose egos aren't strong enough to bear imagined or real defects.

A last word on this subject: get the right doctor. All those who perform plastic surgery aren't necessarily plastic surgeons. A licensed doctor can theoretically perform any medical procedure. Make sure your doctor *specializes* in the procedure you are interested in, and is board-certified.

Now that I've catalogued the various remedies for wrinkles, let me just reiterate the old adage about a stitch in time . . . The time to care for your skin properly is now. The time to stop smoking (and not just to prevent wrinkles) is now. I am *not* an advocate of costly creams or injections, or even more costly surgery, in lieu of daily skin care.

I'd like to conclude this discussion about wrinkles by pointing out that a total absence of wrinkles is a sign of ill health. Extreme tightening of the skin may be a sign of a disease called scleroderma. Most people who have scleroderma don't have a wrinkle on them. They don't have wrinkles where they're supposed to have them. That's one of the things doctors look for when we look at your hands—do you have all the wrinkles you're supposed to, such as over your knuckles and at your elbows? You're supposed to have some wrinkling of the face as you age, as well. If you smile you'll wrinkle some. In scleroderma the skin is so taut it's wrinkleless.

SKIN COLOR CHANGES

Even on normal smooth skin, there are changes with age. So-called age spots or liver spots occur most frequently on the hands of individuals well beyond their thirties. But you can see age-related pigmentary changes in your skin by our decade. There is a coalescence of pigment, a slight unevening of skin color. It's frequently found on the hands or arms, essentially in the most sun-exposed areas. It's nothing to be concerned about, and there's not much that can be done for it.

We are also prone to a variety of growths that range in color from almost bright cherry red to a dark brown. These are the sorts of things that women in their thirties see one day and panic over. They will come in to me and say, "This appeared—what is it? Do I need to worry about it?" Almost always, the answer is no. Many of these growths have some hereditary basis; if your mother had similar changes, you shouldn't be alarmed. Some of these growths can be treated chemically, but most are around for the duration, unless you have them surgically removed. Of course, any spot that grows quickly, has a blue or gray cast, or bleeds should be evaluated by a physician. So should spots that have a variegated color or an irregular border.

STRETCH MARKS

Stretch marks result from tearing of the subcutaneous tissue, the layers of skin that lie just below the surface. They can occur anywhere that rapid or excessive growth of either fat or muscle exceeds the elastic properties of the skin. Initially, stretch marks appear purple or red, but eventually they turn white.

Since our skin in the thirties is a bit less stretchy than it used to be, our tendency toward stretch marks may be expected to increase. Of course, if we don't stretch our skin out, we won't have to worry about them. But a thirty-year-old woman who gets pregnant can figure on getting more of them than she would have a decade earlier.

We might take comfort in the thought that, contrary to what most of us believe, men can get them too, particularly if they work out extensively with weights. All that bulky muscle stretches the skin too fast.

Unfortunately, there is no remedy for stretch marks. If you keep your skin in good shape—supple and not overly dry—you may minimize their appearance. Occasionally rubbing a stretching area with oil may also help. But there is no sure preventive. Once they appear, nothing can make them vanish except time, which allows them to become steadily paler, until eventually they become invisible except on minute examination.

Once you've developed stretch marks, they will reoccur every time you stress that area, so you'll see the road map of your second pregnancy overlaid upon that of your first.

THE OFFENDING SUN

The biggest offender of all against skin is the sun. If you want to look like an alligator suitcase by your forties, lie in the sun unprotected every day during your thirties. Suntanning is the ultimate short-term payoff situation. You look good the day afterward, but the net result is wrinkles and much worse. Women in their thirties are heir to enough wrinkles through nature's gentle nudge that they don't need any help from the sun. So we, more than any other age group, should be careful on the beach and the rooftop garden.

Most dermatologists see red if you question them about sun exposure. Advertisements that say "Get a tan and keep the man . . . develop a deep, dark, sensuous tan . . . make the most of your summer" and so on abound, but dermatologists don't buy advertising time, and what they would have to say doesn't sell products.

Thirty-year-old women should have one overriding concern about sun and skin. That is to consider the carcinogenic potential of sunbathing, past, present, and future. Sun exposure is a tan now, pay later situation. You pay the price much later for what appears to be something fantastic now. And your sunny past may have already hit you with a serious wallop that's waiting to emerge as wrinkles and other problems. Every day you get closer to the payout period.

Your skin actually has sun memory. Dr. John A. Parrish, a dermatologist at Massachusetts General Hospital, has recently finished a study that finds that the skin has a "memory" of past sun exposure.[5] In other words, each new exposure isn't new; there is a cumulative effect. The study confirms that you don't have to burn to do genetic injury to the makeup of your cells. Even if you're careful never to get a sunburn, only a tan, you still have caused damage to your skin. So it's important to always use a sunscreen. Creams, lotions, and gels containing PABA or PABA esters are most widely used. Zinc oxide, which acts as an opaque barrier to keep radiation from reaching the skin, is another common sunscreen. Zinc-based screens work best on limited areas of vulnerability, such as the nose, cheekbones, and lips.

Manufacturers of commercial sunscreens are required to specify the "sun protection factor," or SPF, of their product on the label. This value is determined by comparing the amount of time required to produce redness of the skin through their sunscreen product to the amount of time required to produce the same amount of redness without any protection. SPF values range from 2, minimal protection, to 15, super protection.

One factor not listed on the label is the substantivity of the sunscreen. This means the ability of the product to remain effective under the stresses of sweating, swimming, and prolonged exercise. Substantivity of screen relates to both the absorbing agent and the vehicle used. Recent studies suggest that certain formulations of PABA with other chemicals may have a greater substantivity level than PABA by itself. In addition, products that use a cream as a vehicle may be more resistant to removal than those using an alcohol base. Whichever sunscreen you use should be applied one or two hours before you face the sun, and then reapplied generously while you're out there, particularly after sweating or swimming. Remember: no sunscreen offers total protection; if you tan at all, you're harming your skin. But the screens greatly reduce the impact.

Before we leave screens to ride off into the sunset, here are some cautions about PABA problems. PABA may stain clothing yellow, and can produce allergic reactions in women who are allergic to benzocaine or procaine products. A woman who is allergic to thiazide diuretics or to sulfa drugs may also have a reaction to sunscreens that contain PABA or PABA salts. Imagine the unhappiness of spending an entire day on the beach sore and itching, only to come home and find everything in your beach bag turned butter yellow from the PABA.

Not only does the raging solar furnace's ability to tan your hide vary with the sunscreen you use, but sun tolerance varies from woman to woman. Physicians classify skin into four types according to how much sun it can stand. Type 1 skin is described as always burning very readily and never tanning. Type 2 skin also burns very quickly but does eventually tan a little. Type 3 skin burns but gradually tans, and lucky type 4 skin burns minimally and tans readily.

Frequently women with skin types 1 and 2 will have very pale skin and light-colored eyes and hair. They may or may not freckle. These women will have exceeded their sunburn threshold after just twenty to thirty minutes of noontime summer sun, while women with type 4 skin may not develop redness (which, by the way, we doctors dub erythema) even after forty-five minutes of exposure.

Myths about how to achieve the best, deepest, darkest tan abound. The most common is that sun preparation X is better than preparation Y in promoting a tan. This is entirely false. No suntan lotion or sunscreen *promotes* tanning. Rather, all sunscreens *protect* against sunburn, while the various mineral oils, baby oils, and lotions stuffing the tanning displays lubricate the skin without promoting even a wan tan. Products such as Coppertone QT contain a compound called—take a deep breath—dihydroxyacetone, a colorless chemical that reacts with the skin to produce an orange-yellow-brown coloration. This coloration may last for days or weeks, but it doesn't look much like a natural tan and provides very little protection against sunburn. In other words, with fake coloration you could wind up "tan" and sunburned at the same time.

Another myth about tanning is that you can't get a tan in the shade or on a cloudy day. Most of us, by the time we are thirty, realize that we can be out of direct sunlight on a bright day and still get enough reflected and scattered sunlight to cause a sunburn. This is particularly true if we lie near water or bright sand. Likewise, a hat offers protection from direct sunlight but may still allow reflected sun to hit the face. Of all causes, water probably increases reflection the most. With the sun directly overhead, water may reflect nearly 100 percent of the ultraviolet rays into our faces; if the sun is not directly overhead a much smaller percentage of ultraviolet radiation is reflected. Sand reflects perhaps 25 percent of UV radiation. Snow is also an excellent reflector, bouncing 70 to 90 percent of the light, as do white-painted surfaces or sheets of aluminum—so consider all aspects when you protect against sunlight.

Altitude also affects the intensity of ultraviolet light. Each increase of one thousand feet in altitude adds 4 percent to the intensity of the sun's burn-producing ultraviolet rays. If you are a mile high (assuming you aren't someplace terribly smoggy, like Mexico City), the ray intensity is 20 percent greater than it would be at sea level. In other words, you'll tan—and burn—faster up high, so you need to be that much more careful in the mountains than on the beach.

Technically, what happens to the skin upon exposure to ultraviolet light is an inflammatory reaction in the cells that leaves them scarred. Actual degeneration of connective tissue in the skin occurs with prolonged sun exposure. It is hard to avoid the bottom line that if you tan a lot when you are young, you wrinkle a lot when you are old. Even worse: the areas that show aging first, such as around the mouth and on the neck, are more sensitive to the aging effect of sun than the rest of us. Unprotected exposure will make them look older sooner. Therefore, if you must have a tan, it's better to protect your face and perhaps just tan your arms and legs.

Nobody listens to us doctors on this subject. Tanning is simply too popular. Unfortunately, the old joke among dermatologists is still true, if not very funny (doctors have a peculiar sense of humor about medical subjects). Question: What do you call white people who live in the sun? Answer: Patients. The unanswerable fact on sun exposure is that you can have either a constant tan now or smooth skin later—but not both.

It seems appropriate to mention the worst thing the sun can do to your skin—produce skin cancer. At least skin cancer generally doesn't maim or kill you. Most skin cancers look like a sore or ulcer and usually don't spread beyond their original site. If untreated, they can cause serious trouble internally, but generally women notice the sore early and it can be removed, hopefully leaving a minimal cosmetic defect.

There is an excellent and fairly new topically applied prescription drug for sun-damaged areas, called 5-fluorouracil. Available as a cream or solution, 5-fluorouracil is an intriguing chemical that seeks out disorganized and cancerous skin tissue. It selectively destroys the errant cells while leaving surrounding tissue relatively untouched. The drug can even tell if certain areas that look fine now will show signs of sun damage in the near future. When damaged and disorganized cells are destroyed, fresh new skin will grow, and eventually an even skin tone will be restored. Results with 5-fluorouracil are best on the face and scalp, and less impressive on the hands and forearms.

LIPS

Lips, for all their suppleness, are tough. Aside from the occasional cold sore, lips heal up remarkably well, remaining soft and smooth far longer than other kinds of skin.

Lip skin is significantly different from the rest of your hide. If you looked at epidermal cells from your lips under a microscope they would appear flattened. For this reason, lip skin is thinner and more sensitive both to changes in interior chemistry and influences in the environment. That's why kissing is so involving.

Like the rest of your skin, your lips serve as an interface between you and the outside world. They are often exposed to sun and weather, exotic foodstuffs and the substantial variety of chemicals found in modern health and beauty products. For all this, the lips remain amazingly durable. It's interesting to note that, of the pair, the lower lip suffers the greater share of problems, mainly because it gets more sun exposure. To prevent sun damage to your lips I recommend that you use an emollient like Chap Stick with sunscreen. It's invisible but keeps lips from getting badly sunburned.

If you treat your lips kindly and take simple precautions like this, your lips should remain youthful through this decade, the next, and for years beyond.

HANDS

Hands are among the most exposed of our body parts. We slam them against things and dump them into hot, dirty water. The wind whips at them. We cover them with dirt or ink or snow.

As a result, hands tend to reveal the wear and tear on our bodies more than just about any other part of us. A certain amount of weathering over time is inevitable. The ladies of olden times were forbidden to do anything with their hands lest they lose their soft smoothness. We want to lead active lives. Work, exercise, gardening— virtually any activity will take its toll on our hands. What we want to avoid are calloused, hard-seamed, grainy hands that destroy the image the rest of us attempts to convey.

Dryness is hand enemy number one, and preventing it should be our first priority. Surprisingly, reducing hand washing and using a good hand cream still might not be enough to prevent dry hands at all times. Those of us who are working with babies and cooking meals, or who are office workers (especially around Xerox machines), can get especially dry hands. When we are in particularly drying circumstances, we should use a nifty, inexpensive item called a fingercot.

A fingercot looks like a rubber thimble. You use it to prevent cracked and excessively dry fingertips. Place a bit of cream or ointment on the fingertip, pull on a fingercot, and go back to work. The light, snug fingercot won't interfere with your activity at all, while it moisturizes your parched fingertips.

One of the most widely accepted myths about hand care concerns the soothing properties of white liquid hand lotions. Although they smell good and soothe for about five minutes, they ultimately dry the skin. Hand lotions cannot provide lasting protection because they evaporate and their alcohol base strips existing moisture from the skin, leaving the hand drier than it was in the first place. Creams or ointments are preferable.

HAIR

Your hair, like your fingernails, is extremely responsive to your internal milieu. You can tell a number of things about yourself by examining your hair. Hormonal changes, in particular, affect hair. If your thyroid is overactive, for example, there may be a thinning of the hair. You may even lose some hair, and what you have may become much finer and oilier than it was in the past. If, on the other hand, your thyroid is underactive, you will have very dry, brittle hair. Those of us with inadequate diets tend to have hair that breaks readily, is dry, flyaway, or frizzy; in extreme cases, naturally straight hair will start to grow in curly. Hair changes don't require tremendous internal shifts. Some occur simply through time. Like the skin, the hair becomes drier with age; it loses some of its sheen and luster. This change is the result of diminished oil production by hair follicles.

The hormonal changes that accompany our increasing age may result in thinning hair. The hormone with the worst effect on hair is the "male" hormone androgen. All of us produce androgen in our ovaries and adrenal glands. As we grow older, our naturally high level of estrogen—the female sex hormone—begins to fall. Most often this occurs after menopause, but sporadic deep drops in estrogen levels sometimes affect women in the thirties. Hair follicles find themselves undefended against the existing androgen, which had been tolerated without notice until then. They shut down.

So sensitive is our hair that problems that ordinarily are considered insignificant can ruin it. A few doctors today feel that a subclinical symptomless deficiency of iron may cause hair loss in a few women of our age. A subclinical deficiency wouldn't have any apparent effect at all. But since hair follicles are the most rapidly metabolizing structures in our bodies, any deficiency affects them first. You can feel fine, be vigorous and energetic, and still have a subclinical iron deficiency that could cause your hair to fall out. However, iron deficiency is an extremely uncommon cause of hair loss.

To properly test for iron deficiency you must get two tests—a serum iron test and a serum total iron-binding capacity test—both of which can be made from a small sample of your blood. The serum iron test measures the amount of iron in your bloodstream; serum total iron-binding capacity establishes your blood's capacity to hold iron. A normal ratio of iron capacity is 1 to 5; if yours is 1 to 7 or more and you're losing your hair, you might have a subclinical deficiency. Take iron supplements and see if the problem subsides. However, there is a natural time lag between the introduction of any substance into our systems and any noticeable effect on our hair. So, it may take at least a few months for iron therapy to show positive impact.

Problems other than hidden iron deficiency may be causing your hair to thin prematurely. Malnutrition, for example, a condition that can afflict the diet faddist among us, definitely causes hair to fall out. Fad diets tend to eliminate whole blocks of necessary vitamins, which harms our metabolically sensitive hair. Even worse, some dieting women haven't had a balanced meal in years. They skip from one bizarre diet to the next, heedless of the cumulative damage they do to their systems. Eventually, that damage etches visible effects on their bodies.

Physical shocks, illness, and some medicines can also foster hair loss. If your hair is thinning, you should probably avoid chemicals and medicines as much as possible. Even such common medications as cortisone, antithyroid drugs, borates (found in boric acid and mouthwashes), aspirin (sad but true), excessive amounts of vitamin A, amphetamines, and some antibiotics can cause hair to fall out in some circumstances. Beginning or ending oral contraceptive pills can cause temporary hair loss.

Any substantial shock to the system can be followed in about three months by some degree of hair loss. Anything from childbirth to being hit by a bus could qualify as a major shock.

What causes healthy young women to lose hair most often, however, isn't illness or physical trauma; it's stress. Not only will stress wreak havoc with your heart and your skin, but even your hair suffers when you rage against the outside world.

Some women suffer from a nervous, stress-related condition known as trichotilomania, in which they sit and in agitation twirl, pull, and eventually yank out strands of their hair. After a long enough bout of this behavior, victims begin to get thin patches. Incredibly, they almost never realize that they've been pulling out their hair. In fact, sufferers often react violently to the suggestion that they are their hair's own worst enemy. Hypnosis is probably the best treatment for this unconscious bad habit.

No matter what anyone tells you nothing can make hair grow faster. You can make your hair look thicker and richer, though, by coating the outside surfaces with protein. Simply add egg whites or powdered plain gelatin, along with a small amount of lemon juice, to your ordinary shampoo. The resulting lather will feel thicker, and so will your hair.

Hair is one of the areas of our bodies where preventive care shows to best effect. Since hair is so sensitive to changes, any positive habits we acquire—regular shampooing with mild shampoo, frequent gentle brushing, protecting our hair from intense sun or blustery weather—will show up as brighter, shinier hair rather quickly. And if our hair has grown dull and dispirited, a return to a sensible regimen can bring it back around in next to no time.

No one knows why humans develop gray hair, but what it amounts to is that the cells that are responsible for pigment formation lose their ability to synthesize pigment. This occurs at different rates in different women and at different rates in different hair follicles, so we typically don't turn gray all at once. Why, with sudden trauma, you can turn gray "overnight" is entirely unknown.

Contrary to popular notion, body hair turns gray, too. The process is just slower. Pigment will continue to be synthesized, but body hair does turn lighter with time. Eventually all of your hair will be white. It won't happen until you are very elderly, though.

Is there anything anybody can do to help slow down hair graying? Nope. At the same time most of us won't confront extensive graying until our mid-forties. However, if salt and pepper hair bothers you, buy some dye.

EXCESSIVE HAIR

In this modern era of airbrushed photography and unusual camera angles, we see women in magazines every day who have no excessive body hair, and don't even seem to have any hair on their arms or legs. As a consequence, many of us with perfectly normal hair patterns become concerned that we have excessive amounts of hair. It is not at all abnormal for us to have a few hairs around our nipples or to have some extension of hair up the middle of our bellies, particularly just after pregnancy. In addition, the spread of hair from the pubic area onto the beginning part of the thigh is entirely within normal limits.

On the other hand, extra facial or body hair associated with loss of cyclical menstrual patterns is cause for concern. This, along with such symptoms as balding in a male pattern at the temples, changes in body proportions, or deepening of the voice, may indicate the presence of endocrine abnormalities.

Our hair does not grow continuously but rather in a cyclical fashion, with phases of activity and inactivity. These phases are termed the anagen or growing phase, the catagen or involutional phase, and the telogen or quiescent phase. The length of the hair is determined primarily by the duration of the anagen phase. Scalp hair, for example, will remain in a growing phase for two to six years and then gets a relatively short rest. Other hair, such as forearm hair, has a short growing phase and a relatively long quiescent time, leading to short hairs. Hair on the scalp seems to grow continuously because each hair follicle acts independently of its neighbors, without any overall pattern, so that some hair is always growing. We can't see that some strands are not growing or are in a resting phase. Occasionally, the strands synchronize and for a very short but startling period of time it looks like regions of our head are going bald, but this time of shedding is generally very limited and is followed by a normal growth phase—and an enormous sigh of relief.

Synchronicity can also be caused by any severe illness, high fever, or even severe emotional stress. Sometimes such a situation occurs three to four months after childbirth. It has also been seen in association with severe caloric restriction such as occurs in anorexia nervosa.

Another interesting characteristic of hair growth can be understood from studies of castration. (Please, don't draw Freudian conclusions from this.) If a male is castrated before puberty, he will never grow a beard; however, if castration occurs after puberty, when the beard has fully developed, the hair will continue to grow, although more slowly, and will be of a finer texture. What this indicates is that once a pattern has been established or hair follicles have been stimulated, hair will persist in its original growing pattern despite withdrawal of the initiating stimulus. This is important for women to understand because it explains one of the most frustrating facts about hair problems. If a hormonal imbalance is found as the cause of excessive hair growth in women, it will take months, even years, for the hair growth to respond to treatment and decrease. Doctors can resolve the hormonal changes rapidly with medication, but the hair will persist in its stubborn path for a few months no matter what we do.

While they're waiting, I suggest that my patients with endocrine problems pursue additional, more immediate, forms of aid. Plucking will remove a few stray hairs, but the hair will regrow again in three to six weeks. Wax can be used to entrap protruding hairs and then pull them off the skin as a form of mass plucking. However, like plucking, this method is painful, and it can result in scarring if there is any infection of the hair follicles. Hair can be bleached with hydrogen peroxide to make it less apparent. A 20 percent by volume peroxide (it actually contains only 6 percent pure hydrogen peroxide) solution will make dark hair less obvious. Shaving is a satisfactory, if repetitive, method of removing hair from most parts of the body. It's quick, easy, effective, and does *not* result in a stimulation of additional hair growth, despite myths to the contrary. However, the hair that regrows after shaving does have a bristly appearance and feel to it. (Please note that breast hair should never be shaved or plucked; bleaching is okay, however.) Finally, there is a variety of chemical depilatories such as Nair and Neet to consider. These are compounds called thyoglycolates that chemically degrade hair. They are generally less irritating than the old sulfide types of depilatories, such as Magic Shaving Powder.

The only method of removing unwanted hair permanently is electrolysis. There are two types of electrolysis: one is galvanic low-voltage current, and the other is a short wave current, which is quicker but can result in scarring. Electrolysis is painful and may result in temporary local irritation or in pitlike scarring, but in the hands of a competent operator it will produce excellent and permanent results. For women with severe hair growth, electrolysis can be pursued on a gradual basis, as the budget allows, and combined with other means of treatment until the problem is under control.

NAILS

Our nails grow fastest during our second decade, and more slowly thereafter. Also, as we age, more calcium accumulates in our nails. This, contrary to popular belief, does not make our nails harder. Rather, it makes them more brittle. By the same token, eating gelatin does not have any known beneficial effect on nails. Like hair, nails are almost pure protein; gelatin is also pure protein, which is probably why the belief in its benefits has persisted for so long.

Nails are incredibly porous; they can absorb one hundred times as much water as an equal amount of skin. That's why they hold polish so well. Nail polishes, by the way, are tested so extensively that there's rarely a danger in using them, though occasionally quick-drying polishes can dehydrate and crack your nails.

Sometimes nails change color because of changes or problems in body functions. For example, a Vitamin B_{12} deficiency can cause your nails to blacken; certain antimalarial drugs can make blue-brown lines appear on nails. Phenolphthalein, a chemical found in both old-time laxatives and cheap wines, can bring on dark gray spots, while arsenic generates white bands. There are many other examples.

The most frequent cause of nail discoloration is a simple bruise. When a nail is struck by something hard, the nail bed bleeds into the area beneath the nail. This trapped blood soaks into the porous nail and makes a stain that stays until the nail grows out.

Commercial chemicals can also stain nails. Photographic developers, for example, may blacken them. And the resorcinol in some nail lacquers can cause red-black discoloration.

Most of these shifts are merely of cosmetic interest, but one nail discoloration bodes very ill for you. At first, it looks like a bruise on the nail. However, unlike a bruise, it doesn't grow out; it simply sits in the same spot under the nail and spreads. Far from being a bruise, this spot is a symptom of malignant melanoma, the only life-threatening form of skin cancer. This cancer is very rare, but terribly dangerous for those who get it. So if you have an apparent nail bruise that hasn't moved in weeks call your doctor immediately.

A woman in her thirties can discover some interesting things by looking at the shape and texture of her nails.

Nails, like hair, reflect thyroid gland status to a certain extent. If your thyroid gland is overactive, there may be a separation of the nail from the nail bed. If you have an underactive thyroid, there may be dryness or brittleness of the nails. One of the classical nail signs is the "spoon nail," which results from iron deficiency. In this, the center of the nail indents like the bowl of a spoon.

The cuticle area is of particular interest to doctors. You can see tiny blood vessels growing there, and abnormal growth may indicate a serious systemic disorder, like lupus erythematosus.

One other item we look at is the way the nail interacts with the base of the finger. Nails have a normal interface angle; if that angle is changed or lessened, the finger is known as clubbed, which may indicate chronic undersaturation of the blood with oxygen.

In many ways, your nails can be an early warning system of deeper body problems.

THE SKIN ON YOUR FEET

I'll talk about problems of aching feet elsewhere. Now, I'll discuss foot skin, which can be affected by fungal infections, rashes, and eczema.

The most common fungal infection is athlete's foot, which is characterized by fissuring between the toes. Athlete's foot and other common foot rashes have been written about endlessly and aren't any worse for us thirty-year-olds than for anyone else. But one foot rash has particular impact on us, because of the kind of shoes we wear. It is characterized by a rash on the top of the foot without the characteristic fissuring between the toes that is associated with athlete's foot. In a surprising number of cases the rash is caused by an allergy to the rubber construction in the toe of the shoe. The problem is called rubber box toe, and the prescription is to go out and buy a different pair of shoes.

A Tour of the Body
at Its Prime

OUR BODIES ARE in their prime. We can do more with
them than ever before, we respond more acutely, we feel
more deeply, we control ourselves much more effectively. In short, we feel great, capable, and almost sin-
fully healthy, in most cases.

Paradoxically, all this positive feeling derives from a
body that, taken part by part, is slightly past its prime.
By this I mean that most of our body components have
already reached their developmental crest by our mid-
thirties and are beginning their first small steps along
the curve of healthy aging. Our bones, muscles, veins,
and gums may not be quite as perfect as they were in our
twenties. They are older and nominally less effective.

However, while this is a valuable thing to know, it
shouldn't be taken to heart too heavily. Because more
than anything else I can imagine, the body in the thirties
is infinitely more than the sum of its parts. The body includes the person who inhabits all those bits and pieces,
and whatever minor slippage there may have been in

components, the person in charge of them all is markedly improved.

We are now experienced human beings, and we make better use of the physical tools nature gave us than we could earlier in life. We can't feel very many of the changes our body parts undergo during this decade, but we can feel our increased capability at operating our personal living machine. Some of the changes in our bodies, of course, are visible, tactile or experiential, but these represent a challenge for our expanded abilities.

Thus, as you progress through this tour of the body in our decade, remember that we aren't talking here about a whole person; we are focusing strictly on the nuts and bolts. Time determines how these parts change; you determine how you change as a whole person.

HEART

The female heart! Subject of so many insults over the years. Fickle and flighty—our poor hearts should be worn out from the emotional turmoil by the time we're thirty. Actually, in our thirties our hearts are in less trouble than men's. We can suffer a heart attack, but less frequently than men. Our female hormones "protect" us. A thirty-year-old heart is no bigger or smaller than it used to be. Our pulse depends on the cardiovascular shape that we're in. By the thirties it shouldn't have altered very much either. But there may be more fat around it, especially if you've gained weight or if you eat a tremendous amount of fatty food.

There are, however, some degenerative changes of the heart that occur progressively, such as fat deposition in the heart. If you sectioned a thirty-five-year-old heart and looked at it under a microscope, you would see these progressive changes. But they're minute shifts not apt to cause problems during our decade. The heart really is a tough little organ. So you can be fairly certain that in the thirties your heart remains powerful enough to handle almost anything you want it to do.

Palpitations are a minor heart problem worth talking about, because they are not uncommon for women in their thirties. Palpitations may be described as a fluttering or skipping of the heart. They often occur in women who drink too much coffee or smoke too much marijuana, or experience anxiety attacks. While they may result from anemia or thyroid disease, frequently no cause other than anxiety is discovered. Palpitations always warrant a physical examination and evaluation, though, to make sure that there is no serious organic basis for them.

Another trouble that is quite widespread in our age group is the syndrome of mitral valve prolapse, or Barlow's syndrome. Not well described until recently, it seems to be on the rise. The etiology is unknown, but it's found very frequently these days. Its incidence may be as high as 15 percent of adult women.

The syndrome involves a heart valve—the mitral valve—that doesn't close properly after allowing blood through. It can be likened to the valve in a toilet tank—if it doesn't fit tightly, the toilet runs constantly. A whole variety of psychoneurotic complaints have been attributed to women with Barlow's syndrome. It is unclear whether the neurotic complaints are part of the syndrome or caused by knowledge of the syndrome. After all, if you take an otherwise healthy group of women and say, "You have a leaking mitral valve in your heart," and then give them a questionnaire—"Do you feel depressed? Are you anxious? Do you have headaches?"—more of them are apt to come up with a variety of neurotic-sounding complaints than if they hadn't realized that they had an abnormal heart valve. But as far as we know thus far, there's no tremendous medical worry for later life associated with Barlow's syndrome.

Could you be a thirty-year-old woman walking around with this and not know it? Absolutely. Most women who have it aren't aware of it; it's usually picked up only on a routine exam, although it may be accompanied by palpitations or chest pain. The only reason to be concerned about it is because you should take medication, usually penicillin, whenever you have your teeth cleaned, because the faulty valve is felt to be more subject to developing bacterial infection and therefore antibiotics are prescribed.

What about high blood pressure? Is it common among us in our thirties? Rare? No, it's not common, but the incidence of high blood pressure goes up with age. Normal blood pressure increases due to arteriosclerosis or hardening of the arteries. I don't think it is something for women in their thirties to worry about. But each of us should have an annual blood pressure check just to make sure.

KIDNEYS

There is an age-related decline in kidney function that occurs in all of us, and dosages of certain drugs that are excreted through the kidney need to be adjusted for age and kidney function. But that's a relatively minor effect. In the thirties the kidneys are not working entirely as well as they used to, but they're still working very well. As with the aging of other body systems, kidney change is a continuum, and in the thirties the slope of the curve is very slight. Let's say they're working at 97 percent of their youthful capacity, and should cause most of us few problems for a couple of decades.

LUNGS

There is an age-related decline in lung function, again proceeding at a very gradual rate during our thirties. This can clearly be shown by measuring lung volume and breathing capacity at various ages. Ours is minutely less than it was a decade ago. One reason for this is that our poor lungs are kept busy filtering all the debris that we breathe from our polluted air on a regular basis. The lungs are self-cleaning, but despite their best effort the amount of residue gradually builds up. And you can see the difference in lung tissue of an older woman compared to a younger woman. Exercise conditions our lungs, actually improving their operation. Smoking, on the other hand, is exceedingly detrimental.

THYROID

Normally our thyroid weighs 20 to 30 grams, less than an ounce, and is located on the lower part of our neck, wrapped around the trachea, or windpipe. It lies below the larynx, or voice box, and above the clavicles, or collarbones.

Hyperthyroidism, or an overactive thyroid gland, is far more common in women than in men. The most common cause of overactivity is an auto-immune condition known as Graves' disease, in which the entire thyroid gland enlarges and synthesizes an excessive amount of hormone. This occurs ten times more frequently in women, peaking during our twenties and thirties.

Classically, a woman with Graves' disease has symptoms that include weight loss (despite a good appetite), diarrhea or frequent loose bowel movements, nervousness, irritability, difficulty sleeping, heat intolerance with increased sweating, and palpitations. She may be troubled by oiliness of the hair, increased oiliness and smoothness of her skin, and occasionally by irregularity or loss of menstrual periods. A wide-eyed stare may result from hyperthyroidism, and bulging of the eyes may occur with Graves' disease. Thyroid disease may also cause a number of psychiatric abnormalities or personality changes. A woman may cry frequently, or be nervous or irritable, for example. Every endocrinologist has case histories of women who have been seen on psychiatric wards and given psychiatric diagnoses, when in fact they are merely hyperthyroid with severe personality changes as a result.

Once a diagnosis has been established, treatment is initially aimed at controlling the overactive thyroid and then subsequently treating the disease process permanently. The three modalities of treatment include 1) drugs that act to impede the synthesis of new thyroid hormone by the gland, 2) surgical removal of a sufficient amount of thyroid gland, and 3) radioactive iodide which noninvasively destroys the thyroid tissue.

As with many other diseases, treatment is individualized, and the various choices should be discussed between the woman and her endocrinologist. Of course, regardless of the type of treatment, follow-up is very important.

An underactive thyroid gland, or hypothyroidism, may result from damage to the hypothalamus and pituitary of the brain, which stimulate the thyroid gland, or from actual destruction of thyroid tissue itself. The symptoms of hypothyroidism are almost the opposite of those of hyperthyroidism. They include intolerance of the cold, drying of the skin and hair, a lowering or hoarseness of the voice, constipation, weight gain, fatigue and muscle aches, and emotional changes. If hypothyroidism progresses for a prolonged period of time, over months or years, the end point is called myxedema and is quite dangerous, as it may result in coma.

As with hyperthyroidism, hypothyroidism is generally a straightforward diagnosis, and the treatment is relatively simple as well. Treatment involves taking synthetic thyroid hormone or thyroxin on a daily basis, generally for life. Follow-up is important at regular intervals to ascertain that the correct dose is being taken. Normally our thyroid secretes less hormone as we age, so a reduction in dosage may be necessary after a prolonged period of time.

An additional newer topic of concern about our thyroid is that of radiation exposure during childhood. In the 1940's and 1950's it was the vogue to treat a variety of illnesses ranging from acne to birthmarks to tonsillitis or adenoid infections with radiation treatments. Subsequently, doctors discovered that the thyroid gland received scattered radiation when the neck or head was treated, resulting in more thyroid cancer. Anyone with a history of radiation to her head or neck during childhood is at risk for developing thyroid cancer and should be examined very carefully by a thyroid specialist on an annual basis for the development of a thyroid irregularity or nodule.

When this information was discovered about head and neck irradiation many hospitals such as the Cleveland Clinic sent out notices to their patients who had received irradiation in the 1940's and 1950's. However, many hospitals did not, and certainly many private dermatologists never notified their patients, so that it is certainly worthwhile for a woman in her thirties to inquire of her mother whether she ever received any radiation treatments when she was a child.

BRAIN

We're probably all losing brain cells, unfortunately. The age at which that begins is uncertain, but the decline in brain cells is clearly there. It's a normal part of the aging process, and we can't stop it.

A question I'm often asked is whether the brain is severely changed by life stresses and tensions. I don't suspect that stress kills brain cells or anything like that. Our reaction to stress is channeled through our brains, but the impact of that stress we feel is in the Draconian measures the brains order for our bodies to get us through the crisis. The effect of stress on the brain itself is unknown.

Still, the brain is the one organ that seems to keep improving its performance right through old age. As we get older, our brains get more furrows in them. These are thought to be the repositories of our knowledge, thoughts and experiences. It would be fair to say that, as we get older, the brain is one of the places where we definitely want to get more wrinkles.

JOINTS

Sometimes while just walking down the street you'll see a woman who looks very young except for her hands, which look considerably older and lumpier than the rest of her body, and considerably more worn. This happens because subcutaneous fat—the layer that makes us smoother than men—gets thinner as we get older. This loss of subcutaneous tissue makes the hand bones stand out more prominently. With aging it occurs in all of us to some extent, but it really doesn't hit most of us hard until after menopause. However, bumpy joints of the fingers can also be caused by something as serious as rheumatoid arthritis. A variety of arthritic processes may affect the small joints in the fingers. Arthritis of the distal finger joints closest to the fingernail is more characteristic of osteoarthritis, or the type of arthritis that occurs with aging, while an inflammation of all finger joints is more apt to occur in something like rheumatoid arthritis. That distinguishing feature holds as well for the arthritis associated with psoriasis: it frequently affects the distal joints of the finger.

A thirty-year-old woman whose joints hurt persistently needs evaluation, because the situation is clearly abnormal. The physician will try to separate a joint that merely hurts from a true arthritis, a joint that is inflamed, so it's important to notice whether your joints are red, whether they're swollen and whether they're hot, in addition to whether they hurt. Another item to consider is whether the discomfort goes away over the course of the day. If it does, you may have slept on your hand in an odd position, or you may have rheumatoid arthritis, in which stiffness lessens as the joints get going and warm up.

Rheumatoid arthritis (see "Confronting Our Major Worries" for more on this) is a serious worry for us because it has a peak onset in the fourth decade and may gradually get worse. It affects women in their thirties in an insidious fashion, often beginning with fatigue, weakness and joint stiffness before progressing to joint swelling.

From this, the disease may progress, involving any joint in the body. Besides joint swelling, two other symptoms which may accompany rheumatoid arthritis are dryness of the mouth and dryness of the eyes. So, if you're thirty-five years old and wake up in the morning with painful joints and dry eyes and your mouth is dry, you ought to see the doctor promptly.

If your hands merely seem to be getting terribly worn, it's really no surprise. A thirty-year-old woman has been working with her hands for a long time; dishwater, copy machine acid, dirt, and sun all take their toll.

But there are a couple of things that you can do to help your hands. When you're working in water, by all means wear rubber gloves, and not just with hot water, but with cold water as well. Some women are very sensitive to the cold. If you want to be extra careful, wear cotton gloves under the rubber gloves. That's particularly worthwhile for women who have allergies.

Wintertime is terrible for everyone's hands, largely because with colder weather there's less humidity in the atmosphere both outside and inside. Everything dries out in the wintertime. Our hands are particularly vulnerable because they spend a lot of time in water. The continual evaporative process that goes on dries our skin and stiffens our joints. There's very little we can do about it, without becoming a fanatic.

Hands aren't the only joints susceptible to hard work in our thirties. Knees are subject to a variety of stresses and strains, from housemaid's knee (too much kneeling) to runner's knee (too much jogging). Our thirty-year-old knees aren't necessarily getting weaker or less flexible, but they are aging. Cartilage in our knees may gradually dry out, tear or develop cracks as a result of sports injuries. For some women this will bring on knee problems in the thirties; for others, the process works more slowly. That's genetics.

However, as a general rule, a typical thirty-year-old woman has no more need now than before for extra support, like a knee brace, when she exercises. If you've never had any problems with your knees, don't worry about them. If you have a history of weak knees, or if you've ever injured a knee, then wearing a knee brace becomes important, because our knees are subject to a tremendous amount of stress. Our knee joints are supposed to do only one thing, swing up and back. They're not supposed to rotate. However, a variety of sports put a rotary stress on the knees, which leads to cartilage tears and internal derangements. In healthy knees, everything will stretch a little when you ask it to. In our thirties most of us have knees with a bit of stretch left in them yet.

BELLIES

Although I've heard it said time and again, I don't believe women in their thirties are more prone to chubby bellies than teenagers are. The exception is the woman who gains a lot of weight after adolescence. That poundage tends to hang on the trunk, rather than on the extremities. But there's no one out there forcing us to gain weight. And if we don't, our bellies should stay just slightly rounded.

Everybody is familiar with the image of the thirty-year-old guy who marries, goes to work, gets a desk job, and develops a belly that starts to hang over his belt. Happily, that doesn't happen to us. Men add their extra weight right along the belt line. When we gain weight, our estrogens spread it out more. Our whole trunk will get larger with weight gain or obesity, not just our bellies. Estrogen will also tend to spread new weight to our thighs and buttocks. So the old saw that guys put it on their bellies and women put it on their behinds is true to a certain extent.

A sagging stomach in a 30-year-old woman most often occurs right after childbirth. The stretching of the abdominal muscles that occurs during pregnancy may leave your stomach out of shape afterward. After years of being accustomed to a nice, flat stomach, suitable for a bikini, a woman in her thirties who has delivered may find her stomach unrecognizable postpartum . . . and panic. All that's happened is that her muscle tone hasn't returned to normal. Thirty-year-old muscles don't jump back into shape as quickly as younger ones. You will need to do more diligent and extended exercise than for an earlier pregnancy in order to pull your stomach back into shape.

A last word about bellies—did you ever wonder about that funny line that appears on the abdomen of pregnant women? It's called the linea alba, which makes no sense since that means "white line" and this line is darker than the skin. Pregnancy hormones cause it. If you've just had a baby, take a look before it fades.

BUTTOCKS

As I've said, we have a tendency to put weight more on our buttocks and thighs under the influence of estrogen, and if we don't do some sort of buttocks exercise in our thirties our buttocks tend to sag with a decrease in muscle tone.

What constitutes buttocks exercise? Should you bounce up and down on them or something? Well, running is certainly good for the rear as well as the legs. One popular buttocks exercise is the mule kick, where you rest on your hands and knees and pull your knee in toward your nose and then kick out backward. Any kind of backward kick or leg raise uses the buttocks muscles.

One of the best reasons for not letting your buttocks

get out of shape is that a firm muscular rear can much better withstand the onslaught of cellulite that can begin in the thirties. Cellulite is a condition in which the skin doesn't ride smoothly over the underlying fat because the fat isn't deposited evenly; it's separated by little fiber spans into lumpy bunches. But cellulite is not a new kind of material, it's just fat. You can't dissolve it, beat it, or medicate it away. No preparation in the drugstore will eliminate it. So, what can you do? You can reduce. Reducing always decreases cellulite because it shrinks the size of all fat cells. And you can exercise. Increasing muscle tone also clearly improves cellulite problems by smoothing fat distribution.

In response to sagging, some thirty-year-old women will consider wearing a girdle for the first time. Don't. Girdles are a bad idea for anyone of any age, because they interfere with your muscles. You don't use your muscles because you have a girdle there to do the job. It's bad in terms of developing the muscles to maintain your posture or hold your stomach and buttocks in. In addition, a girdle cuts you off somewhere, whether it's a panty girdle that cuts you off where the end of the panty is, a regular girdle that cuts you off mid-thigh, or a long-line girdle that cuts you off above the knees. At some point the elastic ends and you begin. There's a tendency to develop fluid immediately below that point. Your veins and valves have to be extra efficient to return blood to your heart.

Girdles are a cause of broken blood vessels, as well, because some areas of the girdle inevitably fit more tightly than they're supposed to. A girdle is designed for an even stretch but we aren't always made that way. We may be thicker at the top or middle part of our legs than the designers of that particular girdle anticipated. That puts abnormal stretch on the tissues, resulting in broken blood vessels. Girdles are a bad idea, period. If you don't like sag, exercise and lose weight.

Moving to the inside, are thirty-year-old women more likely than younger ones to get hemorrhoids? If your diet isn't good, if you're constipated a great deal of the time, then yes, you may develop hemorrhoids. Certainly with pregnancy and delivery there's a tremendous increase in varicose veins in the legs, broken vessels in the legs, and hemorrhoids. But there's some genetic component to hemorrhoids, too.

Hemorrhoids are dilated rectal veins. They occur as a result of pressure changes in the veinous system. The hemorrhoidal veins are one of three areas in the body with a cross-flow pattern. If blood flow isn't normal through the inner channel, it proceeds through the outer channel, and that results in a hemorrhoid. If you suffer from hemorrhoids, you should try to keep pressure off your buttocks so blood flows easily. Eat a balanced diet and use seat cushions. Also, simple measures such as sitz baths and suppositories provide welcome relief.

SPINE

Our spines compact with age. If you looked at X rays of your back today and fifteen years ago, the shift might startle you. We don't see or feel it happening, and it doesn't generally hamper our movements until really late in life, but it's happening all the time. This compaction occurs partially because there's a decrease in the spine's water content. The vertebrae and the disks in between them begin to dry out. As they do, they shrink. At the same time, there is a tendency for us to become kyphotic—that is, bending forward. What happens is that the front part of the vertebral body loses more height than the back part. Instead of being a perfect square, it tends to become more angular. The stoop doesn't grow pronounced in most of us until old age, but it's starting now. The impact of this on our thirties may take the form of increased back trouble, which is dealt with in the chapter on "Overcoming Our Minor Complaints."

Because back problems of all types become more frequent at our age, it becomes more important for us to maintain good posture and strong abdominal muscles as a good front support system to counteract any incipient stooping. Building up abdominal musculature is very important in helping to relieve the stress on our backs. So, keep up those sit-ups.

LEGS AND THIGHS

We hear it all the time: the first thing to go is the legs. I don't know if it's true, but I do know that the women in my gym seem to be most concerned about losing weight from their thighs, buttocks, and stomachs, in that order. Basically, though, if our activity level remains stable and if we don't gain an ounce from the time we're twenty until we're forty, our legs and thighs won't change drastically. However, if we do gain weight, then some will certainly settle on our legs and thighs. As with our buttocks, exercises are important, but exercise alone without reducing will not result in smaller thighs (or calves or upper arms, for that matter). In fact, if we exercise without losing weight there may be an increase in the size of our thighs as our muscles increase in bulk. So if you're doing your one-hundredth leg raise and wonder why your legs aren't any skinnier, stop and give your enlarged muscles a rest.

While the size of our legs may remain constant through the thirties, broken vessels can appear along our legs, but our thighs are particularly prone to them. This relates to crossing our legs. There's nothing ostensibly wrong with crossing our legs, but if we keep them crossed for a prolonged period of time, blood continually settles in them, which can lead to broken blood vessels.

Pregnancy is another cause of broken blood vessels. In pregnancy, with the fetus sitting near the vena cava —the major vein that drains the legs—and also near the rectal veins that are prone to hemorrhoids, there's a tendency for blood to pool in the veins, which enlarge and finally become varicose. This is exacerbated by hormonal changes during pregnancy.

For many of us even our normal veins seem to become more prominent on our legs as we get older. That's because of the loss of subcutaneous tissue. It diminishes progressively as we grow older, and our veins literally get closer to the skin surface and therefore are more noticeable. But subcutaneous fat loss doesn't pick up steam for most of us until menopause. Before that it's a very gradual process.

VARICOSE VEINS

Most of us continue to have legs we can be proud of through our thirties. But these are also the years when we see the first signs of problems that will bother us more later in life. One of these is varicose veins.

Some 24 million Americans suffer from varicose veins, 80 percent of them women. At one time these swollen, spidery veins were thought to afflict older women only. In reality, the problem often starts in the late teens and gets progressively worse if not treated. In our thirties the veins become apparent to most of us for the first time. There are two kinds of varicose veins: broken capillaries which are called "spiders," and the larger, full-fledged varicose veins. Both can be treated to keep our legs younger-looking and our circulatory system healthier.

A varicose vein has a faulty or incompetent valve at the juncture of the superficial vein and the deeper vein that carries blood to your heart. Blood can back up at these crucial valves, form pools, and stagnate. The result of this blockage is a blue, almost black vein that is often swollen, and protuberant.

In our thirties, varicose veins most often occur as the result of pregnancy. If we keep in shape, the workout we give our veins helps prevent the stagnation that leads to varicose problems. And now is definitely the time to think about establishing patterns to help prevent the appearance of these unsightly blood channels. Once varicose veins have appeared, it takes surgery to get rid of them. But preventing them requires only a small commitment on our part to exercise a little and keep our legs in reasonable trim. If we're pregnant, we should make sure we get off our feet regularly, and we should continue leg exercises.

Varicose veins tend to run in families. To a large extent, the condition is genetically ordained; if your mother had them, you probably will too. Strangely, the veins are more noticeable in men, who have less fat beneath the surface of their skin, than they are in us. But men don't wear skirts, and we are four times as likely to have the problem as they are. During pregnancy female hormones and the growing fetus cause some of our veins to dilate, increasing the appearance of varicose veins. After pregnancy, the dilated veins subside, but they tend to worsen slightly with each succeeding pregnancy and with age in general—the older we get, the more prominent our veins become. Other factors, such as obesity and prolonged periods of standing can aggravate varicose veins but cannot cause them unless you are already predisposed to the condition.

Spiders, the less serious type, seldom present a significant medical problem, but they are not attractive. Initially red, they later turn blue when they become filled with more blood. They're caused by weak walls in our numerous, tiny, superficial capillaries, and are more noticeable in those of us with thin, fair skin. Usually found on the legs, spiders can also appear on our faces.

No matter how large the spiders become, surgery is never required. The best method of treatment for spiders on the face is electro-desiccation. In this procedure an electrified needle is placed in the swollen capillary to cauterize it. Electrodesiccation does not work as well on the legs where the preferred treatment is an injection of a chemical that dries the vein up. The injection usually flattens the vein, and often improves its color, though occasionally it can leave a light brownish tinge of its own. Perhaps that's better than purple.

Although many doctors can perform these procedures, you should go to one who specializes in your particular problem. For that reason, seek out a physician who has had extensive specific experience. Often, dermatologists handle electrodesiccation of the spidery face veins while vascular surgeons perform injections and the more serious surgical stripping of the varicose leg veins.

Both electrodesiccation and injection can be done in the doctor's office. They don't hurt much; you should be able to walk home afterward. Cost for the treatments should be about the same as for a regular office visit.

Spiders usually recur after treatment because an individual's predisposition to weak walls is constant. The problem does not recur in veins that have already been treated, but in the many other tiny veins that weren't originally affected.

True varicose veins pop up in our late twenties and early thirties. Aside from appearing entirely unattractive, they bring the risk of three possible complications. Phlebitis, a blood clot in the leg, can occur at any age, as early as our twenties, and anytime thereafter. Women with varicose veins are ten times more prone to phlebitis than other women. And the use of oral contraceptives exacerbates this tendency, so the pill should be avoided by women with severe varicose veins. Ruptures and ulcers, the other potential complications, generally don't occur until our late fifties or later. Rupturing occurs when the pressure within the vein gets so high that the blood breaks through the wall of the vein. An ulcer, or sore, can also occur over the area of a varicose vein.

Fortunately, most varicose veins never result in serious medical problems, but they may cause symptoms such as heaviness in the leg or fatigue of the leg, which worsens progressively during the day. Impressive relief may be achieved merely by elevating your leg above the level of your heart, allowing the stagnant blood to return to the circulatory system. For more serious varicose vein flare-ups, the only solution may be a varicose vein ligation and stripping. This operation literally removes the offending vein or veins from your leg so they don't bother you anymore. It's a serious procedure and should never be the first choice of therapy for a primary problem with varicose veins. Also, the veins probably shouldn't be stripped until you are through having all of your children because of the likelihood of the problem recurring after each pregnancy.

Before consulting a surgeon, see if the problem can be controlled by regular use of support hose and comfortable low-heeled shoes. If, however, the veins are thrombosed (clotted off), or if there is a family tendency to phlebitis or severe inflammation of varicose veins, they may have to be surgically removed.

In a varicose vein strip procedure, holes are made over both ends of the varicose vein, and the vein is pulled out through the holes. As you may imagine, all this yanking results in a fair number of scars. The scars will be more or less noticeable, according to how you heal. It's a fairly bloody operation, and its effect is only temporary. New veins may pop up in place of the removed ones. Still, for women who have a tremendous amount of pain as a result of varicose veins, even with support hose or a support stocking like a Jobst Stocking, surgery may be the best solution.

Two things you can do right now to ameliorate the problems of varicose veins are try to lose weight if you're overweight and try to maintain muscle tone in the legs, because that improves blood return. Elevating your legs as frequently as possible also helps.

RAYNAUD'S DISEASE

We all get cold hands and feet at some point during the winter, but for millions of women this situation brings on a potentially serious condition called Raynaud's disease, in which the fingers change color and hurt when exposed to the cold. Poor circulation is the cause of the problem.

Raynaud's develops when small arteries in our hands and feet go into spasm in response to the cold. The tightened arteries can't carry sufficient blood to the fingers and toes, so they begin to change color and hurt.

First they turn bluish-white, a direct response to the loss of oxygenated blood. Later, when blood returns, they can turn deep red from the gush. Women with mild cases of Raynaud's can reduce attacks substantially by wearing gloves and socks to bed and by keeping their hands well covered out of doors. But some Raynaud sufferers have attacks that last for many minutes, eventually causing small, painful ulcers to develop on the fingertips.

Raynaud-like symptoms may result from a number of underlying physical problems such as disorders of the connective tissue or of the blood, drug injection, or as a result of exposure to vibrating instruments. Symptoms may also be caused by the aftermath of frostbite, by a general circulatory disorder, obstruction of the arteries, or even by the long-term effects of the pressure from piano playing and typing. The symptoms usually start in adults and may sometimes involve the fingers or toes of only one hand or foot, though usually both hands or feet are affected in a symmetrical fashion.

Primary Raynaud's has no known physical cause, though attacks seem to be triggered by both cold or emotional stress. Strong emotions such as anger, anxiety, and fear induce lowered hand temperatures in all of us which can increase the likelihood of an attack in someone who has the disease.

Cigarette smoking, which constricts the blood vessels, clearly aggravates Raynaud's symptoms. So do certain foods, such as coffee, aged cheeses, peanut butter, and chocolate, that are high in caffeine, tyramine, or phenylethylamine, which also can constrict blood vessels in some Raynaud's sufferers.

No one knows why Raynaud's afflicts more women than men but female sex hormones may be involved. So far, biofeedback appears to be the safest and most effective treatment for Raynaud's. In biofeedback, the temperature of a person's fingertips is monitored electronically so she can detect slight temperature increases and learn how to bring them about. Ten to thirty sessions with a monitor, plus regular home practice, are usually required for success. Once the skills are learned, though, most Raynaud's sufferers can prevent or abort attacks. For severe cases, drugs or surgery may be necessary.

FOOT PROBLEMS

Women seem to experience painful foot problems far more frequently than men, possibly because of genetics and certainly because of the physical insult of wearing high-heeled shoes, which put the foot at a tremendous mechanical disadvantage.

What happens to the musculoskeletal system when feet end up on three- or four-inch heels? The feet are held in a plantar-flexed position—with the toes away from the nose. This tightens the calf muscles and results in a compensatory bending of the knees. In order to keep the center of gravity in the proper place, the hips flex, causing the buttocks to protrude. In order to stand up straight, a woman must increase the curvature of the lower back, arching her upper back, which further emphasizes the buttocks and protrudes the chest. Women in high heels may look good, but everything is out of kilter.

In addition, high-heeled shoes that have thin soles put excessive pressure on metatarsal bones, resulting in pain right on the ball of the foot and thickening of the skin, or callus formation. Further pain results from normal skin being squeezed between the bone and the central hard area of the callus. Relief from calluses may be obtained by using a rough pumice several times a week after softening the skin first with a bath or shower. As the size of the callus is reduced, the pain generally subsides. In addition, a metatarsal pad may be placed behind the affected metatarsal in order to relieve the pressure on the toughened skin. Similar treatment works well for calluses in other areas, such as on the heel or over the top of a toe joint.

Foot pain may also occur after standing for prolonged periods of time. There may be a tired feeling or a burning feeling in the arch of the foot. This occurs most often in women who have relatively flat feet and have jobs that involve a lot of standing and relatively little walking, such as bank tellers and salespersons. Two things can be done to help this problem. First, move from foot to foot to allow the muscles in the foot to help support the arch. Additionally, use a scaphoid foot pad under the arch, as well as an inner heel wedge, which can be inserted into a shoe for better fit. These are less expensive than formal arch supports or orthotics.

Improperly fitting shoes are also a cause of general foot pain, both while standing still and while walking. And if we succumb and try to cram our feet into weird impractical styles this too will cause problems for us. It's easy enough to tell if your shoe is long enough: there should be enough room for your index finger between the tip of the big toe and the end of the shoe. On standing, if the shoe squeezes your foot so that it bulges over the sides, the shoe is too narrow. Likewise, if the shoe is too tight around the forefoot, with our toes bunched up and squished together, it'll hurt. The solution is to buy shoes for comfort, not just for style.

Bunions are an inherited foot disorder that is generally far more common in women than in men. These lumpy bone growths may first be noticed during our teenage years, but generally don't become troublesome until our thirties and forties. While bunion formation is a genetically inherited trait, shoes can aggravate it, so wearing shoes that fit properly over the metatarsal area or base of the toes is crucial. Surgery should be reserved for women with severe cases of chronic pain, or who have difficulty in obtaining any shoes that fit. The vital

fact about bunionectomy—surgical bunion removal—
that some patients don't understand is that it is, in fact,
bone surgery. It's not a casual operation. During a bunionectomy the doctor will remove the abnormal piece
of bone and a piece of the bone sac. You'll hobble
around for a while afterward. I don't think the surgery
is necessary unless the bunions are so uncomfortable,
painful, and disfiguring that you can't stand it anymore.

Female foot pain as a result of jogging is more common today because of the number of women who have
begun running for exercise. Most of the problems of
joggers are just extreme examples of the difficulties
observed in walkers. With each stride of a runner, the
force exerted on the foot is roughly three times that of
the runner's weight. One of the common problem areas
is on the inner edge of the heel. Frequently X rays reveal
a spurlike projection from the heel, often referred to as
a heel spur—yet X rays of women without pain reveal
these heel spurs too, as frequently as in women with
pain. The cause seems to be tightness or contracture of
the calf muscles that is felt across the bottom of the
heel. Treatment should be aimed at strengthening and
stretching the calf muscles. This can be done by standing, bare feet together, approximately arm's length
from a wall, and then leaning forward into the wall with
a straight back. You should feel a pulling sensation in
your calf muscles. As the exercise progresses over
weeks, your distance from the wall should increase. It
may take three to six weeks of stretching exercises
before results appear.

This problem of pain related to a tightened calf muscle may also occur in a woman who switches from high-
heeled shoes to flat shoes. With high heels there is a progressive tightening of the calf muscles, so when you
switch to low-heeled shoes there may be excessive strain
on your Achilles tendon, calf muscles, or bottom of
your foot.

MUSCLES

I suspect that thirty-year-old muscles have become slightly less strong and stretchy than they once were. The effects of a low-activity life may have begun to take their toll. For instance, more thirty-year-old women complain of muscle soreness after exercises than younger women. This soreness is normal and should be expected. If you begin to work out after being lazy in your thirties you're going to be sore, and you should be. If we're prone to more soreness in our thirties it's because the odds are we haven't been working out for longer periods of time than our twenty-year-old sisters. If you have exercised on a regular basis all along then continue . . . bravo!

A lot of us take our muscles for granted in our twenties. Then, when we reach thirty we realize we have to start exercising to keep at the level we've achieved and the sudden return to exercise hurts. But the rewards are certainly well worth the efforts.

If you're out of shape, there may well now be a problem of increased susceptibility to strains and sprains. Those muscles are no longer accustomed to doing what you're going to ask them to do. Someone in good physical condition should be able to ask something of her body and have it respond.

For a woman in her thirties the state of her muscles relates more to her habits than to her age. We can easily do all the things we did a decade ago, if we're willing to work at it a bit.

BONES

In general, our bones are undergoing a continual remodeling process. There is some tendency for them to become more brittle with age. However, that doesn't usually become evident until we hit menopause, when our loss of bone mineral content accelerates. In our thirties, our bones are somewhat more brittle but not enormously so. In fact, the bone changes during the thirties are usually minor. There is an increment of change, but it's quite small. You could study the bones of women who are entering their thirties and evaluate them again as they leave their thirties and say, yes, there is a general decline in bone calcium content and a change in the ligaments. But these aren't things that we notice, and in every respect they're minor changes.

Rather, what is important for us to realize is that we're entering the beginning of middle age. Even though the change today may not be great, we have to begin to prepare for the changes tomorrow in our later years of middle age. That means establishing good patterns and habits now, so that when we are fifty we don't look in the mirror and say, What happened?

What kind of good habits can we establish for our bones? One of the things that we can do is to drink milk or establish some sort of daily calcium source. The two biggest deficiencies in the American woman's diet are calcium and iron. Believe it or not, many women's only calcium source is ice cream; there are a phenomenal number of women who don't drink any milk whatsoever. Osteoporosis, extremely brittle bones in later life, may be worsened by a continual calcium deficit over the years, so it's important to establish good habits in terms of dairy products now.

EYES

With age there is a gradual change in the refractive state of the eye, so that as we age we tend to become farsighted. This can be either good or bad. If you are as I am, nearsighted, you can look forward to that problem becoming progressively less significant as you grow older. However, if you start out being farsighted, it may get worse. Also, with age a gradual deficiency in the eye's ability to accommodate to near objects occurs, so that you can't focus on things that are close to you or read fine print anymore. This may necessitate a pair of reading glasses or bifocals if you already wear glasses.

These changes do start in our thirties or even earlier. If you measure the capability of a woman's eye to accommodate as she enters her thirties and again as she leaves the decade, you would find this gradual change. This shift in accommodative capacity is extremely gradual, however. For most of us, the impact will be a new prescription for glasses or perhaps our first pair of reading glasses. We may notice our eyes tiring more easily if we try to focus on near objects for a prolonged period of time, or you may notice yourself holding this book farther from your eyes in order to see the print. But basically, our sight does make it through our fourth decade well. Glaucoma is rare before age forty, when it begins to occur frequently, and cataracts even rarer.

EYE PROBLEMS

Our eyes, for all their delicate construction, are durable. For the vast majority of us our eyes are just as strong as they ever have been. We are no more prone to eye problems than any other age group, and in some of us longterm use of contact lenses may have actually improved our sight slightly.

In the rare instances, when a woman in her thirties has serious eye complaints, the cause often lies with the mysterious chronic illness multiple sclerosis.

Almost half of all MS victims experience a rapid loss of vision in one eye as the initial symptom of their disease. MS occurs more frequently in women than in men, with a mean age of onset about thirty, so it's something we should be aware of though not afraid of.

MS is an uncommon demyelinating neurological disease, which means that various areas of the brain and spinal cord lose their protective covering of myelin (white matter), resulting in visual loss or double vision, numbness or weakness of an arm or leg, tremors, difficulty in speaking, or loss of bladder control. While the cause of this distressing disease is unknown, the epidemiology has been established and is intriguing. For example, the disease is very rare between the equator and latitudes of 30 to 35 degrees north and south—up to Los Angeles and Dallas or in Europe to Istanbul. The prevalence increases as you go farther north or south. For instance, the risk in Manitoba, Canada, is six times that in New Orleans. Also, your risk of acquiring the disease is determined by where you lived before age fifteen. If you're a Southern belle by birth, you have some protection.

There seems to be an increased risk in higher socioeconomic groups, and a familial tendency as well. The duration and course of MS vary exceedingly, generally with remissions and recurrences over twenty to thirty years. Unfortunately, there is no cure for MS, and treatment with steroids has not been conspicuously or uniformly successful.

EARS

Our hearing diminishes as we age, also. This is a gradual process that begins in our mid-twenties but does not usually become a problem until our sixties or beyond. The structure in the inner ear responsible for receiving sound waves and transmitting them to the brain as neural impulses is called the cochlea. This tightly coiled organ has about 15,000 hair cells in it. Every day we lose a few of these hair cells. The loss occurs first at the base of the curl, where high-pitched sounds are received, so that high-pitched hearing is affected first. The pace of this progressive hearing loss can be ascertained by audiograms, which show a mean decline in decibel perception of about 10 db between our mid-twenties and our mid-thirties for high-frequency sounds.

For low-frequency sounds there is essentially no change from age twenty to age forty. While some decline in hearing is inevitable, one thing we can do to affect this gradual impairment is to avoid noise trauma, which accelerates the process.

VOICE

What about our voice? Is it the same as when we were kids? Probably not. Nor will it be the same twenty years from now. As we age our voices change, largely because of changes in the muscles and ligaments around the vocal cords, which become less resilient. (The muscles around the cords control their length.) Cord length, combined with the tension on them and the pressure of air being forced through them, determines the pitch of our voice. As these muscles age, our voices become deeper. Parenthetically, in the elderly there may be a slight bowing of the cords in addition, which accounts for the weaker, less vigorous voice of the elderly.

However, any marked or sudden change in your voice should prompt a medical evaluation. Your voice shouldn't get hoarse out of the blue. Severe hoarseness can indicate anything from a polyp on the vocal cords to hypothyroidism to cancer. Any unexpected, persistent change in voice warrants evaluation.

TEETH

Our teeth aren't exempt from change. As we age our teeth gradually become more brittle, drier, and somewhat darker. On the plus side, though, is the fact that we suffer fewer cavities, largely as the result of the fact that we haven't as much untouched tooth area to decay in our thirties as we did during our teens and twenties.

Our gums change, too, becoming less elastic and

receding from our teeth, as indicated by the symbolic expression for age, "long in the tooth." This process exposes the roots; combined with periodontal disease, this results in the loss of more teeth than from any other single process. Years of improper tooth brushing may become manifest now as V-shaped horizontal grooves in our teeth near the gum line. Proper brushing and flossing are a must for us in our thirties if we want to preserve our smiles into our fifties and sixties. The prevention of periodontal disease is the key, and this means regular dental checkups and removal of plaque and calcified debris, the medium for bacteria growth that can lead to cavities. In other words, it's still important for us to brush our teeth carefully. If we do, our youthful smile will last for many years beyond our thirties.

Our Sexuality

WHAT IS SEXY to a woman in her thirties? That depends a lot upon the woman. By now we probably know what we like, and it certainly may be different from what we needed when we were younger.

Some of us like expensive cars, others functional cars that take regular gas. Some of us like standard preppy clothes, others the latest from Paris or Milan. Our tastes in men vary in much the same way. In our twenties, I think, masculinity seems like a vast smorgasbord, and many of us pile our plates high. We want to sample a little of everything. By our thirties, most of us would rather order from the menu; we know what we prefer and don't feel as great a need to dabble.

Personally, I'm turned on by competence and intelligence. I cannot stand being with a man whom I consider to be incompetent at the major tasks of his life. And while I may tolerate incompetence in a woman, I rarely will in a man. For me, what's sexiest is success. Nothing succeeds like success. I like a man who is self-assured and self-confident, yet not self-aggrandizing. There's something nice about the successful man who's humble and doesn't beat you over the head with his success. That's what's sexy to this woman in her thirties.

Other women are turned on by problems. There are women who are continually trying to salvage an alcoholic, who are the helpers who are turned on by helplessness. Different things turn different people on. That's what makes life so interesting.

WHAT WE DON'T FIND SEXY

What isn't sexy to our age group anymore is the uncomfortable novelty. Sex on the beach, for example, with a lot of sand getting in your mouth and hair and the rest of you, is not apt to be sexy at thirty, whereas it might have been at twenty. We laughed at the beach scene in *Airplane*, with seaweed covering the passionate lovers, because we've been there and know that's what it's really like. We thirty-year-old women want to embellish our sex now. We are no longer enticed by flopping around in the back seat of a car at a drive-in. Getting dressed up and having an intimate night is of greater importance than it might have been a decade ago.

This is because we are now more apt to have the financial means to arrange things the way we want. The accouterments, the ambience we prefer, may be more affordable. As we mature, the desire to set the mood gets stronger, as does our need to be able to call at least some of the shots in our love lives.

After all, we have a better idea now of what we like and have stronger feelings about what we don't like. I think most of us have resolved our sexual attitudes by the time we're thirty. We are in a better position to know and tell our partner what pleases us. To that extent, we're more aware of what is happening to our bodies sexually in our thirties, and more in control of getting what we deserve.

WHAT WE WANT

A woman in her thirties is more apt to stand up for her own needs than she was in her twenties. She's more cognizant of those needs, first of all, and more apt to say, "This is what I need," or "This is not in keeping with what I want out of a relationship." That doesn't negate the fact that there are still women among us who are desperate for relationships, who are very needy in relationships, and who opt for something that isn't entirely suitable for them. But for many of them, the thirties will be the time when their deepening needs and gathering frustrations will combine to destroy the relationship. Then they are placed in the odd position of knowing what they want but having to look around to find out who offers it.

They also have to go through an awkward adjustment to a social world that has changed in their absence. Married women have a lot of questions about what's going to happen when they go through a divorce. They feel that all of a sudden they're back in a world they have been away from for a long time, and what's worse, that world has changed. It has speeded up in terms of the sexual practices. There's sort of a time warp. When they dated and married, things proceeded at a much slower pace. What do they do now? How do they cope with the crisis? One means of coping with change is to withdraw from it, to not date or go out at all. That is often a response employed in the early stages of divorce. Other women cope by confronting the situation, getting out there and finding out what feels comfortable for them, what they can comfortably live with. Sometimes—often, in fact—that turns out to be different from what they could have comfortably lived with in their twenties.

SHIFTING VALUES

Among the women I know there are a lot of ex-firebrands who in 1968 were on the barricades but now are corporate lawyers. Their style and politics have changed. Their sexual attitudes and needs, the type of man they want, have changed as well. Many of us are bemused to find that we have grown to be reliable, responsible, and conservative in our own Vietnam-tinted way. It is almost as if the winds of our parents' generation have blown over us and made us—in our thirties—more like them than we ever would have thought possible.

None of this should be construed as suggesting that a more settled sexuality is dull. I think the unknown is still extremely sexy for us. We still have a strong curiosity about other people, and unknown situations. Someone who is unknown is frequently more sexy to us than someone who is known.

So often we still experiment. But it's different than what we did when we were younger. Our adult exploring may take shape as serial monogamy, serial relationships or marriages, rather than one marriage forever and ever. We stay together until our curiosity overpowers the stabilizing forces of contentment and commitment. I don't know if it's healthy, but it's definitely the prevalent mode.

One of the problems with sexual experimentation that I hear over and over again from women in their thirties and forties is the question of exploitation that arises as a result of experimentation. Having "sexual freedom" doesn't seem to have helped at all. For the woman who has gone to a disco, or a bar or a restaurant, and then gone home and to bed with someone of her own free will, the issue frequently arises—if she never hears from that fellow again—"Was I exploited?" "Was he using me (more than I was using him)?" It's the old double standard, which, in my opinion, is still alive and well and no different than when we were twenty. This is most apt to happen after a divorce or break-up when a woman's sexual ego is most vulnerable.

When a woman separates or divorces, she may experience a terrifying fear of being single, of being alone, of being on her own . . . forever. This is particularly true if she has always been oriented toward marriage and motherhood, a woman whose sense of value and self-esteem had been largely derived from her relationship to her husband rather than from a career. So, I hear frequent stories from patients about women our age falling in love with the next man who is nice to them as a result of their fear and insecurity about being single again.

Financial dependency may also be an issue for the woman who devoted her twenties to husband and family rather than to building a successful career. A divorce will drastically alter her financial situation, perhaps prompting her to rush too rapidly into a second marriage. However, there are also women who decide that they are really going to have a good time while they are single . . . this time around. These women confront their newly single state and decide to explore the vistas open to them, and utilize their breakup as a chance for emotional growth and learning. And probably for sexual growth as well.

DANGERS OF EXPERIMENTATION

Such a woman may experiment with hanging from the chandelier, and subsequently decide that the chandelier is no fun. Now. And that may be true for a variety of sexual positions and practices. After trying them again, she may decide that she's through experimenting with them, that she has sorted out from the spectrum of possibilities what she enjoys.

But with a new sex partner that can always change. Even though we do settle down, develop sexual patterns and habits, I don't think our minds are ever closed. Change is essential for growth.

There aren't many physical dangers associated with

sexual experimentation in our thirties. Our sexual equipment can usually handle almost anything we throw it. However, the incidence of cervical cancer has been linked to the number of sexual partners we have and our age at first intercourse. Women who change partners frequently are also more apt to be exposed to herpes virus. Cervical cancer is not that common, even among "promiscuous" women, and shouldn't constitute a serious worry for women who have regular Pap smears in their thirties, but herpes is worthy of worry. Herpes is epidemic at the present time because there is no effective treatment, and because women are frequently unaware that their partner has herpes.

Other than the fact that it hurts like hell, there are two areas of concern about herpes. One is the danger of infection of the fetus as it passes through an infected birth canal. The other is carcinoma—herpes seems to increase susceptibility. These are important concerns that should make any of us go out of her way to avoid acquiring a herpes infection.

A woman in her thirties who is worried about getting herpes can try to check it out with each new partner. She may ask, "Have you ever had any venereal diseases that I need to know about?" But so often she feels, "I don't want to ruin the relationship. I don't want to completely blow the mood by sitting up and saying, 'By the way, do you have any venereal diseases?' "

If that's the case, you can ask your partner to wear a condom. For the most part, that prevents transmission of venereal diseases. It's not going to be a hundred percent effective, but it's pretty good. In any case, a subtle way to deal with the situation is to indicate that you're not protected and ask your partner to please use a condom for contraception, which puts off discussing the issue of venereal disease to a later date.

Our discomfort at being straightforward about sexual problems like herpes brings up the fact that, for all our supposed sexual freedom, many of us still cling to old taboos and inhibitions. It may be okay for us to *do* just about anything, healthy or not, weird or not, but we still can't *talk* easily about half of what we do, and we can't discuss the problems inherent in our new freedom any better than we could as schoolgirls.

ON THE SEXUAL CUSP

To some extent I think that this reflects the fact that women our age aren't entirely comfortable with all of the sexual shifts that have occurred during our lives. We may have gone along with them, may have adopted them of our own free will or as the result of peer pressure, but we're not entirely sure that all of the changes have been entirely beneficial.

I think that women who are in their thirties now are caught on the edge of the sexual revolution. Our mothers clearly antedated the revolution; our daughters are clearly going to grow up after the revolution, but we matured right in the middle of it. For example, a thirty-five-year-old woman who at age twenty-five planned to live in a commune with multiple partners, may now find herself thinking, "I don't want all that freedom, thank you, I'd just as soon marry and settle down in a nice little house in the suburbs." She is surprised that some of her mother's attitudes toward sex and living together and permanence are now her own. It may startle her. But if it startles her, how does it affect her partner?

The sexual revolution has posed problems for men as well as for women. Men are now under much greater pressure to perform, to please their partners, perhaps to have sexual relations before *they* are emotionally prepared. With volumes written about foreplay, after-play and sexual etiquette, men are far more conscious of technique than they were previously. This may act as an impediment to sexual spontaneity and enjoyment. The irony of the situation is that most women aren't searching for perfection of technique. Rather, what they want from a man is a lover who is considerate of them, not only as a sexual partner but as a total person. Women, particularly in their thirties, don't want a flawless stud but someone with a deep capacity for intimacy. Many of my patients express ambivalent feelings about seeing their men work so hard to please them. The shoe is now on the other foot. Women are instructing men to "relax and enjoy it." Women comment to me, "Oh, the poor fellow, he clearly has to perform. He has to satisfy me." This is a comment I have heard repeatedly from liberated women in our post-sexual-revolution society.

Sexual satisfaction is important to be sure. And it's nice that our needs aren't being ignored any longer. But I think that the more important issue for us is that of intimacy, of having someone who really cares about us. Sex is a need just as eating is a need, but there is something underlying sex, and that's the need for caring and intimacy, for emotional nurturance.

I think that acceptance of this need for emotional nurturance is still closer to the surface in women than in men. I think that women will frequently admit to having needs for intimacy more readily than will men. Men will admit, however, that they need sex more readily than they will admit that they need intimacy. This is reflected in the differences between male and female friendships. Women generally have closer friends among other women than men do among other men. Men may have friends with whom they play tennis, go fishing, or do things, but women have friends to talk to, to share with, to help support them. I feel that women are still more open about their feelings than men are.

FIGHTING THE ODDS

What about the problems of trying to stay sexually attractive and happy when you're a thirty-year-old woman trying to divide her energy and attention between a husband or lover and children?

It's obviously very difficult, particularly right after having a baby. When a woman has a new baby, especially if she is nursing, all of her hormones are out of kilter with her sexual being. It may be that her motherhood and her sexuality are separate issues, and that to ask her to immediately resume her previous sexuality is to ask the impossible, because biology is forcing her to pay full attention to mothering her new infant.

Many of my patients have described receiving a lot of pressure in this situation, experiencing tension and conflict about being sexually available and interested in their husbands, and yet also emotionally available to their time-consuming new infants. The added factor of a job or career with further demands heightens this conflict. It makes many women feel inadequate. "I can't measure up. I'm worthless on all fronts."

They have a sense that yes, they can't accomplish everything or meet everyone's demands as well as they did before the baby arrived. They cannot be as attentive to their mate as they were previously, or as efficient and interested in their job, after having been awake half the night with a sick child. Something suffers. What frequently suffers is the woman's own self-image. Not only does she not have as much time to devote to her mate and to her children, but she doesn't have as much time to devote to herself and may resent this tremendously. She sees herself as a failure on all fronts. She is torn apart. She does not, she simply physically cannot, do everything 100 percent perfectly all of the time. But accepting less than perfect is extremely difficult for many women.

My advice: delegate. Attempt to delegate authority and responsibility as much as possible. Spread the load around: "Here, you sleep with my husband for the next few weeks." There are societies where that happens, where new mothers aren't bothered by sexual overtures from their mates. The men go off and find other women in the village for sexual satisfaction. In these societies, in fact, ritual expressly forbids the nursing mother from intercourse with the father. The mother-child unit is considered sacrosanct; and the mother is recognized as having purposes other than sex at that time.

In our society, we are more likely to get someone to watch the child. But until recently in our society, there used to be more people available to watch children. We had an extended family. There was usually someone else to share the burden, to baby-sit some of the time. Now, couples are often on their own, miles away from their extended families and close friends, which makes the demands all the heavier. If the pressure falls largely on the woman, and it almost invariably does, she has a weaker support system on which to rely and may feel trapped, conflicted, depressed.

We can help ourselves with the burdens of child rearing in the absence of established family networks by creating support systems of our own. Many women are setting up childcare co-ops and babysitting exchanges, so that friends and neighbors can fill in some of the roles family members once held. I think this is an excellent idea and I recommend it highly to any mother in her thirties.

SEX VERSUS BIOLOGY

What makes our situation with child rearing even more difficult is that physically a woman in her thirties is not designed to be the sole support of a child and a husband at the same time. Biologically, it's intended to be done at a younger age and in the midst of an extended family that shares the work.

In some respects our biological and social lives aren't synchronized today. Biologically, women are probably geared to have children in their adolescent years and twenties and perhaps less so in their thirties, because there's a natural decline in fertility. At the same time, all of the social forces are now brought to bear on a woman to achieve career success at the same pace as a man, which means to work hard in her twenties and early thirties, and to delay having children. Biologically, socially, and culturally, she's out of sync.

ORGASM

Freud can probably be blamed for some of the original misconceptions about the female orgasm. According to Freud, there were two types of orgasms available to women, either a clitoral orgasm or a vaginal orgasm. Freud suggested that a clitoral orgasm was not a complete or mature orgasm and that only vaginal orgasms were indicative of a true healthy female sexual response. Fortunately, Masters and Johnson dispelled that myth showing that there is only one type of orgasm available to us, which is a combined response of both the clitoris and vagina. While orgasms may vary in number and intensity at different times, our neurological and muscular responses are the same regardless of how the orgasm is achieved.

Failure to achieve orgasm may be due to a number of factors, including anxiety, fear of pain or pregnancy, or "spectatoring," a term coined by Masters and Johnson for the woman who cannot put aside distracting thoughts about whether she is responding correctly during sexual relations. The woman wondering whether she loves her mate or whether she is going to respond properly, or at all, is impeded and becomes an observer rather than a participant. Such mental wandering during intercourse has been described most commonly in obsessive-compulsive individuals, women who cannot put off other items of concern. The best mode of treatment for this type of problem is therapy that focuses on visualization of the sexual act in a subjective rather than objective fashion, so that the woman feels involved in the experience rather than apart from it, looking down at herself. Sexual therapy has been shown to be useful not only for spectatoring but also for a number of other sexual problems.

ANAL SEX

What about anal intercourse? It seems to be undergoing something of a vogue. A thirty-year-old woman who just got involved in a relationship may find that the man wants to have anal intercourse. Is this something she should worry about? Would it damage her body? Anything that hurts can do damage, so yes, anal sex can do damage unless both people are very careful. Vaginal secretions facilitate intercourse, but the anus doesn't have lubricating glands, so an artificial lubricant has to be used for anal intercourse. Whether it's butter, as in *Last Tango in Paris*, or something more standard, like K-Y jelly or Surgilube, this is essential to keep tissues from being torn. It is also advisable that the woman ask her partner to use a condom to lessen the risk of infection. You should also refrain from moving directly from anal to vaginal sex.

Internal problems from anal intercourse come from the angle of the woman's internal plumbing. What normally happens is that upon entry the rectum tilts backward toward the tailbone. Any other angle is going to be uncomfortable. The rectum is thereafter straight for a short distance before it tilts. Stretching it beyond this straight area could tear the inside. Cases of rectal tears do occur, but I've never seen one in a woman.

Anal sex isn't any different for a thirty-year-old than for her younger sister. For both, the body parts aren't being used for their intended purpose.

HOMOSEXUALITY

Lesbians don't have the same kinds of problems that male homosexuals do, because of the lack of anal intercourse. Male homosexuals who are penetrated anally are liable to a variety of special medical problems, because they tend to mix anal and oral sex. This may result in venereal problems, and transmission of diseases such as hepatitis and giardiasis, a parasite illness that is rampant among homosexual males.

Lesbians aren't prone to any unique physical problems. Their sexual practice is basically having a friend bring them to orgasm with hands or tongue, and that's no more troublesome than doing it yourself or with a hetero partner.

MASTURBATION

Those women who masturbated in their twenties will probably masturbate in their thirties. But often, I think married people, both men and women, feel guilt about continuing to masturbate. I don't know that this abates when a woman enters her thirties, though in a maturing marriage it may decline.

What's certainly true is that if a woman has a husband who's not there for her sexually, she's quite likely to turn to masturbation. At thirty-five the woman married to a businessman who's out of town two weeks a month may embrace masturbation with fewer qualms than a younger wife would in similar circumstances.

VAGINA SIZE

A persistent sexual myth involves the "proper" size for the vagina. I generally respond to questions about normal vaginal size by asking, "What's a normal height?" Obviously, there is a wide range of height. Also, the vagina can expand from what is actually a potential space, with the walls touching, to an organ large enough to encompass the head of a newborn baby. It is important to recognize that a vagina that is "too small" will distend when the woman is sexually excited and lubricated, and a vagina that is "too large" will contract as excitement progresses, with engorgement of the vaginal walls during the plateau phase of sexual excitement.

What about physical strength and suppleness of the vagina? Does it stiffen as we get older? Aside from having children, which obviously affects vaginal suppleness and strength if you have a vaginal delivery, there is only a minimal decline with age, but it's not really a factor until menopause.

The changes that come with having children aren't permanent, either. They are partially reversible by doing strengthening exercises for the vaginal muscles, which basically means practicing stopping and starting urination. You repeatedly squeeze the opening shut and the muscles get stronger.

After childbirth, it may take a little longer for a women in her thirties to feel sexy again than it would if she were younger. Much of this, though, depends on what her prepregnant state was like—whether she was in good health, how demanding the pregnancy was, how demanding the newborn infant is.

Whether she is going to feel sexy after the pregnancy or not also depends on how her outlook toward her husband has held up during those nine long months— whether he has been supportive during the pregnancy and delivery, and whether he has met her expectations. This is an extremely important issue because frequently both women and men will have expectations about their partner which are unrealistic. Likewise, their expectations of parenting may also be idealistic and unrealistic. Romantic myths and misconceptions abound and are propagated in our society by the advertising media and television. Frequently, women haven't even discussed their expectations with their partners but are nonetheless deeply disappointed when their dreams and expectations are not met.

HIDDEN AGENDAS

This brings me to the notion of hidden agendas. Frequently sex is the hidden agenda that brings a woman to a physician, with the masquerade of a perplexing complaint. That is, what a woman initially complains about isn't always what's really bothering her. I encounter this frequently because women seek me out as a female physician, who will hopefully be more understanding than a male physician, particularly with regard to delicate sex issues. Some female patients have questions about their own sexuality that they have been too embarrassed to ask their male physician for years. For example, a woman who complains for years of frequent nightly headaches, which have previously gone undiagnosed despite multiple tests, may actually be bothered by the fact that her husband wants her to perform fellatio, which she just abhors, and therefore she develops a headache subconsciously as an excuse. On detailed questioning though, the real problem may be brought out into the open and fully explored.

The discussion of sexual problems and concerns remains for most women an emotionally charged area. Most women still aren't open about their sexuality even with a woman doctor. I have encountered tremendous sexual problems which may be hidden until I inquire pointedly about them. This is unfortunate, because it's obviously important for a woman to be comfortable talking about all sorts of matters, including sexuality, with her physician.

Of course, we doctors often don't make it easy. Until recently, we received no training in the area of sexuality at all. In fact, many medical schools still don't consider human sexuality an important enough topic to be part of the medical school curriculum. So it's no wonder that some physicians ask, "Well, how are things at home?" What that's supposed to include is everything: how are things financially, how are things between you and your spouse, between you and your children, and are things okay in the bedroom? It's such a general question that unless a woman is extremely confident about broaching a delicate sexual issue on her own, she is not going to say anything. She is going to clam up and let the problem smolder. It's particularly important for doctors to ask specifically, "Are you happy with your sex life? Is there anything you want to ask about your sex life? Is there anything I can help you with?" The burden falls on physicians to give women the room to talk. We have to be bold and open about the area of sexuality ourselves.

AFFECTION VERSUS EXPERTISE

When women patients in their thirties do open up and talk, I find that their unhappiness with their husbands or lovers doesn't center on technique or stimulation or on number of orgasms, but rather on their emotions, on love and affection, on mutuality in the relationship.

Everyone needs to be loved, to be cared about for themselves as individuals rather than as sex objects— and to love another person. This is particularly true of single women in our age group. In our twenties we may have had a tendency to say about a fellow: "Well, he isn't perfect, but at least he's got a good bod," or something like that. In our thirties, a good bod isn't enough. We want more emotional interaction. Many of us begin to wonder if we're ever going to find a partner who really loves us.

A number of women our age become desperate to find someone and settle down, if we haven't done so already. There is concern that if we're not married by age thirty-five, maybe we'll never be married, maybe we'll be spinsters. Some women would be devastated. Others can shrug their shoulders. But, married or not, everybody wants to be loved and cherished.

My friends in their early thirties who have never married are concerned about it: Will I ever find someone I can love? Should I have chosen Tom five years ago? No, he wasn't perfect, but maybe the perfect man doesn't exist for me.

I think the key to the notion of love for a woman in her thirties is a man's ability to accept her for what she is, not for her face or her figure or her technique in the sack, but for the parts of her personality that will endure past her thirties or her forties—her vitality, compassion, intelligence, and so on.

A thirty-year-old woman wants to be cherished, not merely turned on. She wants a man who radiates the sense that she is irreplaceable. At thirty and beyond, a woman often asks questions she wouldn't have when younger: What if I had a mastectomy—would he still care? What about when I'm gray and my face is a sea of wrinkles? What about when his belly sags over his belt and his head gleams in the sunshine—will he still be there for me when his body is changed?

Thirty-year-olds take the long view in intimate relationships. Even if they know that most relationships won't run the course, they don't want to bother with a lover who doesn't stand a chance. They are investing precious time and energy in a love affair, so they are willing to be more picky and to demand a greater return. They want their lover to be the right kind of man, even if he doesn't turn out to be the right man. This is partly motivated by the very real need women in their thirties have to find a man they might be comfortable having children with before time runs out for their reproductive lives. Fertility is one of our decade's greatest worries.

FERTILITY

Statistics make the decision to have children in our thirties seem simple and effortless. Over the past eight years the number of women having their first child after thirty has almost doubled, from 58,000 to more than 100,000. The number having their first child after they turn thirty-five has increased as well, primarily among college-educated professional women who have consciously postponed marriage and children until after they have established their careers.

Another set of numbers lurks behind the first, however. These reveal that a woman who has her first child at thirty-five runs a 2 percent risk that her baby will be born with a serious birth defect. This is twice the risk faced by a woman who has her first child at twenty-five. In addition, a woman having her first child at thirty-five has a tripled risk of miscarriage early in pregnancy—a risk of 1.5 percent at thirty-five from 0.5 percent at twenty-five—and a distressingly increased chance of discovering that either she or her husband is infertile.

The reasons behind these increased risks are largely simple biology. We are born with a fixed number of oocytes that gradually ripen into eggs available for fertilization beginning at puberty. The older we become, the older these incipient eggs become. And each year increases the risk that one of them will pick up erroneous genetic information and will divide improperly when fertilized, causing a miscarriage or a birth defect, particularly Down's syndrome (mongolism). The quality and quantity of a man's sperm also decline with age, but that process doesn't begin until age forty.

Health problems also play a role in our increased risks. Noncancerous tumors, pelvic infections, high blood pressure, and diabetes all increase with age, and can make it harder to have a child. Numerous past abortions or the use of certain contraceptives, such as an IUD, can also have negative ramifications. Many doctors now recommend against IUDs in childless thirty-year-old patients, because they increase the risk of pelvic infection, and may reduce later fertility.

Finally, over time we are exposed to the largely unknown hazards that toxic substances and environmental pollution may hold for conception and pregnancy. Scientists have just begun to investigate this area, but according to Sherry Selevan, a researcher with the National Institute for Occupational Safety and Health: "It makes sense that if there has been a prolonged exposure to a toxic substance, that it could adversely affect the reproductive process, especially if it's a substance that accumulates in the tissue, like pesticides.'' An English study, for example, found that older women might run a higher risk of producing a child with a birth defect because they had been exposed to more X rays.[1]

TRENDS AND FERTILITY FEARS

Still, for better or worse, the central importance of reproduction for women of our age cannot be denied. A generation ago, our mothers were usually well past their first experiences with pregnancy and mothering by the time they reached thirty. For them, the fourth decade was taken up with child rearing and homemaking. The ambivalence we may feel had long since been settled for them by rigid social rules.

Now, of course, more and more of us are holding off on the decision to have children. Sometimes this is caused by career pressure; in other women by the desire to be whole and mature before taking on additional responsibility. In any event, the result of our waiting is that we are now experiencing many of the concerns once confined to younger women.

In addition, we face particular problems brought on by the simple biological fact that, statistically speaking, a thirty-year-old woman is not as effective a baby maker as her twenty-five-year-old counterpart. This is a case where our genetic heritage and modern life haven't gotten their act together yet. Historically, it was important for humans to begin reproducing as early as possible, so as many children as possible could be conceived to overcome the fearsome odds of neonatal death and early childhood disease. Today these concerns are remote, yet our bodies remain attuned to the genetic time clock. We reach our peak of physical excellence at childbearing much earlier than our emotional peak for child rearing. When we wait until our lives and minds are ready for children, we often delay to a point where our bodies aren't quite as ready as they once were.

ROOTS OF INFERTILITY

Fear of infertility is a frequent concern in childless thirty-year-old women. With effective contraception, women today can be sexually active for years before their fertility is ever tested. One of the drawbacks of some contraceptive agents—particularly the pill and IUD—is that they can affect the reproductive system enough to defer effective fertility for months after a woman stops using them. This causes no end of worry among women our age who waited to have children and then begin to fear that they can't conceive. It's extremely important that we all realize what the chances for fertility really are.

Infertility can be defined as the inability of a couple to conceive after one year of unprotected intercourse. Studies show that 25 percent of normal couples will conceive in the first month of unprotected intercourse, 63 percent will have conceived after six months, and 80 percent after one year.[2] Beyond this arbitrary limit, another 5 to 10 percent of couples will eventually conceive, and 10 to 15 percent of couples are infertile.

The causes of infertility can be broken down into male causes in 40 percent of the cases and female causes in 40 to 50 percent. The remaining 10 to 20 percent of couples have no known cause for their infertility. They are the so-called normal infertile couples. In perhaps 20 percent of couples who come to infertility clinics for evaluation, a combination of factors in both the man and the woman will explain their infertility.

Strangely, in this era of improving health, infertility definitely appears to be on the rise. Several factors probably account for this. One is that many couples are delaying childbearing until the woman has established a career. Also, the higher incidence of venereal disease, with the attendant scarring and adhesions that can occur both in the woman and in the man, frustrates hopes for conception. Last, the use of the pill, with its incidence of postpill lack of periods and long time requirements to reestablish regular ovulation, delays successful baby making for some women.

Clearly, for a woman in her thirties there is a biological clock ticking away telling her to have children soon. Graphs of fecundity indicate that a woman is most fertile at about age twenty-four and twenty-five and fertility declines gradually thereafter, with the curve becoming more steep at age thirty and again around age thirty-five to thirty-six.

TESTING FERTILITY

The first way to test your fertility is to give conception the old college try. If after several months of trying you haven't conceived, check with a doctor. No fad fertility rituals will be of much value for you until you at least know whether the problem lies with you or your partner. Many infertility problems associated with specific diseases can be treated today with therapy, so don't be afraid to bring your failure out of the closet. Remember, if you're in your thirties you want to conceive as quickly as possible. Don't dawdle.

The standard policy in terms of infertility evaluation is not to evaluate a woman for infertility until she's had one year of unprotected intercourse. However, for an older woman whose time is running out, I think that some preliminary evaluation is necessary before that year is up. Someone who comes in at age thirty-six with six months of unprotected intercourse deserves at least a preliminary evaluation.

It's hard for a doctor to remain callous in the face of a woman's real fear that she may not be able to have children. Ten to 15 percent of couples can't have children. That's a fairly high percentage. Women may be absolutely desperate even before they've really given themselves a chance. I hear from women over and over again how devastated and depressed they are when they get their period again, that this month they were sure they'd be pregnant. That happens frequently.

The frustration of infertility is that it's somehow the great hoax. You may have spent the past fourteen or fifteen years of your life concerned about contraception, and now when you discontinue your contraception, you can't get pregnant. That strikes many women as a mean trick. I've had patients say that over and over. And it's true. For further information, an excellent book is *Infertility: A Guide for Childless Couples* by Barbara Eck Manning.

DOWN'S SYNDROME WORRIES

Once the baby is on its way, we thirty-year-olds still have worries to sort through. The biggest fear centers on Down's syndrome, in which an extra chromosome in a baby's genes produces a creature of delightful, bubbly personality but also moderate to severe retardation and short life span. The incidence of babies with Down's syndrome rises sharply with age. The older a woman is when she conceives, the greater the chance of giving birth to a Down's syndrome child. The risk is approximately one in 800 at age 30, one in 300 at age 35.

A test exists today that can tell early in pregnancy whether a fetus is afflicted. It can inform a woman early enough so that she can choose abortion if she so wishes. The test is called amniocentesis, and it has become a topic of such dramatic interest that it was the basis for several recent soap opera plots.

The drama revolves around the fact that in some cases amniocentesis causes spontaneous abortions. A woman trying to find out if she has a Down's syndrome baby could conceivably abort a perfectly normal fetus. This poses a severe challenge: is the knowledge worth the risk?

Obviously, for a woman implacably opposed to abortion amniocentesis makes little sense. Even if she knows the child will be retarded, she is committed to continuing the pregnancy. But the woman who feels deeply that she could not bear to give birth to a retarded child might easily think the risk was worth it.

Most statistics quote a risk of miscarriage after amniocentesis in the first trimester of 1 in 250. It is at approximately age thirty-five that the incidence of Down's syndrome equals this risk of miscarriage. However, even then I raise the question with my patients: Are the two risks equal—to you? That is to say, if the statistical frequency of Down's equals the frequency of a miscarriage, do those two risks carry an equal weight of fear and responsibility? How would you feel if you had a Down's syndrome baby? Clearly, for a woman who is thirty-two, has had difficulty conceiving, and is concerned about the possibility of conceiving again, amniocentesis would be difficult to justify. It could end the only pregnancy experience she might ever have, and the odds are on her side. But for a woman who is thirty-four, has just stopped using birth control pills, and conceived without any difficulty, the risk of having an abnormal infant might weigh more heavily than the risk of having a miscarriage. The odds are equal, and she can always conceive again. There are a few other risks with amniocentesis, with minor complications ranging from leaks of amniotic fluid to low-grade local infection, but by far the major concern is miscarriage.

HOW AMNIOCENTESIS WORKS

Amniocentesis is generally performed between the fifteenth and seventeeth weeks of pregnancy, when there is enough fluid available to be tested and yet still time to terminate the pregnancy before the current legal limits of around twenty-two weeks gestation. Under the guidance of ultrasonography, sound waves that outline the uterus, placenta, and fetus, a needle is advanced through the skin and into the amniotic fluid sac. Several tablespoons of fluid are withdrawn and sent to the laboratory for analysis. Cells shed by the fetus are separated from the fluid and grown in a lab dish while the fluid is tested for a variety of chemicals. Then the lab cells are examined under a microscope. Their characteristics indicate whether the fetus is male or female and whether the chromosomes are normal in number and form. If an extra chromosome can be seen, the fetus has Down's syndrome. Meanwhile, the fluid analysis determines whether there are blood abnormalities such as sickle cell disease or hemophilia. It can also test for alpha fetoprotein, a protein produced by the fetal liver, which reaches higher concentrations in the amniotic fluid of infants with defects such as failure of the spinal cord or brain to fuse properly along the body's midline.

ABORTION

There is no increased incidence of infection after abortion or incomplete abortions for women in their thirties, but there is a question now, with repeated abortions, about cervical incompetence during subsequent pregnancies. Since thirty-year-olds are likely to have had more abortions than younger women, this is a particular concern of ours.

The cervix is all that stands between the fetus and the outside world. It is a muscular organ at the end of the uterus, which holds the fetus and the amniotic fluid sac the fetus is floating in within the womb. If the cervix is injured by forceful dilation during abortions, subsequently it may not maintain its position, leading to a higher incidence of spontaneous abortion in women who have had previous induced abortions with dilation. The question has not been resolved one way or the other.

A thirty-year-old woman must also face the possibility that she may find it harder to conceive again after an abortion. Her fertility is in the process of declining. There is no evidence that an uncomplicated abortion affects fertility, but even so, with every passing month she will be a little less able to conceive. As a result, abortion is more difficult for us to make a decision about now than it was in our teens or twenties.

BIRTH CONTROL

To a certain extent, birth control methods are a reflection of thirty-year-old life styles. For instance, if a woman has completed her family, she's more apt to opt for something like tubal ligation. She may also favor the permanent solution if she knows she doesn't want to have children. The risk of being on the pill does increase with age, so many women in their thirties opt for a different means of contraception.

The most important factor here is that older women are more comfortable with their bodies than younger women. It's very difficult to prescribe a diaphragm for a teenager; she's not responsible enough, and inserting it makes her feel "funny." By the time someone is thirty, she is more mature and a lot more comfortable with her body, so prescribing a diaphragm isn't as difficult. The failure rate of diaphragms for college women is very high, because the women won't use them—they're embarrassed or uncomfortable or unprepared. Women in their thirties are more mature and are probably self-confident enough to say, "I don't have my diaphragm with me"—or to make sure they do have it.

Barrier methods of contraception like the diaphragm are safe and effective and most importantly, virtually 100 percent free of side effects. Some women will experience some local irritation from the spermicidal agents, but this is unusual and changing agents usually relieves the problem. The question of a women's life style is an important one in deciding about a diaphragm. One of my patients was in the habit of going to discos on Saturday nights, and her disco purse was just too small to hold everything: money, keys, lipstick, hair brush . . . and her diaphragm with jelly or cream. The erratic nature of her sexual life style made a diaphragm an implausible choice for her. So she chose an IUD.

IUD

The IUD is relatively safe but does have both nuisance and potentially serious side effects, including excessive bleeding or cramping. Previously, the annoying side effect of heavier menstrual periods with increased cramping led to the removal of IUDs in approximately 15 percent of patients after a year. The new IUDs with either progesterone or copper are somewhat smaller and are removed less often for bleeding and pain. If you already have heavy, crampy menstrual periods, consider something other than an IUD.

A more serious complication is perforation of the uterus, which generally occurs during insertion of the intrauterine device. The exact incidence of perforation is unknown, but it seems to be quite rare, on the order of 1 or 2 per 1,000 users. It is also related to the frequency with which the particular physician inserts IUDs. In this case, familiarity breeds safety. An IUD should be inserted only by a gynecologist, although this goes against the practice of certain clinics. The incidence of perforation is unknown because it often causes no symptoms, remaining undiscovered until the next checkup.

Infection ranks as the second significant complication of the IUD. Several studies have shown that pelvic inflammatory disease (PID) is more common in women who use IUDs than in other women.[3] In one study the risk for a woman using an IUD was five times that for a woman without one.[4] In women who had never been pregnant, the risk of infection was seven times that of nonusers. The incidence of pelvic infection in IUD users declines with age and with increasing duration of use. Also, it appears to be highest in women who have multiple sexual partners. A married woman in her thirties who has had a problem-free IUD for some time faces relatively little risk.

Pelvic inflammatory disease or any type of uterine in-fection must be treated with a combination of antibi-otics and removal of the foreign body, in this instance the IUD. Most infections are easily treated, but some severe infections may result in infertility and, extremely rarely, death. There is also an increased incidence of tubal and other ectopic (outside of womb) pregnancies in women using IUDs, and a higher incidence of septic abortions, with a few reported cases of bacterial inva-sion of the bloodstream and death.

In summary, while intrauterine devices are extremely effective in many women, they can be worrisome. Any of us considering having an IUD inserted should be screened with regard to menstrual cramping and heavy bleeding, evaluated for the presence of fibroid tumors, and warned about the possible risk of infection and sterility.

THE PILL

Oral contraceptives, those potent pills, have become universally available. The pills are virtually 100 percent effective when used correctly, reversible, and easy to take. The problem with oral contraceptive agents is that there are significant bodywide side effects. These have declined with the reduction in the pills' estrogen dose over the years, but have not disappeared altogether.

All oral contraceptives operate by pharmacologically suppressing the hypothalamus and pituitary gland, causing a "false" cycle. They also act to change the cer-vical mucous, making it thick and hostile to sperm. In addition, they alter the lining of the uterus (en-dometrium), making it unreceptive to implantation of a fertilized egg.

An enormous impact of the pill for some women stems from the fact that it induces a pharmacologic or drugged state that is far from normal. It is not, however, valid to compare a woman on the pill to a woman who is pregnant, which is frequently done. The contraceptive steroids used in oral contraceptives are not natural hormones and do not act in precisely the same fashion. Also, the biochemical and metabolic changes resulting from the contraceptive drugs differ to some extent from natural metabolic and contraceptive changes during pregnancy.

The areas of major concern about the pill cover broad, scary territory.

Tumors. The bottom line on oral-contraceptive-related tumors is that there is currently no evidence to support the assumption that the pill causes cancer in either the breast or the uterus. No definitive long-term prospective study has looked at the relationship between the uterus and oral contraceptives. Most medical thinking holds that the effect of estrogen on the lining of the uterus can be diminished by the addition of progesterone, as in current preparations, resulting in a withdrawal bleeding period. This will prevent any precancerous estrogen-induced changes in the endometrial lining.

Estrogen use in long-term high doses does, however, induce breast tumors in specific strains of rats and mice. It does not produce breast tumors in a variety of other animals, including hamsters, guinea pigs, goats, dogs, and monkeys. Thus far there is only speculation about whether estrogens may produce tumors in humans but no hard evidence to suggest that they do. One of the largest studies to date, carried out by the Royal College of General Practitioners, looked at 46,000 women in England who were taking oral contraceptives from 1968 to 1974. It found no higher incidence of breast cancer in those women who took the pill than in those who did not. This has been confirmed by retrospective studies.[5] In fact, there seemed to be a protective effect against benign breast disease, the formation of fibrous breast cysts, which was associated with the progesterone in the pill. This effect became apparent after approximately two years of continuous oral contraceptive use.

The only type of tumor that is known to increase in oral contraceptive users is the liver adenoma. This is *not* a malignant tumor, but it is a significant tumor that can be associated with bleeding, into the tumor or abdomen, that produces severe pain. While these liver tumors are rare, we should all be alert to the fact that severe pain in the upper right abdomen requires prompt medical attention—especially if you're taking the pill. Statistically it seems that the increase in liver tumors occurs after about five years of continuous pill usage. The tumors may regress if the pill is stopped. In any event, women on the pill should be aware of the possibility of severe pain and should make sure a careful examination of the liver is performed at their annual medical examination.

Heart attack. Two retrospective studies in England indicated that oral contraceptive use increases the risk of heart attack.[6] This seems to be an age-related phenomenon, with the risk of circulatory problems increasing with age. The British studies indicated that oral contraceptive use acted synergistically, rather than additively, with other heart attack risk factors such as high blood pressure, cigarette smoking, diabetes, and obesity. In a group of women admitted to the hospital with heart attacks, the study reported, the risk for pill users who were thirty to thirty-nine years of age was 2.7 times that for nonusers. In women from forty to forty-four years of age, the users' risk of heart attacks was 5.7 times that of a control group who were not on birth control pills.

Stroke. Clinical studies indicate that there is clearly an association between the use of oral contraceptives and stroke in otherwise healthy young women.[7] Information on stroke comes from a large collaborative retrospective study in the United States.[8] The current *Physician's Desk Reference* lists the overall risk of death from blood clots in pill users at 1.5 per 100,000 users under the age of thirty-five, and 4 per 100,000 over the age of thirty-five.[9] This can be compared with an incidence of just 0.2 and 0.5 per 100,000 in women who do not use the pill. Don't call the undertaker yet, though; compare all these factors to the overall death rate from pregnancy and delivery, which is way up around 22 per 100,000 women.

Thromboembolic disease. Along with stroke, blood clots in the deep veins of the legs are more common in women who use the pill than in those who do not. In one of the best studies in England, the risk of deep thrombosis in the leg, as this is called, was 5.7 times higher in women using oral contraceptives than in controls.[10] The English study also showed a clear-cut relationship between the risk of blood clots and the dose of estrogen used. A further implication of this study was that women who underwent surgery had a higher risk of postoperative blood clots, on the order of 3 to 4 times that of non-pill-users.

Hypertension. The best study of high blood pressure and the pill showed that the incidence of hypertension was 2.6 times that of controls after five years of pill use.[11] "After the five years, 5 percent of the users had developed statistically significant high blood pressure. That frequency increased with the duration of usage. The high blood pressure that occurs with oral contraceptives is the result of gradual changes in liver metabolism. Hypertension does not develop immediately, therefore, and should be checked for regularly after a woman has been on the pill for three months. If high blood pressure does develop, it won't go away overnight, either. The changes in liver function may take three to six months to disappear after pill use is stopped.

Gallbladder disease. The association between the pill and gallbladder disease was noted in the Boston Collaborative Drug Surveillance Program, which noted a relative risk in pill users twice that of nonusers.[12] In an English prospective study, the twofold increase in gallstone incidence was confirmed; additionally, the report showed a plateau at about four to five years of pill use.[13] The mechanism for increased incidence of gallstones was alteration of the cholesterol saturation of gallbladder fluids, which is presumably related to the estrogen in the pill.

In addition to all of the above, there are still other side effects that may be caused by the pill. These include depression, headache, nausea, gas, breast enlargement and discomfort, plus a tendency to weight gain. Some of these side effects may be eliminated by changing to a different pill. One thing I always tell a patient who elects to use oral contraceptives is that we have more data about the pill than we do about other methods of birth control, that we know the pill has more side effects than the other available means of contraception, but that at least she knows exactly what she's getting into. At the same time, I tell her to remember that there are side effects with pregnancy and delivery, too.

On the other side of the coin, in terms of positive side effects, is the suggestion that benign breast disease is improved by oral contraceptive use and the fact that 90 percent of women with severe menstrual cramps or dysmenorrhea have relief of their pain. There may also be improvement in premenstrual symptoms of bloating, headache, and weight gain, since the pill induces a false cycle.

It is currently agreed that the following kinds of women should never, ever take birth control pills: (1) women who have a very strong history, in either themselves or their family, of stroke, heart attack, or thromboembolic disorders such as blood clots in the legs or lungs; (2) those with severe liver or kidney disease; (3) those with a strong family history of breast cancer, or a suspected cancer in themselves; (4) those with undiagnosed or abnormal uterine bleeding; (5) those with a history of obstructive jaundice during pregnancy; (6) those with a history of congenital abnormality of blood fats (hyperlipidemia).

Other indications against the use of oral contraceptive pills include a history of migraine headaches in the patient or family, a history of high blood pressure, uterine fibroids, epilepsy, severe varicose veins, and any likelihood that the patient may undergo elective surgery.

One final dreary point about side effects of the pill: smoking, age, and the pill all seem to act synergistically—they gang up on the user—so that after the age of forty the death rate in women who are on the pill and smoke is higher than if they were using no contraception whatsoever. I think it is reasonable to urge women who smoke at the age of thirty to consider some alternate means of contraception. I do not prescribe the pill to women over age 35 who smoke. Of course, the age for stopping the pill can vary a bit based on individual factors.

Although the pill is almost 100 percent reliable, many women find the minor side effects disturbing and the unanswered questions about long-term use frightening. For these reasons they frequently look for another answer.

NEW METHODS

One of the answers proposed is the so-called mini-pill, which involves the continuous daily use of a low dose of a progesterone agent only. The exact mechanism of contraception is not known but may be related to an effect on the fallopian tubes. Drawbacks with the mini-pill include the fact that it is less than perfect—there is a 2.5 percent failure rate, and, more significant, there is a high enough incidence of irregular bleeding and spotting so that many women are very dissatisfied with the method.

Another means of contraception is postcoital treatment with relatively large doses of estrogen given within seventy-two hours after unprotected intercourse. Currently, the primary postcoital contraceptive, diethylstilbestrol (DES), is given in doses of 50 mg per day for five days, generally along with some medication to treat the nausea that often develops. In addition, there is concern about the effect of the DES on a fetus should the drug not prevent pregnancy. A DES baby could have a very high chance of being deformed, and therefore women should agree to an abortion if the drug fails to prevent pregnancy. This could deter some women. The morning-after pill, as this postcoital means of contraception is being called, should not be considered a first-line contraceptive means but only a backup if some other contraceptive has failed.

Another means of contraception that is being investigated, but is not currently licensed by the FDA, is the use of Depo-Provera, an injectable progesterone-like chemical. This drug is in an oil base and lasts for at least three months. Virtually 100 percent effectiveness is assured by 150 mg of Depo-Provera given every three months. However, it is important to note that it takes six to eight months for the drug to be totally cleared from the body, and side effects such as breakthrough bleeding, weight gain, and depression may persist until then.

Another new technique focuses on determining whether a woman is ovulating. Her inability to get pregnant can be determined by analyzing her breath or saliva, two researchers reported at a 1980 New York meeting of the American Chemical Society, and the finding could lead to a simple home test to tell women when they are fertile. James Kostelc and George Preti, chemists at the Monell Chemical Sense Center in Philadelphia, suspected that the amounts of certain sulfur-containing chemicals (the prime source of bad breath) vary with the reproductive cycle. A study confirmed their suspicions. They next found that a similar chemical change takes place in women's saliva. This may prove of more benefit to women trying to conceive than to those trying to avoid pregnancy, but in any case, further studies are needed before a home test can be devised.

DO YOU NEED A GYNECOLOGIST?

In conclusion, I want to address the question of how important a gynecologist should be to us. Basically, I believe there is a gynecological fixation among too many women today. Most of the health problems that women have during their young adult years center around fertility, contraception, and reproduction, so they end up in the care of gynecologists, who for the most part do a decent job with all of their other medical problems as well. But just as straightforward medical problems can be handled by the gynecologist, straightforward gynecological problems can be handled by the internist or family practitioner.

For a lot of women, a gynecologist is the only doctor they have. I think that this is unfortunate for two reasons: first, it's relatively inefficient use of the ob-gyn doctor who has spent time in specialized training, and second, other medical problems may be overlooked. Obstetrical and gynecological training involves years of delivering babies, performing cesarean sections, and learning how to perform gynecologic surgery. A gynecologist's training isn't being fully utilized if he or she spends his or her days tending to vaginitis and diaphragm fitting. The other side of the coin is that the internist is better trained to evaluate other problems such as headaches, thyroid, or cardiac problems. Our focus needs to be redirected away from our genitals and toward our whole bodies. Every women in her thirties should have a gynecologist for those specific problems that do revolve around difficulties with conception or contraception but should also have an internist for the rest of her.

Nutrition and Medication for Our Best Health

NUTRITION

WHAT SHOULD WOMEN eat? How does our food affect us? We physicians have finally begun to recognize that women have different dietary requirements than men.

Doctors have long realized that we need more nutrients during pregnancy, but now our differing needs are seen as lifelong and significant. For instance, we need significantly more iron while menstruating and we may need more vitamin C to make sure our bodies absorb the iron properly.

Organized medicine's increasing understanding of our special nutritional needs is illustrated by a recent report on folic acid supplements. At 25 times the recommended daily allowance of 400 micrograms a day, this study found, folic acid can halt and even reverse cervical dysplasia in women taking the pill. (Dysplasia is an abnormality of cervical cells that sometimes progresses to cancer.) The report, from Dr. A. E. Butterworth, Jr., chairman of nutrition at the University of Alabama Medical Center in Birmingham, derived from a study of 47 women, some of whom received 10 mg of folic acid daily, while others got a placebo.

After three months, the women getting the folic acid supplement showed marked improvement. Dysplasia disappeared in 4 of the women on folic acid but in none who received the placebo. And while dysplasia progressed to very early cancer in 4 of the placebo-treated patients, no such progression occurred with any folic-acid-treated women. One of the problems in interpreting this study, however, is that dysplasia frequently disappears spontaneously.

Here are some other areas where our nutritional needs vary from those of men.

SPECIAL NUTRITIONAL NEEDS

Premenstrual bloating. Avoid excessive salt intake, particularly in the week before menstruation begins. As menses approaches, our levels of estrogen and progesterone rise. These hormones cause us to retain salt and water in our bodies.

Premenstrual depression. A daily 30 mg pyridoxine (vitamin B_6) supplement may help. Increased estrogen levels before menstruation apparently can interfere with normal metabolism of vitamin B_6. The deficiency that results can compromise activity of the amino acid tryptophan, with possible effects on the nervous system.

Oral-contraceptive-related deficiencies. A well-balanced diet is the best treatment for vitamin deficiencies. If you suspect your diet is borderline or inadequate, take a low-level vitamin supplement that contains folic acid (400 micrograms [mcg]), pyridoxine (2 mg), thiamin (1 mg), riboflavin (1.2 mg) and B_{12} (3 mcg). Using oral contraceptives can cause marginal deficiencies of these vitamins.

Oral-contraceptive-induced depression and fatigue. A

daily supplement (30 mg) of pyridoxine may help to overcome pill-related impairment of your ability to metabolize pyridoxine.

Pregnancy. We require a daily increase of 30 gm (about 1 ounce) of protein and 400 mg of additional calcium intake beyond the normal 800 mg. (Five glasses of skim or whole milk can supply all the calcium we need.) We also need 10 to 20 mg of iron and 800 mcg of folic acid supplements, to make sure both the fetus and mother get all they require.[1] Our needs for other vitamins and minerals are slightly increased and usually can be satisfied by a balanced diet or basic vitamin-mineral supplement.

Breast-feeding. During this time we need extra calories, some 600 to 800 a day over our normal caloric level. We also require more calcium—a total of 1,200 mg daily. Too few calories may reduce milk volume; milk quality may be impaired by vitamin and mineral deficiencies. However, milk production may also be blocked by excessive amounts of vitamins, especially pyridoxine, B_6. So don't overload.

Anemia. About 40 percent of women between twenty and fifty have some degree of iron deficiency. An iron supplement plus vitamin C may help. While menstruating women need 18 mg of iron daily, a typical diet provides just about 9 mg. You can load up on iron-rich foods, obviously, but vitamin C improves absorption of iron from any foods you eat when you take 100 mg with a meal.

Folic acid deficiency. This is a common, often overlooked cause of anemia, weakness, fatigue, diarrhea, and sore tongue in pregnant women or women on junk food diets. The daily diet should include uncooked leafy vegetables and other folic-acid-rich foods such as fresh fruit. Deficiencies occur when these foods are totally ignored or cooked too long. They arise particularly often among women whose folic acid stores are depleted by pregnancy or oral contraceptives. Folic acid supplements may also be called for.

Cystic mastitis. This is a benign breast disease that affects as many as 50 percent of women twenty to fifty; signs are aching, tender, lumpy breasts. If you tend to develop cysts you should avoid coffee, tea, cola, and chocolate as much as possible because chemicals in these substances appear to foster cyst development. In one recent study, 37 out of 45 women avoiding these substances had complete resolution of cysts and 7 others reported less discomfort.[2] In another study, 600 units of daily vitamin E supplements completely or partially cleared cysts in 22 out of 26 women.[3] Don't prescribe for yourself, though, until you've made sure malignancy is ruled out.

Urinary tract infections. This is a common problem in women. Treatment combines taking antibiotics with drinking cranberry juice and/or vitamin C supplements to make urine more acidic and so less favorable for bacterial growth.

BALANCED DIET

Beyond these situations, a balanced diet for a woman in her thirties is really the same as a balanced diet for any adult. It should include foods from all the major food groups so that you have a source of calcium and vitamin C, protein, and iron, along with lots of fresh fruits, vegetables, and whole grain products. Roughly 20 percent of the diet should be protein, 35 percent fat, and 45 percent carbohydrate.

The key word here is balanced. Forty-five different essential nutrients have been identified as necessary for health. Of these, some fifteen are minerals or trace metals not found in abundance in all foods. It's important to eat a variety of different foods in order to assure proper intake of all of these nutrients. You shouldn't be eating the same items day in and day out, week after week. That is why fad diets that call for intense concentration on one kind of food aren't terribly healthy. One of the big problems with fad diets is that it takes a combination of food substances working together for proper utilization. If you're eating only one food substance, some of that food is wasted, because it can't be properly metabolized in the absence of nutrients contained in other foods. What you need for health is a combination of foods eaten on a regular basis so your body can use them properly.

Red meat is a major part of the diet of many women our age. Is there a real danger of eating too much meat in your thirties? Yes, there is, but it's not just cholesterol. The other concern about a diet high in red meat is that an excessively high protein diet saps calcium from our bones—more about that later. So, for both these reasons, we should probably limit big chunks of meat to one meal a day.

Even lean red meat has some fat, so the whole issue of cholesterol does arise. But cholesterol, in my mind, is a much maligned compound. Everyone thinks of cholesterol as being the bugaboo, the bad guy. Actually there are different "types" of cholesterol or fats—such as high-density lipoprotein—which probably have a protective effect in terms of heart attacks. It's probably the low-density lipoprotein which is the "cholesterol culprit." One of the things we frequently ignore is that our bodies can make cholesterol. If we don't eat enough cholesterol, we will synthesize it. Cholesterol is essential. It's the building block from which we make all of our steroid hormones, and that includes all the female sex hormones, as well as cortisol, which is essential for life. It's also an important structural element in the formation of cells. So cholesterol is not all bad, and it doesn't just come from food.

For instance, there's a condition called familial hypercholesterolemia, which affects 1 in 500 people. If you take those people and eliminate cholesterol from their diets altogether, they still make too much of it.

Because most of us in our thirties have a higher level of high-density lipoprotein than men, our anxiety about cholesterol problems can be much lower. The concern for us is establishing bad habits now that will get us after menopause, when our natural protection diminishes. Cholesterol levels do relate to our risk of later heart disease, though, so we should limit our daily cholesterol intake to 300 mg, about one egg, a day.

JUNK FOOD

Most of us worry too much about junk food. Just what happens when a thirty-year-old woman eats a candy bar or a hot fudge sundae? One factor is that junk food is generally high in salt. It's also frequently high in simple sugars. When you eat a hot fudge sundae, you dump a tremendous bolus of pure glucose into your system. When that happens, insulin levels rise in response to the elevated sugar level.

The sugar rush that accompanies this is sometimes said to be addictive. I don't know exactly what that means, but the physical response to sugar certainly can cause psychological symptoms of a mild sort. When our sugar level increases we generally become a bit more sleepy, and when it declines, we tend to be more alert and awake. This yo-yo affect has been claimed by some to be habit-forming in some women.

As to whether junk food is worse for us now in our thirties than when we were younger, the answer is no, with one big exception. If we're eating a lot of junk food now, it means that our bad habit has continued for some additional ten or fifteen adult years and may easily continue on into our forties and fifties. Then the physical impact will be greater. Also, the excessive calories in junk food begin to have a greater impact now because our metabolism is slowing. More of each candy bar reaches our hips after passing our lips. So, now is a good time to cut back.

Another consideration about junk food is the lack of important water-soluble B vitamins and folic acid. Candy bars and pretzels aren't fortified with vitamin C either. And because we can't store these important water-soluble vitamins in our fat, we need to eat them on a regular basis.

So, meat poses a problem because of cholesterol, and junk food is a problem because of lack of vitamins and excessive salt and concentrated sugar. What about a high-protein diet? That's not safe either. High-protein diets tend to drive calcium out of our bones. The greater the overindulgence in protein, the greater the problem. What would that do to a thirty-year-old woman? Well, the incidence of osteoporosis, the disease in which the bones grow weak and brittle, increases with age. It doesn't become a major worry until our sixties, but it starts in our thirties. By age thirty-five, 10 percent of women show some signs of reduced bone calcium. It's hard for a thirty-year-old woman to think ahead to being sixty and in bed with a hip fracture or broken ribs, but I often see women in their thirties who I suspect are destined to be those patients. Their bones have slowly leached away.

What happens is that sometime in our thirties, our calcium balance becomes negative. We begin to lose it from our bones. That's exacerbated by pregnancy and nursing, so it's important for us to try to maintain a positive calcium balance. One of the factors to consider in the American diet is the extra intake of protein, which leads to some calcium loss. Cut down to about 4 to 6 ounces of meat a day; that's all you really need.

UNHEALTHY HEALTH FOOD

In my opinion, health food regimens and supplements are generally unhealthy. In these diets women consume a variety of compounds that are poorly controlled and understood. I see a lot of health food faddists in my office, and I'm frequently concerned that the symptoms these women complain of are actually being caused by all the exotic foods and pills that they're taking. Scattered reports about toxic levels of arsenic and mercury and what not in a variety of these health food compounds substantiate my worries.[4] I have health-food addicts come in with a variety of psychoneurotic complaints: muscle aches, pains, weakness, fluctuations in energy level, and so on. Many of these are normal body reactions, and the fears about them these faddists have are part of their neurotic self-image. A different mix of foods won't make these fluctuations go away. That is to say, not everyone feels fantastic all day long. We have to accept the natural ebb and flow of energy and strength. If you eat a heavy meal, you feel sleepy. That is a normal response. But some women don't want to feel sleepy; they can't accept anything less of themselves than 100 percent alertness. They want to make the feeling go away. But that's impossible. Sleepiness is a normal response, and gobbling "health" products won't change that response.

One so-called health food that is undergoing extensive analysis in both the United States and Canada is dolomite, which is used frequently by women, including pregnant women, as a daily source of calcium. One study indicated that dolomite also serves as a source of toxic metals, including lead, arsenic, mercury, aluminum, and antimony.[5] Dr. H. J. Roberts of the Palm Beach Institute for Medical Research, writing in the *New England Journal of Medicine*, suggested that it would be "prudent to avoid dolomite and bone meal until data from the scientific study protocols" become available.[6] I agree.

I never fail to be amazed by patients who radiate a tremendous distrust of drugs but will carelessly and calmly consume a variety of herbs and herbal medications, never recognizing that these herbs are in fact drugs.

For example, one of the most commonly used herbs is ginseng root, which was used for centuries in the Orient as a stimulant for elderly people. Now it's sold in a variety of forms in health food stores. Ginseng products include capsules of ginseng, ginseng tablets, ginseng teas, extracts, cosmetics, and dried roots. Some of the commercially available products do resemble the whole root in composition, but some of the tablets, on analysis, have been found to contain no detectable active ingredients. Some of the teas, when analyzed in one study in the *Journal of Pharmacologic Science*, showed extremely low concentrations of active ingredients. And a study reported in the *Journal of the American Medical Association* in 1975 showed that some preparations that had been labeled as ginseng actually contained other chemical compounds such as phenybultazone, a very strong drug capable of severely lowering white blood cell count.

Why do people take ginseng? It has been promoted as an aphrodisiac and age retardant but actually has a variety of unhealthy side effects. For example, Dr. Ronald Siegel, from the University of California at Los Angeles Medical Center, described a ginseng abuse syndrome in users of the drug. He studied 133 ginseng users over a period of two years and reported adverse effects varying from high blood pressure, skin eruptions, and morning diarrhea to nervousness and swelling of the feet. Ginseng has also been implicated in painful swollen breasts in several women and in changing blood sugar levels.

The basic problem with ginseng and other health food products is that because they are not regulated or analyzed under the jurisdiction of the FDA, they are sometimes not as healthy or free of side effects as their promoters claim and users assume. In addition to the ginseng abuse syndrome, there are now case reports of poisoning from other so-called health foods. Several herbal tea preparations have been implicated in causing severe liver damage. An article in the *New England Journal of Medicine*, for instance, reported a case of acidosis in a user of "flower of sulfur," a sulfur product used as a folk remedy for various bowel problems.[7]

VEGETARIANISM

Vegetarian diets come in three flavors: complete vegetarian diets with no meat products, fish, milk products, or eggs; lacto vegetarian diets in which milk, butter, and cheeses are allowed; and lacto-ovo vegetarian diets, in which eggs are okay also. Deficiencies of various nutrients or vitamins are very unlikely except for women who are complete vegetarians.

One of the essential factors in constructing a vegetarian diet is that it contain enough of the eight essential amino acids. Amino acids are the "building blocks" of proteins (which are the structural components of cells and the basis of various enzymes and hormones). Our bodies can make many of the amino acids, but there are eight which are considered "essential" that we cannot synthesize. Milk products, eggs, meat, and fish supply adequate amounts of all of these essential amino acids. Vegetable proteins also contain all of the essential amino acids, but a single vegetable may be low in a particular amino acid. For example, corn has a low tryptophan content. Beans, however, are low in methionine and rich in tryptophan, so that the diet of the Southwest of corn and beans was an excellent diet containing all of the essential amino acids. Nuts by themselves may be low in methionine and lysine. Certain cereals may be low in lysine. The combination, however, of various cereals and legumes (beans, peas and lentils) can provide a very high-quality protein source that is, in every respect, comparable to the protein provided from animal sources (and without the cholesterol). By consuming a combination of various nuts, cereals and legumes, a complete vegetarian will assure herself of an adequate protein source.

Deficiency of B_{12} has been described in complete vegetarians. Complete vegetarian diets, which include no milk or eggs, provide almost no vitamin B_{12}. This vitamin is essential for the synthesis of red blood cells and neural tissue, and there have been reports in the medical literature of complete vegetarians who develop anemia or low blood counts and even degeneration of the spinal cord because of B_{12} deficiency. It is very rare for a vegetarian to develop B_{12} deficiency because our body stores normally far exceed our daily needs. Nonetheless, I recommend that complete vegetarians take B_{12} supplements in order to prevent problems.

Another deficiency that can occur in vegetarians consuming large quantities of fiber is that of various trace minerals, particularly zinc. Phytates in fiber may decrease the absorption of these minerals. Generally, if the diet includes milk products or eggs, it will also contain enough trace metals. A third deficiency is that of iron. Lima beans are an excellent source, containing over 2 milligrams of iron per half cup serving. Pumpkin seeds are a good source of iron as well, but it's difficult to consume a cup of pumpkin seeds per day. Therefore, if you have any question at all about the adequacy of iron in your diet, you should take an iron supplement.

VITAMINS

Okay, I'm not keen on health food—what about vitamins? Is there a need for them in our thirties?

I believe that the health claims made for various nonprescription vitamin products have probably been overstated. In fact, too much of some vitamins can be harmful. Vitamins can be divided into two types: fat-soluble, such as vitamins A, D, and K, and water-soluble, vitamins B and C. The water-soluble vitamins have no known toxic dosages, but the fat-soluble vitamins do have toxic effects when taken in excess because the body cannot excrete them as readily.

An excellent example of the dual character of vitamins is vitamin A: both deficiency and excess are harmful. Vitamin A is important for vision, and one of the earliest symptoms of vitamin A deficiency is night blindness. On one level it has been shown in some experimental studies to protect against the carcinogenic effects of the aromatic hydrocarbons found in cigarette smoke.[8] Another study of vitamin A showed an increased incidence of various tumors of the colon in rats that were fed a diet deficient in vitamin A.[9] Still another report, in the medical journal *Cancer*, showed an increased incidence of lung cancer in men deficient in vitamin A.[10] Currently studies using vitamin A as a cancer treatment in experimental animals are under way. The catch, however, is that the doses of vitamin A used would be toxic for most of us.

The recommended daily allowance (RDA) for vitamin A in adult women is 4,000 international units (IU) per day. A normal balanced diet contains anywhere from 7,500 to 10,000 IU per day, roughly twice the RDA. The toxic dose for vitamin A is on the order of 50,000 IU per day, but has to be consumed over a long period of time, perhaps a year. Yet increasing numbers of women seem to be taking this much or even more vitamin A and harming themselves.

One study, by the way, showed that emulsified vitamin A is even more toxic than the conventional form—a single dose of a million IU may cause acute vitamin A poisoning.[11] Vitamin A overdosage might mimic some common skin problems; internally it can cause chronic liver disease. Typically, women who ingest excessive doses of vitamin A have dry, coarse, scaly skin. There may be cracks or fissures at the corners of the lips, scaling of the scalp, and loss of hair. The nails may become brittle and break easily. A low-grade fever, fatigue, and insomnia may occur. If you've been gobbling vitamin A and show these symptoms, a firm diagnosis can be made on the basis of a serum or blood vitamin A level test. See your doctor.

If you eat yellow vegetables regularly, you're getting enough vitamin A.

Yellow skin may occur from eating excessive amounts of carotene. Some vitamin-A-rich foods, such as carrots and squash, also are high in carotene. There doesn't appear to be any other injurious effect from the high levels of carotene. The yellowing can be distinguished from jaundice because the whites of the eyes remain white and the coloration is usually strongest on the palms and soles. Stop eating so many carrots, and skin color will rapidly return to normal.

Vitamin D is very interesting, also. In the past decade our concept of how the body uses vitamin D has been tremendously broadened, bringing the realization that vitamin D is not really a vitamin but a hormone. If a woman is exposed to adequate sunlight she doesn't need a dietary supplement of vitamin D. Via a unique process of activation in the skin, ultraviolet light converts a chemical made from cholesterol in the body into vitamin D itself. Only if you live in the dark and don't drink milk is there a need to worry about vitamin D deficiency with its attendant bone mineralization problems. If you do need extra D, milk and milk products can be supplemented with vitamin D. While the daily requirement for vitamin D in adults has not been established, the National Research Council of the United States has recommended an intake of 400 IU per day. Vitamin D, along with parathyroid hormone, is important for the normal control of calcium and phosphate metabolism in the body and normal bone mineralization.

Vitamin D overdose, like vitamin A overdose, occurs only after chronic ingestion of excessive amounts of vitamin D, on the order of 50,000 to 100,000 IU per day for months. Because vitamin D is fat-soluble, the excessive amounts are stored in the body fat and released slowly into the bloodstream rather than being excreted promptly. There are no reports of toxicity from vitamin D as the result of excessive sun exposure; that's presumably because of natural protective mechanisms that impede the release of vitamin D from the skin. Vitamin D excess is related to high levels of calcium in the blood and urine. Symptoms include lethargy, loss of appetite, constipation, and kidney stones or kidney failure.

Vitamin E, another fat-soluble vitamin, and currently the pretty baby of vitamin faddists, actually consists of several compounds called tocopherols. The RDA for vitamin E is 15 IU per day, which is easily met, as the substance is plentiful in many foods, including vegetable oils. There are currently no known overdose symptoms documented for vitamin E. However, because the other fat-soluble vitamins, A and D, can be toxic, it seems prudent not to take excessive amounts of vitamin E. The temptation to overdo might be large. Vitamin E has been touted as a stimulant for sexual performance, as a protector against lung damage caused by certain cigarette-smoke hydrocarbons, and as an effective agent in slowing aging.

This claim for vitamin E is very interesting. It's based on the fact that vitamin E is an antioxidant, which means that it interferes with, or inactivates, certain active chemical substances that are formed in cells as the byproducts of oxidation. It is clear that these free radicals can interact with protein in the cells in order to form age-related pigments. Nonetheless, it is unclear what these aging pigments have to do with aging itself. Animal studies have shown a decline in aging pigments following supplemental doses of vitamin E, but there was no change in the important parameters of health performance or the death rate due to aging in the test animals.[12]

A report in the *Journal of the American Medical Association* stated: "Right now you can go to the drugstore and buy thousands of grams of vitamin E and take as much as you want, not knowing that it may affect you profoundly. It may change your lipids; it may, and probably will, alter some of your steroid hormones. At least at the dosage levels we prescribed, which weren't all that high, vitamin E is not a benign vitamin that you can take like vitamin C if you think you're getting a cold. It is—and we need to stress this—a pharmacologic agent."[13]

Vitamin C has engendered a tremendous amount of controversy in recent years, with the claim that megadoses of this vitamin—1 gm or more per day—will either prevent or minimize the symptoms of the common cold. However, controlled studies showed no significant differences in either the frequency, the severity, or the duration of the common cold in patients treated with placebos compared to those treated with vitamin C.[14] Large doses of vitamin C aren't needed for any other reason, either. Large doses *can* interfere with the absorption of vitamin B_{12} or cause scurvy to develop in the infants of mothers who have taken excessive amounts of vitamin C during pregnancy. So, no megadoses, please, particularly if you're pregnant.

Vitamin C deficiency (scurvy) is an unusual disease in the world today; the vitamin is present in milk, organ meats, and fruits and vegetables. Interestingly, humans, other primates, and guinea pigs are the only mammals unable to synthesize vitamin C from sugar. The need for vitamin C in our diets is actually a result of a genetic defect in our handling of carbohydrates.

VITAMIN PILLS

What about the daily vitamin and mineral supplement? I tell my patients that a normal, balanced diet ordinarily provides all of the vitamins and minerals necessary for good health. If a woman eats a varied diet containing leafy green vegetables, yellow vegetables (such as squash or carrots), fruits, whole grain cereals or nuts, some source of vitamin C (such as citrus fruits, parsley, or green peppers), a source of calcium, and either meat or fish or a combination of lentil and beans for protein and iron, then all of her requirements have been met. A supplemental vitamin or mineral preparation is superfluous. However, if a woman eats a skimpy breakfast and fast food for lunch and dinner, then a vitamin supplement is a good idea. The brand doesn't matter much. So-called natural vitamins are essentially the same as synthetic vitamins. If in doubt about your diet, take a vitamin; one a day won't hurt.

Various drugs we take can interfere with our body's capability to absorb or utilize vitamins and minerals. For example, mineral oil will result in a deficiency of the fat-soluble vitamins A, D, and E by causing them to be malabsorbed. Alcohol leads to a deficiency of folic acid, magnesium, protein, and thiamine. Various anticonvulsant medications can change the metabolism of vitamin D and calcium leading to bone disease. And diuretics may deplete us of sodium, potassium, calcium or magnesium by increasing the excretion of these minerals through our kidneys.

TRACE METALS

A current dietary notion is that we all need supplements of trace metals, inorganic compounds our bodies use in their processing chores. Trace metals are one of the reasons why you should consume a balanced diet, and why it's not enough to eat a piece of chicken and a salad day in and day out, because chicken alone may not contain a wide enough variety of these trace metals—zinc, selenium, cobalt, and many others. The body does have a requirement for these things, but the exact amounts are poorly understood, and some of the requirements are unknown. So the question remains, Is a thirty-year-old woman doing herself any good by taking high doses of trace metals?

Well, zinc has been used in a variety of surgical studies to promote healing. There's a very interesting study of hermorrhoid surgery patients that evaluated this question.[15] (Can you see all these patients with their bottoms up in the air, watching the progress of their hemorrhoid scars?) Zinc was shown to be helpful in promoting healing, but it's unclear whether those people were zinc-deficient or whether zinc in excess did the trick.

I don't see any purpose in consuming excess amounts of zinc or any other trace metal until more is known about them. All of the metals can lead to toxicity if taken to excess.

SALT

Some 35 million Americans have hypertension (high blood pressure), and not all of them are high-powered male executives. Women can get it just as easily. Is the culprit in hypertension, as some researchers believe, excessive salt? Perhaps, but it hasn't yet been proved. Rather than being a cause, salt may merely set up the conditions necessary for hypertension to develop.

Many of us consume twenty to thirty times as much salt as our bodies actually need. Historically, this excessive salt intake is a relatively recent development, having occurred in the past 200 to 300 years. In ancient times, salt was rare and therefore valuable. Roman soldiers in fact were paid in salt. Thus the word "salary" and the phrase "worth her salt."

Many studies show that in societies where salt is low, such as in rural Uganda, in the highlands of Malaysia and in populations in New Guinea, blood pressure does not increase with age as occurs in American society, and hypertension is a rarity. Studies also show that people who are accustomed to living with very little salt in their diet will show a rise in blood pressure when they are exposed to a higher sodium intake. For example, people in the inland villages in the Solomon Islands, who eat very little salt and cook their food in fresh water, have no change in their blood pressure as they age and no hypertension. However, people of a similar genetic background, in a similar village on an offshore island, who do their cooking in salty sea water, have a substantial change in blood pressure as they age and a higher incidence of hypertension.

We do need some salt to function properly. Sodium, along with potassium and chloride, is an essential nutrient that regulates the balance of water in and out of body cells. Without these nutrients, body functions would quickly grind to a halt. But the actual amount of sodium needed to sustain life is 300 to 400 milligrams (mg.) a day—the amount in one-tenth of a teaspoon of salt.

Few of us realize how much salt we consume. Even if you eat no obviously salty foods, such as pickles, sauerkraut, anchovies, or chipped beef, chances are you are packing in incredible amounts of hidden sodium in baked and processed foods, cured meats, and hard cheeses. For example, while 14 potato chips contain 190 mg of sodium and an ounce of salted cocktail peanuts has 132 mg, two slices of packaged white bread have 234 mg, a 1-ounce serving of cornflakes has 278 mg, and a half cup of cottage cheese has a whopping 435 mg.

Should we eliminate salt from our diet? After all, more than 80 percent of the people in the United States do not develop high blood pressure despite a lifelong consumption of a high-sodium diet. This segment of the population would gain very little from giving up all salty foods. However, the 15 to 20 percent of women who are destined to become hypertensive would benefit tremendously by reducing their dietary intake of sodium. Who among us is likely to fit into this group? Those women who have a family history of high blood pressure and had normal to highish blood pressure during adolescence would probably benefit tremendously by eliminating hidden salt in their diets.

Another reason for us to cut down on salt intake is that extra salt can increase our discomfort prior to menstruation. Many of us would feel better with a cutback in salt during the days before menstruation. Less salt means less water retained in our pre-period bodies.

CAFFEINE

Is caffeine unhealthy? We've been drinking or eating it since we stumbled out of the caves, with no obvious signs of illness, but recent research has pointed up some disturbing questions about caffeine's role in a number of health problems, some of particular concern to women.

Cystic breast lumps. Caffeine may promote formation of cysts, particularly those that appear just before menstruation in women our age. Women with cystic breasts might consider cutting coffee, tea and cola from their diets.

Heart disease. For most of us caffeine won't cause serious heart problems. A direct link between the stimulant and heart disease has never been shown. However, if you have a tendency toward heart problems, the additional work caffeine puts on your heart may speed problems along. And some sensitive individuals may develop high blood pressure after drinking a lot of coffee. If you get heart palpitations, cut down on caffeine.

Ulcers. Since caffeine stimulates stomach acid secretion, women with ulcers or "acid stomach" should avoid it. It won't help to switch to decaffeinated coffee—apparently all roasted grain beverages, with or without caffeine, increase acid flow.

You should probably cut down on or even eliminate caffeine from your diet while pregnant or nursing, because high doses of it have been found to cause birth defects in animals. The FDA has called for studies to determine if caffeine poses a danger to the human fetus. Studies are in progress; for now the FDA advises pregnant women to avoid coffee, tea, and cola, the same way it advises them to avoid alcohol, cigarettes, and other drugs. Because the first three months of pregnancy are critical to fetal development, eliminating caffeine when you first start trying to conceive is probably prudent.

If you're nursing, two or three cups of coffee spaced throughout the day probably won't cause problems, but drinking much more than that may allow enough caffeine in your breast milk to make your baby restless and "colicky." The best time to drink coffee or tea is just after you nurse so that by the next feeding most of the caffeine will be gone from your system.

How much caffeine is too much? Reactions to caffeine vary enormously among us. Some of us find that a single cup of coffee sends us through the roof, while others can drink cup after cup and still sleep like logs. In any case, a hyper, "speedy" feeling means you've exceeded your capacity.

SUGAR SUBSTITUTES

Since 1970, when the FDA banned cyclamates as a sugar substitute, there has been a flurry of concern about artificial sweeteners. Saccharin clearly is a carcinogen of relatively low potency in rats. However, the problem of extrapolating from rats to humans led the FDA and Congress to pass the Saccharin Study and Labeling Act in 1977, putting an eighteen-month moratorium on a saccharin ban.

Now the results of major new studies are in, and in general, they found no increased risk of bladder cancer among most users of artificial sweeteners.[16] Only heavy users. Those who consumed six or more servings of saccharin (the equivalent of two or more diet beverages) per day had an increased risk.

An unanswered question concerns fetal exposure to saccharin. With what is known today, it's prudent for pregnant women to avoid saccharin. It's interesting to note that most of the subjects in the saccharin study were over sixty-five years old and had consumed much less artificial sweetener over their lifetime than we will in our lives. It's probably too soon to judge the effects of lifelong consumption of large amounts of a weak carcinogen.

Clearly, more research into nonnutritive sweeteners needs to be done. Saccharin will be replaced only when there is a suitable alternative. On July 15, 1981, the FDA approved a new artificial sugar substitute for use in various dry food products such as drink mixes, puddings, gelatins, and cereals. This new sweetener, Aspartane, consists of two amino acids, aspartic acid and phenylalanine. It is said to be virtually indistinguishable from sugar in taste and has 1/10 calorie per teaspoon, compared to 18 calories per teaspoon of sugar.

Although Aspartane has survived the final round of testing, it will probably only partially replace saccharin as a nonnutritive sweetener. This is because it is unsuitable for cooking or baking, as it denatures at high temperatures. In addition, if it is in contact with water for long periods of time it loses its sweetening ability. Nor has this sweetener been free from controversy. FDA approval of the sweetener was delayed since 1974 because of an animal study showing that it might cause brain damage. Additional intensive studies failed to show any indication of brain damage, but the sweetener probably should be avoided by women who have phenylketonuria, a metabolic disease. Currently Aspartane is marketed freely in France, Luxembourg, and Belgium.

FASTING

A great mist of misinformation clouds this practice. A lot of fad diets advocate occasional fasting to cleanse your body out, and some women are doing it because it's the ultimate diet: instead of trying to cut down all the time, they eat normally and then fast a couple of days a month.

I don't understand exactly what "cleansing your body" means to advocates of fasting. Nonetheless, I suspect that it relates in some fashion to a preoccupation with bowels, with "retained feces" that are considered a culprit, a toxin to the individual. Fasting will result in weight loss, but much of this weight loss is due to fluid and is immediately regained when you resume eating. What does happen when you fast is that you begin breaking down your muscle as well as your fat. Ketone bodies such as acetoacetate and hydroxybutyrate increase. Also, blood uric acid levels rise, but gout rarely results if kidney function is normal.

Ketones do suppress appetite, but they can have injurious side effects. Ketones have been shown to have effects on the heart, occasionally resulting in an increased incidence of ectopic or unusual heart beats or disturbances in the cardiac rhythm. Obviously, everyone who diets has a high ketone level. But in normal individuals, there are counter-regulatory forces, particularly insulin, which come into play so that the situation doesn't get out of control. In diabetics, where insulin is inadequate, it's these same ketones, which are acidic, that make victims so sick. At the same time, I don't think that fasting would be any more dangerous for us in our thirties or forties than it was in our twenties. A short-term fast is generally well tolerated, but I wouldn't fast if I were pregnant, certainly. Ketones have been associated with significant lowering of intelligence quotient (IQ), so I wouldn't recommend fasting for a pregnant woman.

HOLISTIC HEALTH

How important do you think this holistic business is? I do believe the idea that your mental attitude is etched in your face and your body, that you feel younger when you're in harmony, has some validity, but not to the extent that holistic enthusiasts would profess. I doubt if we're going to genuinely look significantly younger if we merely feel and think younger, but I do think that our attitude is crucial in coping with daily stresses and major life stresses as well. And when we cope better, we feel better.

Our attitude does influence to some extent how we age, but at the same time, there's obviously a large component of aging uninfluenced by behavior and attitude, which is largely immutable. A lot of our aging pattern is derived from our genes, and there's nothing we can do about it.

Within the boundaries of our genes, though, the idea of being happy and contented with our lives in order to keep ourselves "healthy" has some validity. We may not find truth or eternal youth, but we can greatly reduce our chance of developing major diseases, like heart problems or ulcers, through our outlook.

I don't have any bone to pick with nontraditional or holistic medicine (in fact, I applaud the focus on seeing the *whole* person), but I would merely stress the importance of maintaining ties with traditional medicine so that no stone is unturned. And I'd counsel caution: the sign on the door doesn't always rate a carpet on the floor, if you can determine what goes on the sign. As a doctor, I can hang out a shingle that says I specialize in neurosurgery or cardiovascular surgery without having had any training to that effect (of course hospitals would not grant me operating privileges). The same is true for holistic practitioners. They can say whatever they please about themselves and may not have any training or any regulatory body that's overseeing them. So, be a skeptical customer for your health's sake.

MEDICATIONS

Even the best-fed individual, the most prudent sensible dieter, from time to time needs medication for minor gripes. The range of medicines available to us today is staggering, and our medicinal patterns are quite unique. Here is a brief tour through the basics of medication for women our age. Keep in mind that it covers a lot of ground very quickly; before you select a medicine for any serious problem, you should check with your doctor.

DMSO

DMSO, an industrial solvent that has garnered much publicity lately for its supposed pain-killing benefits, can be harmful and carries the potential for tragedy. It relieves pain without influencing the cause of the pain. Physicians who deal with it have seen a variety of pains treated ineffectively with DMSO when conventional therapy would have been of value. I've seen cases of arthritis that have been treated with DMSO, where the immediate pain was relieved, but the joint was destroyed. One of the most vital things to do in patients with arthritis is to see if destruction of the joint can be avoided. Because DMSO relieves pain, patients may ignore symptoms that require medical attention, because they don't feel anything. Currently, DMSO isn't licensed for medical use in most states, but this industrial solvent can be obtained through a variety of nonmedical sources. I would not recommend using it for anything whatsoever, without close medical supervision.

NARCOTICS

Many narcotics can produce nausea—codeine is a particular offender in that regard—and it's not infrequent for a patient to come in complaining that she is allergic to codeine when in fact all she has had is nausea. A few people are allergic to narcotics, but the reaction goes beyond simple nausea.

ANTIBIOTICS

You don't "build up" an allergy to an antibiotic, contrary to popular belief. Antibiotic allergies can appear suddenly, out of the blue. That is to say, you can have been given penicillin five times in the past without any untoward effect, and then on the sixth occasion can develop an allergic reaction and hover near death. No one knows why this happens.

TONICS

The tonics that are supposed to make people feel better and younger are really just vitamins in alcohol. The part that makes you feel better is the alcohol, which is a muscle relaxant and central nervous system depressant. Aside from that, tonics probably have some placebo effect as well. Some people like to take them, and if it does no specific harm, I don't object. Is there such a thing as a genuine tonic? A tonic that actually loosens you up, actually will retard some of the aging changes that are going on? I'm afraid not. If there were one, I'd be taking it.

CORTISONE CREAM

Cortisone cream, if used for a prolonged period of time, will lead to atrophy of the skin—making it thin and papery. If you're not careful, the end result of cortisone cream treatment won't be a good one; that's why more potent mixes of cortisone remain controlled as prescription drugs.

As it turns out, nonprescription cortisone cream contains a weak steroid at a very low dose. But I suppose that if you had layers of it on a particular area over a month's time, you might have some atrophy of the skin as a result.

So if you're using nonprescription cortisone cream, don't just keep slathering it on all the time. If the problem doesn't respond after a few days, it needs to be evaluated by a doctor. Cortisone is useful because it decreases inflammation; if you have an itchy insect bite or something of that sort, it might be useful to put a little hydrocortisone cream on it. But prolonged use is to be avoided.

LAXATIVES

The problem with laxatives is that they can be abused. Too many of us don't eat bulk foods; we don't eat fiber foods. In fact, we tend to eat a lot of constipating foods, such as hard cheeses, chocolate, and nuts, and then we rely on a laxative.

The bowel musculature doesn't actually atrophy, but it doesn't do its job as well as it should. If the muscles aren't used on a regular basis, they lose the capability to perform their function as well as possible, and have to be retrained. Many adult women rely too heavily on laxatives and enemas to do the job. When I have a patient like this my job is to help her change her patterns to allow her to recognize the "call to stool" and not ignore it. When she feels she has to go, whether it's in the morning after a cup of coffee or in the evening after dinner, she has to make time in her life to respond, rather than suppressing the urge.

Fortunately, a variety of laxatives now available allow the colon to do its work on a stool that is increased in bulk, as with bulk laxatives, or decreased in hardness, as with stool softeners. These don't stimulate and irritate the bowel muscles as old-fashioned laxatives do.

DOUCHES

Medicated and scented douches have joined the familiar vinegar preparations on the drugstore shelf. Do they have any particular value to us in our thirties? My answer is no. In fact, I don't think they have value at any age. The classical vinegar douche's only job is to restore normal acid pH to the vagina. Women who eat a lot of sweets have more sugar in their vaginal cells, which sets them up for more frequent yeast infections, and douching with a dilute vinegar solution can help. Also, some women are particularly prone to getting yeast infections after intercourse, because semen is alkaline and upsets the normal pH in the vagina. Simple douches may be useful for them too.

Excessive douching though is not healthy. Someone who douches every day is not improving her health. Quite the contrary—the normal protective vaginal cells are being washed away, and she is actually increasing her chances of having problems. The scent doesn't add anything valuable and may increase the chances of an allergic reaction.

PAINKILLERS

There are currently dozens of painkillers available on the market, both alone and in combination with other drugs, so it may be difficult to choose among them. The difference in most pain medication revolves around the choice of aspirin or acetaminophen. In controlled studies of mild to moderate pain there was no clear-cut advantage to one over the other.[17] Likewise, no controlled trials have shown that one brand of plain aspirin or plain acetaminophen is any better than any other brand.

The major differences between aspirin and acetaminophen revolve around cost, with generic or non-brand-name aspirin generally being cheaper than acetaminophen. Also aspirin, in addition to having analgesic and antipyretic effects, has a distinct antiinflammatory effect, which acetaminophen does not have. Generally, I recommend aspirin rather than acetaminophen to most women because of this additional antiinflammatory capability.

It is unclear whether buffered aspirin has any significant advantage over nonbuffered aspirin. It is clear that buffers added to aspirin do increase the pH, leading to a quicker time of dissolution of the aspirin and presumably more rapid onset. However, whether the buffers produce a meaningful decrease in gastric acidity is a matter of some debate. Buffered aspirin solutions like Alka-Seltzer do probably provide the quickest means of analgesia because the aspirin is already in solution, and the peak serum level is achieved more rapidly than if the aspirin tablet must first disintegrate before being absorbed. However, trials of buffered aspirin solutions versus plain aspirin tablets or buffered aspirin tablets have failed to confirm a more rapid or effective analgesia for the solutions. Aspirin also exists in a variety of combinations, including combinations with acetaminophen, as in Excedrin. This is no more effective than optimal doses of either aspirin or acetaminophen alone.

DRUG ABUSE

In our pressure-filled lives, the comfort of medications sometimes leads to their abuse. Tranquilizers like Valium and Librium (benzodiazepines) carry a particular tendency for abuse by women. It is said that in general women tend to abuse prescription drugs more frequently, and men abuse illicit drugs more frequently. It is hard to know just how widespread this use is, but it's clear that the drugs are "best sellers" and reap large profits for their manufacturers.

The amount of medicine that constitutes abuse varies from woman to woman. The potential for abuse varies according to the prescribing habits of the physician as well. For example, the physician who prescribes a hundred Valium at a time for a woman is, in my opinion, doing her a disservice. My own feeling about tranquilizers is that they are useful and often necessary adjuncts during periods of acute stress, or in chronic situations of anxiety where there isn't any immediate escape from the problem. But on a day to day basis, I feel it's best to learn to cope with the stress in your life.

How do you know if you have a problem? Is popping Valium once or twice a day something to worry about? Yes, it is. I think you do have a problem. Not so much because of the medicine's physical effect, but because it's a crutch. And the question that should concern you is why do you need this crutch on a daily basis? Why can't you walk without it?

Perhaps your reason for taking Valium still exists. But perhaps it doesn't. Your drug gobbling may have become just a bad habit—like anything else may become a habit—that needs to be changed. The amount of true physical addiction to benzodiazepines is less than it was to some of the older compounds like barbiturates. You could die from barbiturate withdrawal. No one dies due to withdrawal from a low-grade Valium habit. So in the absence of overwhelming stress, you have no reason to take it, and certainly no physical reason not to stop cold turkey.

Stopping a drug cold turkey is easier said than done, however. The habit can't just be tossed aside. Perhaps you should ask your doctor if there are any groups nearby of reformed pill users who can lend you support. Quitting is so much easier if you know you're not the only one going through the throes. If asking your doctor is a problem, call the city department of human services or the nearest major hospital with a drug treatment facility.

ACUPUNCTURE

In recent years acupuncture has become one of the most controversial means of controlling pain. The four-thousand-year-old Chinese treatment is based on ancient Taoist philosophy. Man is described as consisting of two forces (yin and yang) that affect the total energy balance, or chi. Acupuncture diagnosis is pursued by exploring in a ritual fashion twelve different radial pulses, and therapy is based on the relationship of the five basic elements of fire, earth, metal, water, and wood. There are more than four hundred carefully described acupuncture points, and treatment consists of inserting very fine needles into several of these points. The acupuncture points are located along twelve paired and two unpaired lines of force that are said to traverse the body from head to toe.

All of this sounds quite unscientific, which is perhaps one reason why physicians have been reluctant to accept acupuncture. However, recent scientific explanations for the basis of action of acupuncture have come from laboratories in Sweden, Canada, the United States, and the People's Republic of China, so now physicians whose patients suffer chronic pain that hasn't responded to the usual methods and treatments are warming to acupuncture as a reasonable alternative.

One hypothesis, called the "gate hypothesis," postulates that one type of sensory input may be inhibited by another type occurring in a different type of nerve fiber. (This is the basic principle underlying the use of transcutaneous neuronal stimulation, TNS, which works via stimulating electrodes attached to the skin.) Another theory is that acupuncture works via the release of brain neurotransmitters. In animals it can be shown that acupuncture induces a release of endorphins and can slow the reaction to obnoxious or noxious stimuli. Naloxone, which blocks the effect of endorphins, endogenous opiate-like compounds within the human brain, will block the effect of acupuncture. Researchers at the NIH have confirmed that endorphins are released into the cerebrospinal fluid of rats after stimulation of the ear via acupuncture.[18] Fascinating.

Clearly, more work needs to be done to answer the many unanswered questions that currently exist about acupuncture. However, there seems little doubt that acupuncture may bring relief for those of us who haven't gotten relief from other methods. It may well be worth trying.

Hopefully, by the time we have reached our thirties, our minds are still open to new avenues of treatment like acupuncture but are closed to nutrition nonsense and fraudulent food fads. We should have the sense to keep things out of our systems that we aren't certain about. Sensible nutrition and medication maintain our most precious asset, our health.

Overcoming Our
Minor Complaints

I BELIEVE THAT, overall, women feel better during their thirties than during any other decade. We have achieved an enviable balance between physical condition and mental control. When we were younger our bodies might have been a bit zippier, but we didn't understand them as well or handle them as capably. When we become older, the inevitable small shifts wrought by time will make retaining the mastery we now have more difficult.

But in this decade, the elements harmonize. I can't tell you how often I hear women of our age say that they never felt better in their lives. That they never understood themselves more fully and were never more aware of their bodies' capabilities. It's an exciting special feeling for this unique time in our lives.

At the same time, in our thirties we also understand our body's foibles more fully. This is simply another facet of establishing dominion over ourselves, another step in our process of self-discovery and understanding. In this decade we see what nagging problems our bodies are heir to, what bothersome situations turn up frequently.

The knowledge we gain of what bothers us provides us with a golden opportunity to examine these problems and work to overcome or at least limit them. Now is the time for us to learn as much as we can about any small problems we regularly face so that we can establish patterns or begin practices that will cut down their impact later in our lives and make us that much more aware of ourselves and comfortable with our bodies.

PREMENSTRUAL SYNDROME

From two to fourteen days before menstruation, many of us feel bloated. Our skin breaks out. Our breasts become sore and tender. We may feel extremely listless, anxious, restless, tense, depressed, or energized. We may, in fact, experience any of more than fifty symptoms that all add up to what doctors have dubbed premenstrual syndrome (PMS).

Until recently, doctors have shied away from discussing this wide-ranging condition for four reasons: The line between mild pre-menstrual impairment and the full-blown syndrome has not yet been drawn; doctors didn't think the condition was serious enough to warrant major inquiry; women were reluctant to discuss their troubles; and symptoms were so varied—even within one woman's experience—that studying PMS was extraordinarily difficult.

Sweeping this problem under the rug was a mistake. Generations of PMS denial gave rise to the "raging hormones" theory which says we are out of control half of each month, making us unfit to serve as pilots or presidents.

Happily, more of us are now willing to talk about

PMS. Medicine has already accepted the reality of menstrual cramps and come up with effective treatments. Now equally serious attention is focusing on the rest of our monthly cycle. In April, 1981, the *Journal of the American Medical Association* published an article entitled "Premenstrual Syndrome: An Ancient Woe Deserving of Modern Scrutiny" that called PMS "the newest women's health issue in the United States."

And attention is growing. In Madison, Wisconsin, and Boston, educational and informational organizations and clinics have sprung up. Premenstrual syndrome is now accepted as a mitigating factor in crimes committed in the United Kingdom. In France, the syndrome is grounds for a plea of temporary insanity. It's only a matter of time before PMS is used as a legal defense in the United States.

What exactly causes PMS, and how harmful are its effects? Most doctors agree that PMS is a physical problem caused by a hormonal imbalance. If there are accompanying psychological or emotional symptoms the cause is still physical. However, stress can make matters worse.

Some women suffer so severely from PMS they feel "out of control" just before their periods. They are candidates for hormone treatment. Most of us, though, recognize our symptoms and compensate, just as people learn to function at work even if they are tired. Vitamins, diet changes, and exercise often help, but nothing cures PMS.

We tend to get the same kinds of symptoms each month. Some of us grow tired, some sleep and eat more, and hang around the house. Others become anxious, agitated, and insecure. Still others have only the physical symptoms—headaches and bloating. A tiny lucky minority even have more energy and feel better than normal right before their periods.

It's important, before you consider treating your own PMS, to be certain you have it. Rate your moods and behavior each day in a calendar or date book. Of course, mark when you menstruate and also note when you are particularly cheerful or down in the dumps, when you feel well, when you feel rotten. If the same patterns appear just before your period, and at no other time, for three consecutive months, you probably have PMS. However, you only need treatment if your symptoms pose a greater problem than you can cope with.

Every PMS expert has a pet theory; experiment with the different approaches to see what works best for you:

If you feel jumpy and have sore breasts, cut out caffeine. That means no coffee, tea, colas, or chocolate.

Reduce your salt intake just before menses to minimize water retention.

Take a vitamin B_6 supplement. Some doctors believe that B_6 deficiency sets off a hormonal imbalance that can affect mood.

Increase your potassium intake by eating ripe bananas and peanuts and drinking fresh orange juice. One idea is that PMS may be caused by a potassium/sodium imbalance.

None of these therapies has been proven in adequately controlled clinical trials, though, so don't be discouraged if your case doesn't respond to these home remedies.

THE "RAGING HORMONE" THEORY

Our hormone levels do vary with our menstrual cycles, but there's no difference between the "raging" of our hormones in our thirties and what went on in our twenties. The exception to the rule is that some women, a small percentage of women, will undergo menopause in their thirties. (The average age of menopause is 51.) That's quite unusual, but it does occur. And, obviously, that wipes out cyclical hormone variations.

Over the years, most of us become accustomed to our hormonal tides, but for some of us in our thirties, it's difficult to continue coping with the internal fluctuations and lack of control. Frequently I'll have a woman in my office who may have had a tough time with PMS during her twenties but somehow can't continue to cope with it in her thirties. Then, what I look for when someone can't cope with something that's been there for a long time is what's going on in the background, what's the psychological milieu, what's changed for that woman. The problem often is in her life, not in her body.

How does pregnancy affect this? Does having a child even out our systems or do hormones rage the same after pregnancy as before?

PREGNANCY, HORMONES AND LACTATION

During pregnancy itself there are marked hormonal changes, particularly in the female sex hormones that are present in ever increasing amounts during pregnancy. The marked increase in estrogen that we experience during pregnancy has been linked to feelings of enhanced well-being and a lowered risk of mental illness. The hormone progesterone, which is produced by the placenta, changes also, rising tenfold during pregnancy. This hormone has been postulated to have a calming effect, producing both relief of depression and drowsiness in one study of women conducted at Stanford Medical School. So, the pregnant woman is hormonally encouraged to feel good, to be calm and relaxed.

With delivery, all this changes, and our hormones plummet. This precipitous decline in estrogen and progesterone can be likened to the fall of hormones we experience before the onset of menstruation, and, just as prior to menstruation many women become more tearful, emotionally labile and depressed, so do post-partum women. These "post partum blues" are most apt to develop three to four days after we deliver and are clearly related to the change in our hormone levels. Statistics indicate that we are at increased risk of developing a psychological illness during this time and in fact for the first three months after delivery.

If a woman elects to bottle-feed her infant, her hormones gradually return to normal over the next six to eight weeks, and she begins to cycle again, with normal monthly hormone fluctuations.

If, however, she decides to breast-feed her child, then another hormone, prolactin, comes into play. This hormone results in lactation and suppresses a woman's normal menstrual cycle. Prolactin, like progesterone, has been postulated to have a calming effect. In fact, many women report feeling very relaxed during and after nursing, and, interestingly, ambitious, hard-driving career women may note that their competitive edge is dulled somewhat by breast feeding.

URINARY TRACT INFECTIONS

Because our urethral opening from the bladder is near our vaginal and anal openings, and is short (only about an inch and a half long compared to a urethra of eight or nine inches in the male), we are particularly prone to get urinary tract infections. One woman in ten has one at any given moment. The urinary tract itself consists of the kidneys, the ureters, which carry urine from the kidneys to the bladder, and then the urethra, which carries urine from the bladder out of the body. Most commonly, urinary tract infections affect the urethra and bladder and are known as urethritis or cystitis. It's not known why some of us never develop a urinary tract infection and others have several infections per year, but it is clear that there are several factors which do predispose us to infection. One is clearly prolonged sexual intercourse. The term "honeymoon cystitis" was coined to describe infections that occur when a woman first begins having sexual intercourse. However, if a woman acquires a new sexual partner or resumes sexual activity after a long hiatus—as some of us do in our thirties— the likelihood of developing a urinary tract infection increases. Pregnancy can also be a factor.

Sometimes irritation from a diaphragm causes painful urination, forcing a switch to another contraceptive. Other causes of painful or difficult urination include wearing skintight jeans, inserting a tampon incorrectly, and bicycle riding or jogging with a full bladder. Those of us prone to dysuria, as painful urination is called by doctors, should be careful to empty our bladders before doing anything that might conceivably irritate our urinary tract. We should also avoid such cleansing irritants as bubble baths, scented douches, and feminine hygiene sprays.

With urinary tract problems, prevention is absolutely the best medicine. After using the toilet, you should always wipe from front to back to avoid spreading anal germs toward the urinary path. Rinsing the vaginal and anal area with a stream of water is even better. Having both you and your sexual partner wash your perineal regions and urinate before intercourse, and again within ten to fifteen minutes afterward, also reduces the possibility of infection. It also helps if you drink a glass of water before and after intercourse to help wash out your bladder. Urinating after intercourse is probably the most important of all these measures. In addition, a single prophylactic dose of an antibiotic, taken daily or after each episode of intercourse, can block the recurrence of urinary infections in women who get them from sex. Ask your doctor about the many possible antibiotic treatments.

Urinary tract infections can be excruciatingly uncomfortable. Urethritis announces itself with a burning pain at the end of the urination and an increasingly urgent need to urinate. The initial twinges of a urinary tract infection will become more severe after several hours, with a frequent urge to urinate and perhaps only small amounts of urine coming out, increasing pain, and occasionally bloody urine. If the infection has spread to the bladder with cystitis, crampy lower abdominal pain may develop. If the pain spreads to the back and is accompanied by fever, chills, nausea, vomiting, or diarrhea, then pyelonephritis (inflammation of the kidneys) has occurred and prompt medical attention is necessary.

Diagnosis of a urinary tract infection involves a urinalysis that looks for white cells, red blood cells, protein, and bacteria, as well as a culture of the urine to determine what the offending organism is and what types of antibiotics it will be sensitive to.

Some women have "silent" urinary tract infections. Their lab test is positive but they have no symptoms. Within a year, however, one-third of these women develop undeniable symptoms of infection. Silent infections should probably be treated just like those that cause symptoms. A urinalysis test at your annual exam can detect a symptomless infection before the problem progresses.

Recent studies have shown that many women with symptoms of cystitis or urethritis can be cured with a single dose of an antibiotic, such as 3 gm of amoxicillin or 2 gm of sulfisoxazole.[1] If there is any indication that the kidneys are involved or if a woman is pregnant, single-dose treatment is not recommended. Occasionally, antibiotics must be taken for ten days to two weeks. If your physician recommends a full course of antibiotics then the full course should be taken, although your symptoms may subside after twenty-four hours. With severe dysuria, a urinary analgesic such as Pyridium, which colors the urine orange, may also be prescribed. Recovery can be hastened by drinking lots of fluids and emptying the bladder frequently. A follow-up culture, generally done a week after the antibiotic course has been completed, is essential to insure that the infection has been entirely eradicated.

In the book *Cystitis* (Warner Books, 1980), Angela Kilmartin, whose own recurrent urinary infections wrecked her career and almost ended her marriage, describes her own first-aid measure for nipping an attack in the bud (keep in mind, though, there isn't much scientific proof of its value): Immediately upon feeling the first twinges of an infection, she states, drink a pint of water with one teaspoon of baking soda mixed in. Follow with eight ounces of plain water every twenty minutes for the next three hours; then slowly ease up on your water guzzling. Each subsequent hour repeat the bicarbonate in a glass of water regimen. Some doctors believe the water without the baking soda would work just as well. Don't try any of this if you have high blood pressure or heart disease.

Relapses do occur, and when they do you must be reevaluated to ascertain whether the organism is the same as before or different from your prior infection. All too often we take antibiotics left over from a previous urinary tract infection, don't obtain relief, and only then go for treatment. This is a problem because the antibiotics may impede the growth of organisms in the testing culture, hampering diagnosis, while not adequately treating the infection. If you have several recurrences of urinary tract infections, you may need a more thorough investigation to determine whether a congenital abnormality, kidney stone, or other structural defect may account for the persistence of bacteria. Most recurrent infections in women are due to entry of new organisms, however, in which case they may be candidates for prophylaxis.

Occasionally symptoms similar to a urinary tract infection may result from a vaginal infection. Herpes, for example, may form vesicles or blisters near the urethral opening that cause pain on urination. Yeast infections caused by the *Candida* organism may lead to irritation of the urethral opening as well.

Pregnancy definitely increases urinary tract infections, and may increase the incidence of silent infections in the urine. This happens because there is pressure on the bladder and the bladder is displaced by the growing fetus.

Speaking of vaginal infections, you might be wondering if they get worse, or better, as we get into our thirties. They probably don't change too much from a medical standpoint. We're no more susceptible to vaginal viruses and bacteria; we aren't more resistant, either. We may be more adept at dealing with these problems because we've had a longer time to get used to them. The same would be true for urinary tract infections. By our thirties we know what kinds of things to avoid and how to cope with the drudgery of infection.

Some patients, though, come in with their first urinary tract infection at thirty-five or thirty-seven and have absolutely no concept at all of treatment or prevention, because they've never had to deal with it before. These women are stunned. They don't know what to do and they react to the discomfort most severely. I can only suggest that they stay calm and face an embarrassing, uncomfortable situation with as much grace and good humor as possible.

BACK PAIN

Millions of women suffer from back pain. Most of us have awakened at some time and moaned, "Oh, my aching back." Incidentally, eight out of ten of us will experience back pain sometime in our lives. Each year over 200,000 Americans have surgery in the hopes of curing or alleviating back pain. The problem, basically, is that people walk upright. Our bones and backs are still meant for a four-legged existence, but we insist on walking on our hind legs. Our genes are still a few million years behind us. This puts our spines at a mechanical disadvantage. On top of this, our sedentary life weakens the support muscles of our backs and abdomens, which makes for even more stress on our poor backs.

Trauma is probably the most frequent cause of back pain. Every day thousands of women injure their backs because of overzealous athletic attempts, injudicious lifting, or a fall. These injuries are so common among us largely because so many of us are in poor physical condition at the outset. Unfortunately, common sense is not too common; frequently a woman will come in to see me complaining of low back pain after having decided to rearrange the furniture by herself or to engage in a strenuous game of tennis on the weekend after not having exercised in weeks.

Acute lumbar strain, as this grief is called, really hurts. It may come on gradually over a period of days or may happen suddenly as a result of one wrong bend, lift, or reach. Suddenly, the muscles and ligaments that support the vertebral column become overstressed and strained, and they go into spasms so intense that sometimes they feel like rocks to an examining physician. The best preventive measure is simple: Keep your back in shape. Don't let the muscles atrophy. Moderate bending and stretching exercises can banish back pain from your life.

Degenerative disk disease or herniation of a disk must be distinguished from the more common acute lumbar strain just described. Normally the vertebral column is composed of blocks of bone—vertebrae—stacked one on top of another and separated by softer fibrocartilage structures called disks. A complicated set of ligaments and muscles surrounds the vertebral column and the disks, providing flexibility and support for the spinal cord and the nerve endings running through it. The disks act as cushions, and normally they have two parts: a softer area, the nucleus pulposus, surrounded by more fibrous tissue, the anulus fibrosus. Repeated minor trauma to the disk may result in enough tears of the anulus fibrosus so that eventually even a very tiny shock can cause the softer part of the disk to jut into the vertebral body either above or below the disk or into the spinal canal itself. This rapid herniation of the soft center through the hard outer membrane causes teeth-grinding pain. If the protruding material presses on a nearby nerve, classical sciatica occurs, and the pain grows even more severe, radiating along the buttock, back of the thigh, lower leg, or foot.

Evaluation of a woman with low back pain involves a physical examination and a careful medical history. The doctor will examine her while she bends, sits, and stands. Knees and ankles will be tested, as will muscle strength and sensation. If there is a question of referred pain from another part of the body, abdominal and pelvic examinations may be performed as well. Most frequently the cause is acute lumbar strain and tests are not ordered. However, if there is any suggestion of metabolic or degenerative disease, a variety of tests may be ordered. But please note: X rays are not routinely ordered in cases of back strain. If your doctor asks for one, particularly before examining you, question her about her reasons.

The best treatment for a painful lower back is bed rest. Most back strains are relieved by adequate rest. You should stay in bed with your knees bent up, and get up only to go to the bathroom. It's a crashing bore, but it works. You may have to lie there one or two weeks before you feel better.

Once the acute attack is over, exercise to prevent future problems. You don't actually exercise your back, but rather your stomach.

The point of exercise is to strengthen your abdomen so these front muscles can take some of the stress off your back. The pelvic tilt is one of the best maneuvers for this. Lie on your back, bend your knees, and then tilt your pelvis so that the small of your back flattens against the floor. You'll feel it across your belly immediately. You can also do a pelvic tilt while standing. As you stand, thrust your pelvis forward as if a string were tied to the front of it. You want to achieve the opposite of our common but back-straining posture with the buttocks thrust backward and the breasts thrust forward. Another comfortable posture for backs is to stand at a bar with one foot resting on something. The folks who designed taverns knew what they were doing.

If an acute herniation of a disk does not subside with bed rest, heat, and sedatives in the hospital, then surgery may be necessary. Doctors feel surgery is indicated in patients who have repeated attacks of sciatica and progressive changes in the leg muscles. During surgery the herniated disk material is removed, and the disk space is explored for any other degenerative disk fragments. A spinal fusion may be performed to stabilize the spine if there is enough evidence of progressive degeneration.

A newer, less invasive treatment for herniated disks is a technique called chemonucleolysis, which was pioneered by Dr. Lyman Smith. This procedure involves injecting a herniated disk with chymopapain, an enzyme derived from the leaves of the papaya plant. The enzyme is also present in meat tenderizers and has been used for years to make meat more tender. Centuries ago, Polynesians were wrapping meat in papaya leaves in order to tenderize it. The stuff works much the same way on the tough tissue in our backs. It breaks down some protein complexes in cartilage, and when injected into a degenerated disk it dissolves the soft nucleus pulposus, relieving the pain.

Initially, it appeared that the risks of chemonucleolysis were small. Allergic reaction was reported in fewer than 1 percent of patients so treated, and infections were rare. There were a few cases of paralysis after injection, but that was probably because the procedure was not performed properly. The advantages of chemonucleolysis are that your hospital stay is much shorter and your chance of success is on the order of 70 percent.

Despite this, the Food and Drug Administration withdrew chymopapain from the market in the United States in 1975 because of questions about its worth. The study on which the withdrawal was based showed no difference between injection of chymopapain into a disk and the injection of just the substance in which the chymopapain was dissolved.[2] In addition, a question arose as to whether injecting or dissolving an intervertebral disk could result in subsequent narrowing of the spinal column and horribly painful entrapment of a nerve root in later life.

Currently there is a triple-blind study being done in the United States to settle the controversy. This FDA approved study involves the use of either the enzyme chymopapain, a plain salt solution or the diluent solution being injected without either the patient or physician knowing what is being injected. The results of this study will take several years to be completed and assessed. Little comfort, I know, but that's the best I can offer.

Pregnancy, by the way, increases the risk of having a lumbar strain by shifting your center of balance forward, which increases the stress on your lower back. Low back pain is also very common in women who have had multiple pregnancies with excessive weight gain and who then fail to lose the additional weight or recondition their abdominal muscles with postpartum exercises. They tote around an additional ten or twenty pounds of weight that adds to the stress on their backs, and their abdominal muscles aren't prepared to share the strain.

BREAST PAIN

Pain in the breast may occur at any age and may be sharp, dull, stabbing, aching, constant, or fleeting. It may start in the back and shoot around the breast, ending in the nipple area. It may do just the opposite, starting in or beneath the nipple, involving the entire breast or just one segment of it. It may occur in one breast or both. Much anxiety can be avoided if women are aware that breast pain may have nothing to do with the breast at all. It may be what is known as referred pain, or pain radiating from another part of the body. For example, breast pain may be one of the earliest symptoms of several common conditions, such as bursitis of the shoulder, degenerative arthritis, or a slipped disk.

Unfortunately,. it is not always possible to find a clear-cut cause for breast pain or a simple treatment to relieve it. Women who worry that breast pain reflects something sinister should bear the following in mind: if the pain occurs in monthly cycles that parallel the physiological changes in the breast during each menstrual cycle, the chances are that the pain is linked to normal physiological phenomena.

Most lumps in the breast, both benign and malignant, are painless (with the major exception of a cyst that enlarges rapidly and causes discomfort as it pushes normal breast tissue aside), and the absence of discomfort has often contributed to a delay in diagnosis.

Retraction or puckering of our breast skin or the nipple leaves no room for doubt. Get a medical opinion. Cancer is one common cause of this visible sign (the skin appears to be drawn together in very tiny ripples), but so are a number of benign breast conditions. Retraction of the skin occurs because the tissues are reacting to inflammation, to infection or to invasion by malignant cells. If these changes happen to take place behind the nipple, the nipple itself may become distorted or inverted. (Nipple inversion is not uncommon and is a completely normal occurrence, but when it appears for the first time, it should be called to the attention of a physician.)

Nipple discharge is another symptom that often provokes anxiety out of proportion to its actual significance. Nine times out of ten, nipple discharge in a woman who is neither pregnant nor nursing is due to a perfectly harmless physiological cause or to a correctable condition. It is true that nipple discharge may be a sign of cancer, but for women this symptom is far down the list of cancer warnings. (Nipple discharge in men more commonly signifies malignant disease.)

Crusting or erosion of the nipple surface that does not improve after application of a bland ointment or cream, or after gentle washing with warm water and soap for a few days, should be checked by a doctor. One very important reason is that there is a form of cancer (Paget's disease) that affects the nipple first. It begins as reddening, roughening, or thickening of the nipple surface. Since at this stage there is no lump, patients rarely suspect how serious the condition is.

Dilated or enlarged veins running over the breast are generally harmless. They often occur during pregnancy and lactation. However, it is important to watch for this change in the blood vessels, since in rare instances they may become more prominent because of a tumor lying beneath them.

LACTOSE INTOLERANCE

The sugar component of milk, lactose, may cause a variety of abdominal symptoms including cramps, bloating, and diarrhea in the condition known as lactose intolerance. In this condition there is a deficiency of the enzyme lactase that splits ingested lactose into glucose and galactose in the small intestine. If lactase is deficient, the sugar is subsequently fermented in the colon to become various organic acids and gas. It is these that lead to the abdominal distension, pain, diarrhea, and flatulence. Most of us won't ever suffer lactase deficiency; among those of us who do the cause may be either congenital or acquired, but in either case it generally does not cause symptoms until our twenties or thirties. If you are black, Oriental, Native American, Indian, or of Mediterranean descent, you have a higher chance of suffering this condition than the rest of us.

While many women with lactase deficiency are aware that milk and dairy products will give them symptoms, a surprising number are not. Also, because lactase deficiency is frequently only partial, many women will be able to tolerate a scoop of ice cream per day with minimal symptoms, but not one spoonful more.

Lactose is present in large quantities in milk and milk products such as yogurt and soft cheese, but not in hard cheese. It occurs in other products where you might not expect it, such as puddings, pie fillings, some bakery goods, and such dry foods as dehydrated soups, instant potatoes, powdered soft drinks, and instant breakfast drinks. Lactose is also found in tiny amounts in some medicinal tablets and capsules.

Recently a commercial lactase preparation that can be added to milk has become available in the United States for treatment of lactose intolerance. This product, called Lactade, can be purchased without a prescription and added to milk and then refrigerated. Four or five drops of the enzyme preparation in a quart of milk will break down 70 percent of the lactose in 24 hours; eight or ten drops will break down 90 percent. The shelf life of milk treated with this preparation is the same as that of milk which is not treated.

MALABSORPTION OF CARBOHYDRATE IN WHEAT FLOUR

While malabsorption of the sugar lactose has been known for some time, a recent article in the *New England Journal of Medicine* by Dr. Michael Levitt from the University of Minneapolis evaluated the possibility that malabsorption of other dietary carbohydrates might also lead to abdominal pain, gas and diarrhea in otherwise healthy individuals.[3] He showed that seventeen of eighteen healthy subjects who ate wheat starch in the form of either macaroni or bread made from *all-purpose* wheat flour failed to completely absorb the wheat flour as compared to a low-gluten wheat flour or white flour that was almost completely absorbed. It was suggested that women who are tagged as having "functional bowel symptoms," that is, bowel complaints of cramping, diarrhea and gas, who have been evaluated and not found to have any organic basis for their illness, might try a wheat-free diet in an attempt to obtain relief. He likewise mentioned that constipated women might benefit from a diet high in wheat, a suggestion which was supported by additional research that showed that normal women had an increased volume of stool while ingesting a high-wheat diet.

BULIMIA

For some of us, eating is like being on a roller coaster. When we see food we want it—all of it. After we eat, the repercussions of what we've done hit us, and we want to get rid of it all again, immediately. We begin to binge, then purge ourselves by vomiting. Once the cycle begins, it can become a habit.

This is bulimia, an eating disorder that is also called

bulimarexia, or the gorge-purge syndrome. Those who suffer from it are predominantly average-to-slender women in the twenties and thirties, students and career women with interesting lives.-They are preoccupied with food and with their weight, and are regularly seized by the urge to overeat, and then purge themselves of the calories by vomiting, taking laxatives and/or diuretics, or fasting for several days, sometimes with the help of diet pills.

The syndrome is not new, but victims have recently begun admitting to it in increasing numbers. Dr. Craig Johnson, director of the Anorexia Nervosa Center at Michael Reese Hospital's Psychosomatic and Psychiatric Institute in Chicago, says he uncovered bulimics in 1980 while screening college students for a study he was conducting. To his surprise, over 20 percent of his sample were active bingers and purgers.

Since his findings on bulimia were published, approximately five thousand women have asked the institute for help and information. Most of them had been gorging and purging anywhere from three to fifteen years, and had not previously been victims of anorexia nervosa, the better-known "starvation disease," which, Dr. Johnson feels, "in numbers pales compared to bulimia."

Classic anorexics are usually teenagers who starve themselves to skeletal thinness; in the process, they frequently cease to menstruate, lose their appetites, and even jeopardize their lives. Bulimics, instead of turning away from food, as anorexics do in times of stress, turn to food for solace. In some cases, abrupt changes or traumatic events may trigger the syndrome. Sometimes dieting causes such an overwhelming focus on food that the woman snaps, binges, then purges to overcome this fault and the cycle begins.

No one knows the extent of the phenomenon; it has not been studied long enough. But Dr. William Davis, director of the Center for the Study of Anorexia in New York City, suspects that more than 5 percent of adult females are bulimics.

If you feel you may be bulimic, or tending toward bulimia, see your doctor immediately. If she's no help, write: Anorexia Nervosa Center, Michael Reese Hospital, Psychosomatic and Psychiatric Institute, 2929 South Ellis Avenue, Chicago, Ill. 60616, or the Center for the Study of Anorexia, 1 West 91st Street, New York, N.Y. 10024

TOXIC SHOCK SYNDROME

Since the withdrawal of Rely tampons from the market, there has been a decline in interest in toxic shock syndrome, which was first described in 1978 as a distressing, acute "flu-like" ailment with fever, rash, vomiting and diarrhea that seems to strike tampon users out of the blue, and that can progress to include lethargy, confusion, "shock lung" and kidney failure. Studies of cases that occurred during the initial scare have revealed some basic facts about the disease that are of interest to us.

The condition appears predominantly in menstruating women who are under thirty years of age, although there are a few case reports of toxic shock occurring in men too. Many doctors think this is due to maturity, rather than to anything physical, as younger women are more likely to abuse tampons, which is one of the suspected causes of toxic shock syndrome. Another possibility is that the staphylococcal bacteria (which make the toxin responsible for toxic shock syndrome) become less active as we get older. But, while your chances of getting the syndrome decrease with advancing age, you are not really free from risk until you stop menstruating altogether. So don't ignore symptoms even if you are thirty-nine or forty, or older.

There is some concern that toxic shock syndrome has been unrecognized in the past and may occur in a minor variation as well. This is probably the most important consideration for us. Do you develop a headache, fever, eye irritation or muscle aching during your period while using tampons? Do you get a "cold" at that time? You may have a running battle with a low-grade form of toxic shock syndrome and might well be advised to consider another form of menstrual protection. At least it would be wise to forego tampons during the night in favor of pads, and to change tampons frequently during the daytime.

PAINFUL MENSTRUATION

Menstrual cramps improve after pregnancy, so in olden days paternalistic gynecologists would recommend that you get pregnant in order to relieve your cramps. The advice was sound, I suppose, but that's a heck of a way to solve a simple problem. So, you took your choice: you either got pregnant or took strong narcotic pain medications or birth control pills, but in recent years chemicals called prostaglandins have been implicated as the culprit in causing dysmenorrhea.

Treatment is now directed at inhibiting the synthesis of these prostaglandins, assuming that the pain has no identifiable organic cause, which is generally the case. A variety of prostaglandin synthetase inhibiters are available. Aspirin is the most common inhibiter, and many women will find that just taking aspirin on a regular basis is sufficient to allow them to function normally. The other agents used to inhibit prostaglandin synthesis include ibuprofen (Motrin), mefenamic acid (Ponstel), indomethacin (Indocin) and naproxen (Naprosyn). These agents are clearly more effective than aspirin in treating severe pain. However, they may have some side effects.

In a controlled trial with 51 women over three successive menstrual cycles, Dr. J. C. Morrison of the University of Tennessee Health Sciences Center (Memphis) and other physicians compared efficacy of an inhibiter drug with that of an analgesic, Darvon, and an inert placebo.[4] Complete relief was experienced by 31 women while on Motrin, compared with 7 on Darvon and 1 taking the placebo. Normal daily activities could be pursued by 49 on Motrin and later by 40 on Darvon.

If you do have a baby, your cramps improve afterward because your uterus has stretched out and then returned to a larger than pre-gravid size. Since it's not so tightly packed, it's going to be less subject to all of the hormonal influences that cause cramping.

For those of us who haven't had children, cramps may increase as we move into our thirties, because we may develop fibroids, benign tumors that obstruct certain areas of the uterus, or endometriosis.

FATIGUE

Fatigue is fatiguing. The sensation of being tired leaves many women spent and low. I think that most patients who come in complaining of fatigue have unrealistic expectations of what they should be able to accomplish in the world; they may be overworked or depressed.

Not looking forward to getting out of bed, not looking forward to going anywhere, not looking forward to taking care of yourself or your family, feeling tired all the time, despite the fact that you're sleeping excessively—these are the symptoms of depression. Fatigue is frequently a manifestation of depression. Certainly a woman can complain of lassitude and have leukemia, but that is exceedingly rare. For the most part, complaints of fatigue, when evaluated thoroughly, have no organic basis.

That doesn't mean that sometimes there isn't a subtle organic cause for fatigue that remains undiagnosed. I fully believe that occasionally we may have a subclinical viral infection or be exposed to a small dose of some sort of toxin in our environment that causes us to feel tired, but more often, I see someone who comes in with a variety of complaints including fatigue, and note after note from previous years shows that she has always complained of lassitude. That woman is usually chronically depressed, or may suffer fatigue or depression when placed under stress. That's the true cause of fatigue.

I think there are two types of tired, good tired and bad tired. The kind of tired I've been talking about results from doing nothing all day, from boredom or malaise—that's bad. But then there's the kind of tired feeling that comes from having a lot of physical exercise during the day. That's genuine—that's good tired.

Women in their thirties sometimes feel that both types of tiredness are signs that they're getting old. They may not give themselves credit for all they accomplish.

Obviously, at some point we do accomplish less as we get older. Clearly ninety-year-olds don't do what twenty-year-olds do. We age every day. Some of us have unrealistic remembrances of what went on in the past and unrealistic expectations of what we should be able to accomplish in the present. That's particularly true for women who are trying to combine everything in life. We want it all; we can't wait; we want to have a family and a job and friends and a social life—but we don't realize that it's grueling, that there needs to be some time for self, some time for separateness, or we'll feel perennially exhausted.

Well, if much fatigue is basically a symptom of the blues, is there any sign of tiredness or something that goes along with tiredness that is really a danger sign that you should worry about?

Yes, two things: fever and weight loss. Of course, any other symptoms, such as change in bowel habits or abdominal pain or severe headaches are important, but the two big ones that physicians are going to ask about are fever and weight loss. Even low-grade fever may be significant. Feeling hot or a little bit sweaty in the afternoon may be due to a low-grade fever, a tip-off to some underlying infection such as mononucleosis or hepatitis or malignancy causing that feeling of lassitude. And, as most of us know, inexplicable weight loss is always a concern.

BOWEL PROBLEMS

In American culture there's a paradox in terms of bowel movements: people are obsessed about how often they have a bowel movement, but they never pay any attention (particularly when the physician wants to know) to what the bowel movement looks like. Despite their fixation, they may be totally oblivious to gross blood in their bowel movements or to bowel movements that are yellow and full of fat—unmistakable problems. Some women just don't look before they flush. Yet I have patients who can tell me instantly how frequently they go, and are often quite concerned about whether they move their bowels perfectly every day.

There is certainly no "norm," no optimal number of times per day or per week to have a bowel movement. It's an individual matter, based to some extent on your internal setup as well as on how much fiber and bulk you eat. Most of us know that people who eat a high-bulk, high-fiber diet have more bowel movements and seem to have a lower incidence of colon cancer than heavy meat eaters. One of the hypotheses is that toxins formed as a result of bacterial action are in contact longer with the lining of the bowels, perhaps initiating cancerous changes.

It's probably advisable to consume a high-bulk, high-fiber diet, not only to prevent constipation but also perhaps to lower the risk of colon cancer. That's about the only concern a woman in her thirties should have about her bowels. You don't have to be absolutely regular in order to be healthy. And there is no perfect stool.

ALLERGIES

Allergies often don't make much sense.

At the age of thirty a woman suddenly becomes allergic to hot dogs. Or a woman who has always been allergic to cats gets a kitten, yet her anticipated sneezing and itching don't appear. Some of us are allergic to soft-boiled eggs but not hard-boiled eggs. And hay-fever victims can sometimes react to cantaloupe as well as to ragweed. Why? Doctors are only just beginning to understand.

Almost everyone comes into contact with pollen, for instance, so why doesn't everyone have hay fever? The average person inhales pollen without consequence. But the hay-fever sufferer's body makes a mistake, reacting to the pollen as a harmful substance and producing a special class of antibody called immunoglobulin E (IgE) to combat it. These in turn cause the release of histamine, one of the chemicals responsible for producing such symptoms as itchy, watery eyes, fits of sneezing, and mucus buildup in the nose. Some sufferers also experience fatigue, loss of appetite, and irritability.

Hay fever (seasonal allergic rhinitis) tends to run in families; there is no way to prevent it and no way to predict whether an individual will be affected. While some people develop hay fever as children, others have no symptoms until they reach their late teens or twenties. For some hay-fever sufferers, the symptoms get worse over the years; but usually they grow far less severe around middle age.

Allergies such as hay fever are a peculiar medical situation in which we are, in a sense, too healthy. Our body's immune system is working too well, causing reactions to too many foreign materials, protecting us so righteously that we are miserable.

By the time we reach our thirties most of us have learned to cope with our childhood allergies. In fact, most of these become less severe as our bodies settle down. But new allergies can crop up at any time, and many of us will experience our first serious allergic reactions during this decade. So it's important for us to understand, as clearly as science is able to explain it, what is going on inside us to make this happen.

Our immune system produces a virtually infinite array of antibodies designed to link up with different foreign particles. Most antibodies circulate freely in the bloodstream, helping to destroy invaders and flush or eliminate them from our bodies. But one antibody, IgE, behaves differently from all others. Instead of floating freely, its Y-shaped molecules are embedded in certain cell membranes. When an allergen particle comes along it combines with the upper regions of two adjacent IgE molecules, bridging them and drawing them together. This tugging alters the membrane, causing the cell to release histamine and other powerful chemicals. Allergy victims have from ten to one hundred times as much IgE as other people.

Two types of white blood cells, T cells and B cells, figure in IgE production. The B cells actually produce the IgE, while the T cells make substances that control the production rate. Under normal circumstances, the buildup of IgE in the body produces a negative feedback reaction that causes production to cease. In allergic people this feedback loop has gone haywire. Once production starts, the body has an extremely difficult time turning it off again.

For years scientists struggled to identify what the Iago behind allergic machinations might be. In the 1970s one offender was identified as leukotrienes—a family of unusual sulfur-bearing compounds that are a hundred times as potent as histamines in generating inflammation and swelling and in contracting involuntary muscles. They figure heavily in asthma and anaphylactic shock, and their effects last longer than those of histamines. Current research at Harvard is aimed at developing antileukotrienes, which researchers consider the most promising possible treatment for allergy in the future.

What can we do now? Well, get rid of the cat, vacuum up the dust, buy an air purifier, try antihistamines. For short, intense attacks, a steroid nasal spray or inhaler can help, but long-term use of steroids may be dangerous. For the truly miserable, allergy shots are worth a try. But if they do not help within three years, doctors advise quitting.

There is, however, one last bit of hope: after we turn forty, our immune systems become less energetic, and allergies may simply fade away.

THE COMMON COLD

The common cold is just that, common, largely because there are hundreds of types of viruses that can cause colds and because they are relatively contagious. Because colds are caused by viruses, they are not amenable to treatment with antibiotics. This cannot be overstressed.

The symptoms of the common cold are well known to all of us. They include sneezing, a stuffy or runny nose, sore throat, hoarse voice, weepy eyes, and perhaps a dry cough. Generally these symptoms are accompanied by a feeling of malaise with chills and low-grade fever under 100 degrees. Headache, muscle aches and pains, and disinterest in food are not uncommon.

No matter what we do for a cold, the virus will run its course. We can expect to be sick from 5 to 14 days. However, there are a number of things that we can do to alleviate the distress of the symptoms caused by the virus and to assure that a complicating bacterial infection doesn't occur. Most importantly, rest. If you feel tired, rest. There is no doubt that the body needs more rest than usual as it's busy fighting the virus. In addition, it is important to drink adequate amounts of fluid to replace the excess losses occurring through nasal secretions and sweating. In addition, it is important to drink adequate amounts of fluid to replace the excess losses occurring through nasal secretions and sweating. A variety of over-the-counter cold preparations are available without a prescription to ease the symptoms of a cold or upper respiratory infection. Decongestants are useful for runny noses. What they do is constrict the blood vessels to decrease the amount of secretions. Sudafedryne is one of the most common decongestants appearing in a variety of combination preparations as well as by itself. Decongestant drops may produce a rebound phenomenon when they wear off. Therefore, it is probably best to stay away from nasal sprays or drops. Also, decongestants can be dangerous for women with high blood pressure, as they do constrict blood vessels elsewhere in the body besides the nose.

Antihistamines may also help a runny nose. They dry nasal secretions. One side effect of antihistamines is that they may cause sleepiness, so that it is important not to operate machinery or drive after taking antihistamines, particularly if you are unaccustomed to taking drugs. Chlorphenaramine is a prototype antihistamine and can be taken as 4 milligrams every 4 to 6 hours or in longer-acting preparations. Aspirin or acetaminophen (Tylenol or Datril) can be very effective in alleviating the muscle aches and pains and headache of a cold.

A number of over-the-counter remedies contain a variety of other products, including vitamins, tranquilizers, or caffeine to counteract the sedative effect of antihistamines and various cough suppressants or expectorants. But in general a combination of an antipyretic such as aspirin, a decongestant such as sudafedryne and an antihistamine such as chlorphenaramine are sufficient for most cases of upper respiratory infection. Various antihistamine products may make some women feel sleepy or disoriented, and the decongestants may make you feel racey, so in general it's best to take the medications separately rather than in combination.

Some symptoms that may go along with what seems to be a common cold or upper respiratory infection actually indicate that there is a bacterial infection requiring the services of a physician. In general, any earache or persistent pain in the sinuses, cough that produces discolored, yellow, greenish or rusty sputum or cough without other symptoms of a cold, or sore throat without other symptoms of a cold requires evaluation by a physician.

Temperature over 100 with an upper respiratory infection is unusual. However, with influenza there is frequently high fever over 100 degrees. Unfortunately, there is nothing that can be done to prevent the common cold; not even wearing a mask, as the Japanese frequently do during cold season, will protect you. In regard to the flu, however—and the terms influenza and flu should be restricted to upper respiratory infections that are clearly epidemic in nature and are characterized by a more sudden onset, typically with headache, muscle pains and fever higher than with the common cold—influenza vaccination may be preventive.

Influenza vaccination, or the flu shot, is prepared by growing viruses in eggs, purifying them, and killing them. The vaccine is prepared from the antigens of the most recent type of influenza. One of the problems with the vaccine is that the flu virus is constantly changing, and if a major shift should occur from one year to another, then the protection afforded by the vaccine is diminished. In addition, influenza vaccination is generally safe but not entirely so. The Guillain-Barre Syndrome paralysis that followed the use of the inactivated swine flu vaccine, has not been shown to occur with more recent influenza vaccinations. However, there may be an illness similar to flu produced after vaccination, and fatal reactions may occur as well. The current recommendation of the United States Public Health Service is that routine yearly immunizations with a polyvalent influenza vaccine be performed in high risk groups such as diabetics or in women with a respiratory ailment such as asthma.

HEADACHES

Headaches have the distinction of being the major complaint in half the patients seen in a typical doctor's office. Every one of us has had a headache at some time in her life. There is no specific age-related information about headaches, except that you can develop migraines at any point in your life. So just because you didn't have migraines in your twenties and you now start having severe headaches, that doesn't mean you have a brain tumor. You may have a late-blooming migraine syndrome.

A headache in itself is not a disease. Rather, it is a symptom that may indicate a variety of disease processes or may be part of a larger disease process. Headaches are complex, and their diagnosis and treatment may not be simple or straightforward. In the vast majority of cases, the headache is not found to have an organic basis other than tension.

Headaches can be classified in six types: (1) vascular headaches, including migraine headaches and migraine variants; (2) tension headaches; (3) headaches associated with pathology within the skull, such as tumors, infections, or aneurysms; (4) headaches associated with pathology outside the skull, such as problems with the eyes, ears, nose, or bones of the neck; (5) headaches associated with trauma; (6) headaches associated with other systemic disease processes, such as fever, high blood pressure, or infection.

Most valuable to the doctor trying to determine the cause of your headaches is your personal history. Your physician may try to obtain a profile of your headaches, including the time of day when the headaches occur; relationship to meals, if any; the duration of the attacks in seconds, minutes, hours, or days; the severity of the attacks, including what types of activities must be forgone; the speed with which the pain reaches a peak, subsequent fluctuations and speed of offset or decline of pain; the location of the pain; the response of the pain to various acts, such as changing posture, going to the bathroom, and taking various therapeutic agents such as aspirin; and any associated symptoms such as fever, numbness, loss of body function, confusion, or visual changes.

One type of vascular headache the doctor may be trying to focus on is the classical migraine headache. Migraines encompass a complex of symptoms, more common in women than men, characterized by periodic throbbing headaches that often are confined to one side of the head. The life history profile of the sufferer of classic migraine headaches actually begins before she is even born, because migraines usually run in families. Also, migraine sufferers frequently have a history of illness-related headaches or motion sickness in childhood.

The classical migraine headache has two components. The early component is constriction of blood vessels, during which the patient may notice numbness or weakness or visual changes with bright scintillating points of light. Then comes a second phase, during which the headache itself develops, generally over an hour or two. The pain may last four to six hours or even longer. There may be nausea and vomiting with the onset of the headache.

Common or ordinary migraine headaches may be preceded by some vague, premonitory symptoms lasting hours or days. This premonitory phase corresponds to the vasoconstrictive phase of the blood vessels. With vasodilation, one side of the head begins to throb in association with dilation of the cranial blood vessels. As the throbbing increases, the pain may become excruciating and may be accompanied by nausea, vomiting, diarrhea, chills or increased urination. Occasionally the woman may awaken with a full-blown headache, but more commonly the headache will build up over a period of hours. The headache may persist for several days or may be relieved by sleep. There may be a stuffy or runny nose on the effected side as well. Sometimes common migraines are confused with sinus headaches because of the tearing of the eyes and nasal stuffiness. In the third phase of a common migraine, the headache becomes steady, dull and nonthrobbing. It may be associated with nausea, vomiting, sweating or chills. Frequently a low-grade pain in the back of the neck or scalp may persist after the headache has abated.

Classical migraine headaches may flare up during the first few months of pregnancy, while ordinary migraine headaches will diminish.

Is there a typical personality of the migraine patient? For some time there was an insistence in medical literature that a migraine personality existed, characterized by inflexibility and shyness during childhood, with subsequent perfectionism in the adult, rigidity of personality, and a pervasive meticulousness and inner tension. Sufferers were said to be prone to migraine attacks during a so-called letdown period after days or weeks of hard work and stress. Weekends and holidays were felt to be common times for periodic attacks. Patients were described as being sensitive to any emotional stress and as having poor coping mechanisms for dealing with stress. However, additional studies have not confirmed these ideas, and the relationship between work, activity, and headaches has not been consistent.

The exact chemical compounds that cause migraine or vascular headaches are still a matter of intense investigation. Currently, interest has been focused on a number of chemical substances such as serotonin and neurochinin that have been shown to affect migraines. In one study of migraine patients it was found that they excreted an increased amount of certain catecholamine chemicals derived from serotonin.[5] Doctors feel that the substance serotonin may be released from blood platelets and cause the intense vasoconstriction that leads to headaches.

Another study looked at neurochinin.[6] Researchers isolated this factor by injecting small amounts of salt solution under the skin in various parts of the body or across the headache area in migraine patients during headache attacks. They then withdrew some of the fluid and analyzed it for a variety of substances. They found a high concentration of neurochinin and were able to relate this directly to the intensity of the headache. In addition, they found that neurochinin, when injected into the skin, caused dilation of the blood vessels and increased leaking of capillaries.

Once a diagnosis of migraine headache has been made, the goals become prevention and relief of the acute attack. Prevention revolves around identifying the possible trigger factors and then eliminating them. Occasionally certain foods can be linked clearly to migraines. Particular offenders are certain hard cheeses, chocolate, alcohol, nitrites in preserved meats (such as cold cuts and hot dogs), and monosodium glutamate (MSG). Emotional and environmental factors may also trigger a migraine but are more difficult to avoid.

The mainstay of migraine treatment today is clearly ergot alkaloid medication. These drugs prevent the blood vessels from expanding and therefore, to be most effective, need to be taken before the headache throbbing becomes established; it is important to time the ergot preparation to avert a headache. Ergotamines can be taken by mouth, by rectal suppository, or by injection. There is, however, a tremendous danger of habituation or overdose with ergot preparations because of the question of whether a headache is beginning or not. If you guess wrong repeatedly, you may overdose and make yourself as miserable as the headache would. Side effects of ergot preparations include numbness and tingling of the fingers and toes, muscle pains in the arms or legs, weakness of the legs, itching, swelling, and occasionally disturbances of the heart rhythm. Therefore, they must be carefully prescribed by your physician. Other medications used to treat migraine headaches include antidepressants, steroids, and diuretics. Diuretics are particularly valuable to those of us who develop migraine headaches with the onset of our menstrual periods.

Tension headaches are caused by contraction of the muscles of the scalp and at the back of the neck. Sometimes the headache doesn't really feel like a pain but rather like a fullness or pressure, as though there were a tight band across the head. These headaches may be persistent, barely allowing the sufferer to sleep at night and then reappearing the next morning, perhaps for days or even weeks at a time. Treatment for this type of headache generally includes heat and muscle massage along with either muscle relaxants or simple pain medications such as aspirin or acetaminophen. Ergot medication provides no relief for a tension headache, as the cause of the headache is not vascular, that is, in the blood vessels.

Headaches occasionally may be associated with intracranial abnormalities such as aneurysms, tumors, or abnormalities of the intracranial blood vessels. I think that most women, when they come to a physician with a headache, want relief and at the same time reassurance that they don't have a brain tumor. The chances of having a tumor are, of course, remote. Characteristically, headache associated with a brain tumor is generally intermittent in the early stages but increases in both duration and frequency over time. It is usually in the same location each time, and frequently is affected by changes in position, coughing, or straining.

Headache may also be caused by infection in the ear, nose, sinus, or eye. Sinus headaches are usually accompanied by a stuffy nose, tender sinuses, discharges of pus, and perhaps fever. Surprise, surprise: rarely are eye troubles or visual woes the cause of a headache, except in elderly people with glaucoma.

The headache that occurs after head or neck trauma may be quite severe and continuous. It may occur immediately after trauma, but more frequently may not begin for several weeks after an injury. With time, they will eventually go away.

HEALTH ABOVE ALL

After reading about one problem after another, you may end up feeling as if there are a lot of things wrong with you. I want to dispel that notion immediately.

All women face a dizzying array of potential problems and nasty little things their bodies can do to them. In reality most of us suffer from very few problems. Nobody has to worry about all of the ills noted in this chapter. For the vast majority of us, one or perhaps two concern us personally; the rest we can be interested in as troubles our friends and sisters are coping with.

The important point to remember is that we aren't beset by incessant problems in our thirties. To the contrary, we are strong enough to battle off almost everything that nature can bring our way. On those occasions when we do have a small problem, understanding and diligence can help us master the situation. Meanwhile, don't waste your valuable time worrying about a problem you don't have.

Changing Our Habits

WHEN WE ARE very young we can abuse our bodies with impunity and they will always snap right back. It's easy to build up the feeling during our youth that we can do what we want with ourselves and never have to pay for it.

Now, as most of us I'm sure have already begun to realize, we must begin to rein ourselves in a little. Now is the time of life when we first begin to feel our excesses, when strains and overexertions give us a hint of how time will eventually slow us down.

To a certain extent this realization simply builds character. Our lives, our habits begin to mold us into distinctive individuals. Our mannerisms, even our personal attitudes may be centered around certain habits that we think are particularly clever or revealing. But there is a group of widespread destructive behaviors, many of which are lionized by the young, that have few benefits but carry the potential for future complications for women our age. The key in confronting these bad habits is to remember that now is the time when we can and should take them in hand and get them under control. We are young enough and strong enough to conquer them, and they haven't yet had too much time to work against us. In another decade, we won't be as strong. So, think about these issues carefully. Do you really want to continue your bad habits? Or should you, as a competent, vital woman in your thirties, jettison them and assert your desire to do only what genuinely pleases you as a knowledgeable adult?

SMOKING

I pester women who smoke because it is an obvious health hazard that can be stopped. No one enjoys smoking initially. The habit is acquired only with painstaking efforts to keep from choking. Once started, however, it surely is addicting.

I know quitting is very hard. I realize that many of us worry about its effect on our weight and our social compatibility. But remember the joy of fresh air in your lungs, the improved power and stamina you'll achieve. The enhanced youthfulness you'll experience physically and emotionally after stopping cigarette smoking is so exciting and so important for your body that it is surely worth a special effort. And so much good help is available today. Smokenders programs have helped many women. Hypnosis has worked for others. Every community now has supportive programs to help us quit. Your local American Cancer Society chapter will be only too glad to put you in touch with all of them.

What are the risks of smoking for us? The major ones are an increased incidence of cancer and heart attack. Smokers have a twenty times greater chance of developing lung cancer than do nonsmokers. They also have an increased incidence of cancer of the bladder, mouth, larynx, and pancreas. Their risk of heart attack is two to three times higher than in nonsmokers. And they face a greater chance of getting emphysema.

They also face an increased risk of wrinkling. This is clearly seen in women who smoke heavily. Dermatologists have begun to notice that women who smoke very heavily are more apt to develop fine facial wrinkles as they age than women who do not smoke.

Women who smoke increase their risk of miscarriage and of having children below normal birth weight.

The risk of smoking extends not only to the woman who smokes but also to those around her. It is clear that cigarette smoke adversely affects the smoker's non-puffing companions. A study in the *American Journal of Epidemiology and Public Health* found many more acute respiratory illnesses in children whose parents smoke; the more cigarettes smoked per day by the parents, the greater the number of days of illness of the children.[1] In addition, a study in the *New England Journal of Medicine* showed that workers exposed to the smoke of co-workers had a measurable change in lung function as if they themselves had smoked between one and ten cigarettes per day.[2]

Unfortunately, as the ad says, women have "come a long way." Seductive advertising has now made it chic for us to smoke as excessively as men. Lung cancer in Connecticut between the years 1945 and 1949, when smoking was not socially acceptable for women, was five times greater in men than in women. By 1974, that difference had dropped to less than two to one. And in 1975, Connecticut statistics in the "Tumor Registry" indicated *more* cases of lung cancer in women in our age group than in men.

The bottom line on smoking is that if you want to be fully healthy, at some point you have to quit cold turkey. Cutting down is helpful but doesn't abolish the habit.

Smoking is an addiction. Smokers are physiologically dependent on the nicotine in their cigarettes. (This is in addition to the psychological dependence and the sheer force of habit of smoking.) If deprived of nicotine, they suffer withdrawal. Nicotine is most addicting when it is inhaled into the lungs. It is less addicting if absorbed from the mucous lining of the mouth or nose, as occurs with chewing tobacco and snuff.

In smoking, nicotine is inhaled into the lungs, where the blood picks up the nicotine and carries it directly to the brain. When nicotine levels later drop in the brain, withdrawal begins. The initial phases of cigarette withdrawal are marked by irritability followed by nausea, headache, and other physical symptoms. It has been shown that nicotine produces changes in brain wave patterns, hormone levels, blood pressure, heart rate, delivery of blood to the skin, etc. On withdrawal there is difficulty concentrating on anything but the craving for cigarettes. The severe symptoms abate after one or two weeks. However, craving may continue for years in some reformed smokers.

Is there a safe cigarette? A smoker may switch to the lowest-tar, lowest-nicotine brand available in the belief that she is now at lower risk. This may not be true, because she may compensate for the lower dose of nicotine by smoking more cigarettes, puffing more frequently, or inhaling more deeply. Also, the composition of tar may vary in "lower-tar" cigarettes. Tar is an aggregate of particles in cigarette smoke. More than 200,000 substances have been identified in cigarette smoke. Low-tar cigarettes may have less favorable mixes of these substances in the tar.

The major carcinogens in cigarette smoke are hydrocarbons, but there are also a number of so-called tumor promoters and tumor accelerators present that probably greatly enhance the smoke's ability to cause cancer. The destructive effect of smoking results from a number of very strong irritants to the lungs and to the lining cells of the lungs, which have small hairs called cilia. Some components of cigarette smoke damage the cilia. Normally the cilia function to move mucus and debris out of the lungs, but smoking actually paralyzes them so they cannot perform their job properly. This is one of the reasons why cigarette puffers develop the so-called smoker's cough, particularly in the morning, when the cilia have had a chance to recover somewhat and begin to clean up the mess.

Women who smoke actually seem to be different kinds of people from nonsmokers. Studies show that women who smoke drink more alcohol, coffee, and tea than women who do not smoke.[3] In general, they weigh slightly less and experience menopause sooner than non-smokers. They can't perform as well at exercise tests and show a small increase in their blood cholesterol level.

If a woman cannot quit smoking altogether, I think it is essential that she stop during pregnancy. It is irresponsible to subject the fetus to the variety of drugs and toxins in cigarette smoke. Infants whose mothers smoked during pregnancy weigh on the average at least half a pound less than do infants whose mothers did not smoke. In addition, maternal smoking during pregnancy has been related to an increase in early fetal and neonatal deaths. Don't take your habit out on your baby.

MARIJUANA

Marijuana is one of the world's most interesting plants. Throughout the centuries, it's had a variety of uses in rope and hemp, as a fiber in garments, shoes, and paper, in weapons such as strings on archers' bows, and as a pleasurable intoxicant. Fifty years ago, the extract was on every pharmacist's shelf; the plant has been illegal only since 1937. But marijuana seeds may still be found in packages of mixed birdseed.

Most of us probably know the basics of how marijuana works. But there are important factors many of us may not have heard of. Unlike alcohol, which is water-soluble and changes our behavior briefly, THC, marijuana's active ingredient, has a far slower disappearance rate. It lingers in the body for days after absorption, as long as thirty days, in fact.

Marijuana is absorbed differently when taken by different means. Fifty percent of the active ingredient is absorbed into the bloodstream when smoked, whereas only five to ten percent is absorbed into the bloodstream if the THC is ingested, as in baked food.

Smoking marijuana may trigger epilepsy or palpitations. There may be prolonged adverse reactions with visual distortions, recurrent "highs," or anxiety attacks.

Various marijuana chemical agents seem to have some effect on cell interaction and cell synthesis. These components disturb cells that are rapidly turning over, such as white blood cells. This could prove to have disturbing long-range health impacts.

Studies from Harvard Medical School indicate that marijuana smoke is more destructive and detrimental than tobacco smoke to the defense system of the lung, which normally works to prevent you from getting pneumonia.[4]

The most unsettling offshoot of smoking marijuana for us is a tie to menstrual irregularity. One study showed that the incidence of abnormal menstrual cycles was higher in women who smoked marijuana at least three times a week than in nonsmokers.[5] The marijuana smokers suffered abnormal menstrual cycles 38 percent of the time, as opposed to only 12 percent of the control subjects.

Animal studies on marijuana in the brain are rather interesting, as well. The limbic system of the brain, which is responsible for emotions and control of pleasure and memory storage, can be altered permanently in animals given marijuana. One study showed permanent brain wave changes in the limbic structure of rats that had been treated for six months with THC.[6]

There's probably some direct neural effect of THC on the human brain centers that control behavior. For this reason psychiatrists are in agreement on one thing: patients prone to schizophrenia and other mental abnormalities should not use marijuana.

After long-term high-level use of marijuana, stopping may cause some withdrawal symptoms, including irritability, body aches, nausea, and hyperactivity.

Pregnant women should definitely avoid marijuana, not only because of the toxic effects of THC, but because it is an unregulated compound and a variety of other unknown toxic substances may be mixed in with the marijuana, some of which can harm the fetus.

COCAINE

Cocaine, you may be surprised to know, is an effective medicine, used therapeutically to both decrease blood flow and anesthetize membranes, particularly in the nose and mouth. But the street form of the drug is something else entirely. No one knows what's mixed in with a batch of cocaine. It may be strychnine; it may be arsenic; it may be LSD; it may be sugar. One of my concerns about street drugs is the fact that they are so impure; you don't know what you're getting. You may be getting something that you really don't want, that can really hurt you.

What does cocaine do to you if you do actually use it? It leads to a vasoconstriction of the mucous lining of your nose and mouth. With prolonged use it can result in a hole in the nose, a perforation between the nasal cavities, because of continued irritation and loss of blood supply to the tissues. It also results in an increase in heart rate and blood pressure, which can cause problems in a woman with heart disease or high blood pressure.

When a thirty-year-old woman takes cocaine, does it have any immediate effects on her face or on her body that she should worry about? The only immediately noticeable effects are constriction of the blood vessels and an increased state of excitement. The jumpiness brought on by the drug can lead to exhaustion and all the negative ramifications that come with it. Overdose can result in delirium, convulsions, and even death in rare instances.

The long-term effect is the dangerous one. Cocaine has a phenomenal potential for abuse, for addictive abuse, despite all you may have heard about how safe it is. People who need to feel up and high and good, who crave that rush, can get hooked on it. That's an expensive and perhaps lethal hook.

Finally, a word about the substitutes promoted as legal alternatives to cocaine. The use of these substitutes has escalated as magazine ads claim the products are "just like the real thing." But they're not: several products, such as Coca Snow Incense and Coca Snuff, contain caffeine combined with citric acid, a nasal irritant. Others, such as Snort and Snuff Iceberg, contain local anesthetics. As often happens, someone gets rich on deceptive advertising, and you may have an adverse reaction.

STRESS

I include stress as a bad habit because it doesn't arise from how we live but from how we react to how we live. It is a danger sign that tells us we are overburdened by the external environment. The level at which our burden might become too great varies widely from one person to another, and even within one person in varying circumstances. But once it is reached, clear, unmistakable signs appear that warn us to relax, lighten up, stop taking everything so seriously.

The first response to stress is the "flight or fight" response. A rush of adrenaline accompanies stress. This brings a constriction of peripheral blood vessels so that blood is available to our deeper organs and muscles. The response arises from our past, when stress indicated a *fight*, in which a cut would bleed less if the blood was shunted toward the muscles and away from the skin.

There is also an increase in heart rate, an activation of our emergency mental faculties to make us more alert and awake in case *flight* should result from the stress. Endorphins are released. Hormone levels change.

The problem for us arises when there is no release from the stress on an hour to hour, day to day, week to week basis. If stress is not relieved or contained by coping mechanisms, then fatigue and exhaustion gradually ensue. Our hands and feet may feel chronically cold; we may have headaches or notice stiffness of our neck and shoulders.

If we press on in the face of these important physical warnings, we are doing ourselves harm. But pulling back is hard because stress is a hidden ailment. It is never its own cause. To reduce stress we must search through our lives for the situations that are overburdening us, and change them. This is extremely difficult because if they were happy or unimportant circumstances they wouldn't be causing stress in the first place. In that sense, we are caught up in a tautology. To root out stress is stressful.

This problem has grown much worse for women recently because we have been set adrift in a social and business world without fixed rules. We are doing things women never did before and are forcing the world around us to change. In the long run this is certainly good, but right now it means we are all performing without a net.

I think that we today have more burdens placed upon us than in the past. A woman's role in the past was very clearly defined, and with the loss of that definition has come a lot more stress in terms of deciding what we want to do with our lives and how we can meld all the various pieces together. There's more stress for men as a result of these changes, too, because men can't decide what's expected of them. There are a lot more roles available for everybody, and the result is social-psychological confusion. These are exciting times for us, but difficult too.

The thirties are one time for making binding

decisions—our decade of choice. Decision making is always a stressful process; today it is particularly so. We are now striving for equality with men in the labor market, and at the same time trying to fulfill our goals in terms of relating to others, having husbands and having children. All this subjects us to a lot more stress. We are exposed to the same physical and emotional hazards of the work environment as men, but we have a number of additional problems and pressures created by conflicting expectations of what our role really is and what our work in life involves.

There's the Framingham heart study, for example, which showed that with the increase of women in the labor force from 28 percent in 1950 to 42 percent in 1978, there was an increase in female coronary artery disease.[7] The study implies that women are more prone to achievement-oriented Type A behavior than we were in the past, because we have a lot more things we have to accomplish. I've certainly seen this among my colleagues and friends who are in the midst of their career—they have all of the stresses on them that men do, and then some. My friends in academic life are expected to write papers, doctoral theses, and so on while they're busy being pregnant; my working friends are expected to deliver their babies and be back at work a day later, or at least after the weekend, and go on with life as usual. These role conflicts impose an extra stress on these women. The old adage about knowing someone who's busy reading the newspaper and brushing her teeth and eating breakfast at the same time is common today. That's the Type A woman, and she's all around us—the person who is acutely aware of time and how much needs to be accomplished in the small amount of time available.

This affects us heavily in the thirties, because that's often when we assume our large responsibilities and face our toughest choices. It's a time of career growth for women, as it is for men. I have friends who have decided that they simply don't have time now to get married or have children. In the background the biological clock is ticking away for them. They must have families soon, or forget it, but they have to fulfill themselves in their jobs as well. After arriving at whatever degree of professional education they deemed necessary, they want to use that education and establish themselves in the professional world. They want to make their mark. These conflicts and choices put huge strains on a woman's body.

No one totally understands the effects of chronic stress on our bodies. They may not be all bad, however. Some amount of stress is not only tolerable but also essential to well-being, according to Dr. Hans Selye, one of the original writers on stress. Events that are stressful to one woman may be ignored by a second and regarded as a welcome challenge by a third. The same stress that mobilizes some of us to greater efficiency confuses and disorganizes others, and causes still others of us to withdraw. What constitutes an excessive amount of stress varies from woman to woman, according to her ego strength, coping mechanisms, cultural influences and tolerance level.

Some stresses are self-induced, for example, as in the woman undergoing labor or in the mountain climber on an arduous climb. In both instances, a long-term gain is anticipated as a consequence of a short-term stress. Some situations are stressful to all of us, such as the threat of death, while others are stressful to a very few of us, for example, a woman with claustrophobia at a crowded party.

STRESS DURING PREGNANCY

Animal studies and clinical observations have suggested for some time that stress during pregnancy can affect offspring. Among the possible results in animals are cleft palate, harelip, aberrant sexual behavior, irritability, hyperactivity, and eating problems. Recently, stress during pregnancy was found to exert an even more serious effect. A team at Cornell University Medical College in New York City found, in work with rats, that stress can alter the way embryonic nerve cells express their genetic potential.[8] In other words, stress can actually alter the way a fetus's cells operate. Stress causes chemical changes that affect the production of adrenaline compounds. So the old saw about staying placid during pregnancy appears to be true. Theoretically, stress could harm the child.

COPING MECHANISMS

The first step in coping with stress is to recognize and acknowledge that the stress exists, to say to yourself, "Yes, I have a headache or a stiff neck or whatever, because I feel pressured as a response to this particular situation, because I am under stress." The next step is to acquire more information about the situation, to determine what you can do, if anything, to alleviate the pressure. The third and most important step is to relax, which allows you to focus more clearly on the problem and possible solutions. Finally, you can either take action to change the situation or, having relaxed and gathered more information, reappraise the situation and decide that it's no longer stress provoking.

An unhelpful coping mechanism that we all occasionally employ is denial or withdrawal, the "ostrich syndrome," in which we hope that the problem will miraculously disappear while we have our heads calmly stuck in the sand. While a certain amount of denial may be helpful initially in a stressful situation, in the long run it is disadvantageous because it prevents us from taking positive action.

Another mechanism of coping is to assert yourself in a positive fashion before the stress occurs. You may be able to anticipate a potential demand or conflict and then avert it. If you anticipate a time crunch, start earlier or omit a low-priority item from your day. Leave free time during your day to deal with unexpected events; set priorities for the day, the week or the month. Assert yourself.

STRESS REPERCUSSIONS

Here are some specific physical ills related to stress and what you might be able to do about them.

Tense jaw. This is an instinctual response—we tense our jaw muscles as a fighting response to threatening situations: meeting deadlines or meeting in-laws. Jaw tension can result in neck pain and ringing in the ears. To relieve the pressure, hang your mouth open and push it gently back and forth until you find a pain-free position. Massage your jaw and relax.

Aching neck and shoulders. These result from dense knotted muscles and can be relieved by neck rolls. Sit comfortably, close your eyes, and breathe normally. Tilt your head forward, trying to touch your chin to your chest. Hold this posture for fifteen seconds. Then tilt your head back as far as you can and stay that way for another fifteen seconds. Repeat in both directions, then slowly roll your head in full circles, first clockwise, then counterclockwise.

Rash, hives. Stress can sometimes bring on an itchy pink rash. Antihistamines such as chlorpheniramine can relieve it temporarily. A cold shower or cold compresses placed on the affected area for five to ten minutes can relieve itching and reduce redness. Or you can also reduce itching with an over-the-counter hydrocortisone cream and then mask the redness with cover-up or foundation.

Hyperventilation. This results when we feel a loss of control in response to stress. The only remedy is to consciously reassert control. Sit down, relax, and take long, deep, slow breaths, breathing in through your nose for a count of 3, and out through your mouth while you count to 4 and 5. Numbness or tingling around the lips or fingers with hyperventilation will respond to slow breathing into and out of a paper bag.

Stomach cramps. These are usually a side effect of tension buildup and often respond to deep breathing. If they become more severe during your period, water retention may be the reason, so cut down on salt intake. If you get cramps frequently tell your physician.

ALCOHOL

Alcohol abuse is a growing problem among American women, perhaps partly because working women try to match the drinking habits of their male colleagues, partly because women at home are less content and so drink more, and partly because women can drink more freely than at any time in the past.

Here more than in any other area we can see how our newfound ability to toe the male standard has hurt us. Men have been harming their bodies with booze for generations. Women have always indulged, too, but the social impediments against female consumption were always stronger, so it was harder for us to drink on a chronic basis.

Now, many of us are on the male power trip. Our numbers are too few in the business world for us to remold it into a more female form, so instead we may dive in with gusto, trying to shape ourselves to the male patterns already in place. We want to outboy the boys—and drinking is an important part of that existing network. But booze hits us harder than it does men. Whenever we go out drinking with the boys, we get a little drunker than they do, and put ourselves under a bit more stress.

"For some women the two-martini lunch is no myth," Eleanor Z. Hanna, director of the Alcohol Clinic at Massachusetts General Hospital, said at a 1981 news conference on the problem. "Failure of most women to realize that their tolerance for alcohol is much less than that of men poses a serious health danger."

The larger size of men, compared with women, is believed to be one reason men have a greater capacity for alcohol. Men also maintain a fairly constant level of tolerance for alcohol, while our tolerance can vary because of menstrual cycles and the use of oral contraceptives.

Hanna said more women were seeking help because they realized they had an alcohol problem. "As more women enter the work force and many have more disposable income, the number of women seeking help at alcohol treatment centers is also rising."

Interestingly, a study reported at the Canadian Addictions Foundation Conference in St. John's, Newfoundland, showed female problem drinkers usually did not drink significantly more alcohol at social events than women who did not have problems.[9] Regardless of the occasion, the problem woman drinker averaged only two drinks. However, female problem drinkers went back for that "acceptable" dose many more times during the day than is prudent. Male problem drinkers, on the other hand, will consume three and a half times as much alcohol at each occasion as their normal counterparts.

Our perception that more professional and career women are doing more drinking than they did in the past may be accurate, but I think that previously there were many closet alcoholics among women who stayed at home. Also, I suspect alcohol was supplanted for a time in our generation by marijuana. Now a lot of us have gone back to our premarijuana drinking habits. But it's difficult to know how much people drink. They lie about it to their physicians and to themselves.

Who makes up this hidden alcoholic army tippling away all day long? It's very difficult to know, but I think that closet alcoholism is quite a substantial problem, and a very insidious one. The woman who is stuck at home with the kids can slide into a terrible state, because she may take one drink in the morning to "get her going," and the next thing you know she's downing half a quart a day. It's hard for her to admit that she has a habit, and even harder to kick it.

The signs are visible, however, to anyone who pays a lot of attention. I have patients who come in for something else, and when I look at them, I say to myself, "This woman's been spending her days at home drinking." You don't see gross effects too often when someone's thirty. But you can pick up suspicious indications by the time she's thirty or forty. Generally, people who drink a lot also smoke a lot (although that's not always the case) and the effects of their smoking are harsher; they really look as if they smoke a lot. They may have a hoarser, deeper voice than you'd expect, and more wrinkling. Last, they may have a peculiar contracture or thickening of the ligaments in the palms of their hands, which goes along with being alcoholic.

Their friends can't tell that they drink too much. It's hard to know that even about someone you're close to. People are very covert about their drinking—with their physicians, too. Doctors are so cynical about people's lack of truthfulness concerning drinking that the general rule of thumb is to double the amount someone tells you that they drink. Also, when someone talks about pints and quarts, you know they have a problem. No one says "I drink half a pint" or "I drink a quart" unless they drink to excess.

If you're worried about a friend, ask her whether she drinks too much. If she says, "No, I just knock off a pint a day," you can be pretty sure she has a problem. You should do everything you can to help her: call her doctor, get in touch with the local chapter of Alcoholics Anonymous. Most important of all, let her know you care and want to help her.

I can't emphasize enough how harmful drinking can be. Even if a thirty-year-old woman only drinks socially, the effects on her body can be widespread. And in her thirties and forties these will last longer than they would have in her twenties.

Alcohol is directly toxic to a variety of systems—to all types of blood cells, to brain cells (you lose brain cells everytime you take a drink); even a tiny sip of booze is a direct liver toxin. Alcohol has bad effects on the heart muscles, too. It's poison, pure and simple.

Like the other drugs, alcohol should be assiduously avoided during pregnancy. Alcohol is so devastating to the fetus that a fetal alcohol syndrome has been described. In this, infants are short and have small heads, dislocated hips, cleft palates, and heart defects. Their mental capabilities are affected also. While this syndrome occurs in infants whose mothers drank heavily (two or three ounces a day) during pregnancy, there are effects from much smaller doses of alcohol, even two to three ounces a week. So if you're pregnant, water rather than wine, tonic without the gin.

The effects of alcohol cannot be obviated by a good diet. This was debated in the medical literature for years—was alcohol the problem or were the effects attributed to alcohol actually due to poor nutrition caused by replacing food calories with alcohol calories? Now it's pretty clear that the effects are a toxic effect of the alcohol.

So the more you drink, the harder you're making it on yourself—although some interesting recent work shows that people who drink just a glass or two of wine or beer a day live longer and have less heart disease than people who don't drink at all.[10] So, in moderation, there may be some protective effect of drinking a *small* amount of alcohol a day.

The emotional factors of life in our thirties play a serious role in our drinking. The trauma of divorce and the resulting changes in life style, the adjustment to having children, the stress of an important job—all contribute to the temptation to escape the pressure cooker.

Regarding alcohol, sometimes I wonder if an increase in alcohol abuse isn't one of the negative aspects of the whole women's movement, our move toward independence. In the sexist past the woman who drank in public was thought of as a loose woman, and that kept a lot of women from drinking. Now, we can go into a bar and order a beer like anybody else. That makes it easier for us to drink. We can drink more and be more like men, even though it's bad for our health. But social acceptability isn't an excuse. If a woman wanted to drink to excess before, she did. If she wants to drink now, she does. I don't think that society's attitude toward alcohol has changed. It's still considered something that one may indulge in socially, but not to excess, and certainly not to the point of addiction or alcoholism. And the reasons for drinking haven't changed, either; we're just more susceptible to them now.

I've painted a bleak picture here because I think it's important to realize that just because alcohol is more accepted than other drugs, it isn't necessarily any better for us. At the same time, I don't want to come on like Carry Nation. I think that moderation is the byword we should use for our drinking. We shouldn't drink beyond the point of becoming relaxed; tipsy is too much. And we should maintain control. We should only drink what we want, when we want. We shouldn't drink because it's good for business or because any social partner wants us to. It's our body and our decision. We should make good use of that marvelous social dodge—the acceptable Perrier cocktail. Why ordering Perrier in a bar isn't considered poor form when every other non-alcoholic beverage is, I don't know. But it's a painless way to stay in the social swim without getting smashed.

Confronting Our
Major Worries

LIKE A BRIEF cold wind on a warm and sunny day, the fleeting fear of major physical problems our future may hold whisks past us at times during our thirties. It is not so much that we fear for our bodies today; we know this is a healthy time of life. The whisper of disquiet is over our future.

There's nothing wrong with this feeling at all. Confronting our bodily changes as we age, our inevitable slowing and our ultimate mortality is a healthy, vital process for us to undergo. It is part of maturity and experiencing every aspect of life.

But we should keep in mind that life doesn't just happen to us—we also influence our lives. And major medical problems don't necessarily just strike us randomly, either. We can do things right now to decrease our chances of suffering later in life.

For those serious worries that do affect us during our thirties, we should be comforted by the knowledge that we have a better chance of conquering any problem now, when we are young and vibrant, than many years hence when we may not be as formidable.

We should not pretend that serious problems don't exist. They do. But neither should we face them with a sense of despair or helplessness. We should confront them with knowledge, confidence and the belief that everything that happens to us is part of life—a life we are in charge of and that cannot be stolen from us by any illness until our very last day.

CANCER

BREAST CANCER

Breast cancer remains the leading cause of death due to cancer in women. A woman living in the United States has a risk of 1 in 11 that she will develop breast cancer during her lifetime. In 1980 more than 110,000 new cases of breast cancer were reported in the United States, and there were 36,000 deaths.

During our thirties the rate of cancer climbs. It rises with increasing frequency after the age of twenty right up to menopause, when the incidence levels off until there is a second rise in frequency occurring after age sixty-five.

As with most other malignant diseases, the cause of breast cancer is unknown. For instance, no one knows why Oriental women rarely get breast cancer. However, a number of factors can clearly affect our risk. One is heredity. Lab mice have clearly shown the strong influence of heredity on the development of breast cancer. The same is probably true, although to a smaller extent, for us.

If your mother or sister, or both, developed breast cancer before menopause, your risk is substantial. Your risk is not as great if their cancer appeared after menopause, or if only an aunt or grandmother on either side of the family had breast cancer. Reports indicate a two-to-sevenfold increase in the frequency of breast cancer in family members of women who've already had it.[1]

Estrogens have been implicated as well. While the exact role of estrogens in the initiation of breast cancer is controversial, it is generally agreed that they may hasten the development of breast cancer in women who are genetically susceptible. The risk of breast cancer does increase directly with the total number of years that a woman ovulates. Studies show that breast cancer rates decrease in women who undergo removal of the ovaries before the age of forty.[2]

I can't tell you how to avoid breast cancer, but some factors that place you at a higher than average risk might be worth keeping in mind.

Age. Eight in 10 breast cancers occur after forty-five, but the incidence in women our age seems to be rising.

Childbearing. The risk is higher for those of us who are childless or who will bear our first child after thirty.

Diet. Obese women face greater risk, and so apparently do those of us who eat a lot of animal fat. Dutch women, with their high consumption of cheese, butter, and milk, have the highest breast cancer rate in the world; Japanese women, who eat fish and rice, the lowest.

Benign breast disease. Fibrocystic breast disease—the appearance of lumps in the breasts—is not a proven precursor of breast cancer but some doctors believe women with a tendency toward benign breast tumors may have a greater risk of developing breast cancer later in life.

Previous breast cancer. Cancer in one breast increases your chances of later getting it in the other.

The pill. The relationship between the pill and breast cancer is most confused. One group feels that since the pill appears to reduce cystic disease, which some doctors tie in with cancer, its effect could be positive. Others hold that if you take the birth control pill for more than five years, your chances of developing breast cancer are four times greater than if you hadn't taken the pill; two times greater if you are a former user or have a grand-mother or aunt (not a mother or sister) who has had breast cancer. Some studies suggest that the use of estrogens to relieve menopause symptoms may lead to breast cancer. Some studies suggest that the use of estrogens to relieve menopause symptoms may lead to breast cancer ten or fifteen years later. So, a woman at extra risk for other reasons should avoid taking estrogens.

X rays. Radiation to the chest may be of greater concern between the ages of ten and nineteen than now. But it definitely does increase the risk of breast cancer for us, too.

Keeping track of all these variables is well nigh impossible. You can never be certain if and when you'll get breast cancer. If you do, early detection when the cancer is small can save your life. Keep an eye on body changes that may herald the arrival of a tiny tumor.

The best method is to examine your breasts properly every month soon after your menstrual period. If you do this diligently you're much more likely to discover a tumor when it is small and perhaps can be treated by lumpectomy—tumor removal—rather than mastectomy.

What do you feel for? Lumps, obviously—but no woman's breasts are exactly like another's, especially in consistency. It is extremely rare to find a woman of any age whose breasts feel entirely and uniformly smooth, like pastry dough.

Since all women's breasts are different, you can't realistically expect your doctor to remember exactly how your breasts felt at the previous examination, a year or more ago. By examining your own breasts each month and becoming familiar with the way they feel, you can help fill in the picture for the doctor.

Most of us realize that a new lump or a thickened area in the breast should send us scurrying to see a doctor. But many are not aware that other changes in the breasts may signal trouble requiring prompt medical attention. Most often these prove to be minor problems, but never feel foolish about bringing something unusual

to the attention of your doctor; it's far better to be told
that the condition is inconsequential than to take the
chance of holding back on a situation that could prove
serious.

A case in point is edema of the breast, a difficult-to-
describe condition that has driven doctors to similes like
peau d'orange (French for orange peel) and *pigskin*, a
reference to the fact that both of these natural surfaces
have prominent pores. The edematous breast, too,
features prominent porelike openings in skin that grows
tough and thick like the skin of an orange. Although
benign conditions, such as inflammation or infection,
can produce this development, it most often is due to
cancer. A lump may also be present—a clearer signal of
danger—but not always. All edematous breasts should
be examined by a physician.

A lump in the armpit is another example. It is almost
invariably caused by enlarged lymph glands so the cause
could be anything from a passing infection to invasive
cancer. Enlarged lymph nodes in the armpit can be a
sign of breast cancer even before any lump can be felt in
the breast. Be cautious: if a lump in the armpit is big
enough to be felt, it is worrisome enough to tell your
doctor about.

How often you should take a step beyond self-exam-
ination and have your doctor check your breasts is relative to risk. Obviously if you are a high-risk patient,
you need to go more often. Your own level of breast-
cancer risk is a subject you should discuss with your
doctor.

The lower-risk patient should have her breasts examined as part of her regular health care. These periodic
examinations provide reasonable assurance that any
breast disorder will be discovered fairly early in its
course.

Before age forty, examination once a year should
more than suffice; after forty we should probably get
our breasts checked medically twice a year. Note that
my recommendation differs from that of the American
Cancer Society, which recommends an exam only every

three years until age forty and then every year thereafter. Most specialists recommend a baseline screening mammogram sometime between the ages of thirty-five and forty, particularly for women with large or difficult to examine breasts. Periodic mammography is not recommended until age fifty by the American Cancer Society.

The moderately high-risk woman with cystic disease of the breast in her past or a family history of breast cancer should be examined by her doctor twice a year until the age of thirty-five, and after that, every four months. At about this age, unless it is indicated for a specific reason at an earlier age, a mammogram is also indicated for safety's sake. Likewise, a checkup every four months is usually recommended for those of us with any confirmed mammary cyst. And, after thirty-five, many doctors recommend mammography as well, but only at two or three year intervals.

This high-risk group includes those who have had a demonstrable premalignant lesion in one breast, those who have breast growths called multiple papillomas, and those with a very strong family history of breast cancer.

The highest-risk patient is someone who has already had breast cancer. Most specialists agree that these women should be checked every three months and should have a yearly mammogram. It's better, by the way, to have the same doctor do all your periodic exams.

If, when examining your breasts, your doctor senses a problem, she will turn to an array of more specific tests to check it out, including needle biopsy, mammography, excisional biopsy or ultrasound.

Needle biopsy uses a fine needle to extract fluid from a suspect breast mass in an effort to determine whether it is benign or malignant. The procedure is usually done under local anesthetic in a doctor's office. Often a lump is too small for effective needle biopsy, however. Doctors are far more likely to recommend mammography, an X-ray examination of the breasts usually done by a radiologist, that can indicate a tumor that may be malignant.

As you probably know, mammography has a number of problems. The small dose of radiation it delivers could, if repeated often enough, cause cancer. In addition, an X ray does not always provide a definitive answer. Mammography misses between 6 and 25 percent of breast cancers that are later diagnosed by surgical biopsy. At the same time, it can detect abnormal cells early—without answering the serious question of whether any of those spots will ever emerge as cancer. Thus the test could result in overtreatment. Nevertheless, mammography is a useful tool, if used appropriately.

An excisional biopsy, which is usually performed in a hospital under anesthetic, provides the definitive diagnosis. In this surgical procedure, the suspect lump is excised from the breast and submitted to immediate microscopic examination to determine if it is malignant or benign. In case of malignancy, detailed results, giving suggestions for the most effective treatment, can usually be reported within several days.

A new test uses ultrasound to search for breast cancer. It is based on the notion that the age of a woman and the density of her breasts may determine the best way to screen for breast cancer at its earliest and most curable stages. In young women, like us, whose breast tissue is typically dense, ultrasound is proving highly effective in differentiating between cancerous growths and benign lumps, such as cysts. Mammography continues to work better on less dense older breasts.

"Mammography doesn't detect lesions well in dense breast tissue and ultrasound does," explained Dr. Catherine Cole Beuglet of Jefferson Medical Center, Philadelphia, where two thousand women have been examined with ultrasound.[3] "Mammography is best in older women, in whom the aging process has turned dense breast tissue to fat."

Because women with fibrocystic breast disease have extremely dense breasts, ultrasound may prove of particular benefit to them as well as to women who develop breast lumps during pregnancy, when they shouldn't be X-rayed. If you can determine that a lump is benign, you can wait until after delivery to treat it. Tests are now under way to determine the ultimate role for ultrasound as a breast cancer detection tool.

MASTECTOMY

If breast cancer is diagnosed, there are a number of treatment methods available. These include a variety of surgical procedures ranging from removal of the tumor alone (lumpectomy) to simple mastectomy, in which the entire breast is removed, to total mastectomy, in which the underlying muscle is removed in addition to the breast and dissection of the lymph nodes of the armpit is performed to determine the extent of the disease.

Subsequently, chemotherapy with cancer-killing drugs or radiation therapy may be employed. Hormonal manipulation may also be indicated. As nonsurgical adjunctive treatment of breast cancer has improved, there has been a trend toward less extensive surgical procedures, with excellent short-term survival statistics for women with early-stage tumors. If your doctor recommends a total, radical mastectomy as a one-stage procedure, get a second opinion.

Mastectomy may be necessary but it is terrifying. Not only is the woman who undergoes a mastectomy frightened about her health and well-being, but her sense of femininity has been assaulted. One of the symbols of her womanhood has been removed, leaving her scarred and disfigured—but, hopefully, cancer-free.

In recent years, many prominent women have come forward to openly discuss their experiences with breast cancer. I think that this has helped other women with cancer by lifting taboos and promoting sharing. Counseling and talking with other women who have had similar experiences can help a woman adjust to her disease and disfiguration and decide about possible breast reconstruction.

If you have had the misfortune of going the whole route with breast cancer, you might want to get in touch with one of the organizations or institutions that provide information and, in some cases, counseling for women seeking breast reconstruction.

The American Society of Plastic and Reconstructive Surgeons, Inc., 29 East Madison Street, Suite 800, Chicago, Ill. 60602, (312) 641-0935. You can request three free booklets: "Breast Reconstruction Following Mastectomy for Cancer," "Plastic and Reconstructive Surgery," and "How to Select a Qualified Surgeon." And if you tell them where you plan to have your surgery and what type it is, they will provide the names of three surgeons certified by the American Board of Plastic Surgery.

The Office of Cancer Communications, National Cancer Institute, Building 31, Room 10A18, Bethesda, Md. 20205. Send a postcard with your name and address requesting their booklet "Breast Reconstruction."

The American Cancer Society. Telephone the Service of Rehabilitation Department of your local chapter. Someone should be there to answer questions about breast reconstruction.

UTERINE AND CERVICAL CANCER

Cancer of the uterus can take different forms—either cancer of the cervix or cancer of the lining of the uterus (the endometrium). Cervical cancer can strike at any time. Endometrial cancer is extremely unusual in women under the age of thirty; it generally occurs in women over fifty. It is more common in those of us who are overweight or have used estrogens for a long time. The most important warning signal of uterine cancer is abnormal vaginal bleeding.

Even before any symptoms show, the simple and reliable Pap test, part of your annual checkup, can detect cervical cancer. (The Pap test can't detect endometrial cancer because these cells are too far inside the body.) When detected early enough, cervical cancer can be cured almost 100 percent of the time. The incidence of death from cervical cancer is actually going down, perhaps because women are taking better care of themselves. Because of this decline, the American Cancer Society recently recommended that for women between the ages of twenty and forty years who have had two negative Pap tests a year apart, an annual Pap test is no longer necessary. Three years between Pap tests will do. Many physicians including myself have been reluctant to adopt this three-year proposal, feeling that the additional screening is worthwhile. We fear that the extended period between tests may make some women forget to have a Pap test altogether. In addition, we feel that other evaluations performed on the annual visit, such as blood pressure check and breast examination, should be done annually. Pick your side in the debate. I'd choose the side of overprotection myself.

The cause of cancer of the cervix is unknown, but there are a number of factors that are clearly related to an increased incidence. One is age at first sexual intercourse, as the incidence of cervical cancer is markedly decreased in virgins and in women who delay sexual intercourse until later years. In addition, there is some indication that the incidence of cervical cancer is lower in women who have intercourse with men who are circumcised. An array of different partners has also been implicated as a significant factor in the development of cervical cancer. The relationship between herpes virus and cancer of the cervix is a controversial one. While it has not yet been conclusively proved, I think it is probably prudent for a woman who has had herpes to at least continue with annual Pap smears.

Herpes virus type II is also a candidate for the role of carcinogen in squamous cell carcinoma in situ, abbreviated CIS, of the vulva. Unlike cervical cancer, which is declining in frequency, CIS of the vulva is being reported with increasing frequency. The Connecticut Tumor Registry showed an increased incidence of vulvar CIS from 0.02 per 100,000 women to 0.81 per 100,000 women for the years 1945 through 1975 and then from 1975 to 1979. While carcinoma in situ of the cervix is felt to definitely be a premalignant condition, the same is not true for carcinoma in situ of the vulva, with only perhaps 5 percent progressing to true carcinoma in one study.

AML

The cancer that terrifies me the most is *AML,* an extremely rare form of leukemia. The major reason is that the disease preys on my age group and appears in a very insidious fashion. Previously healthy vibrant women are struck down in the prime of their life with an incurable illness that drains the vigor out of them so fast you can almost see it happening moment by moment before your eyes.

Although rare, AML is deadly, and the people it kills are often our age. I think one of the reasons physicians like me are so spooked by AML is that we treat leukemia during our training. We can identify with these patients and their families and friends. In their age and habits they may be much like us. It's like watching yourself die. And it's terrifying.

ATHEROSCLEROSIS AND HEART DISEASE

Women our age don't have the same knee-jerk paranoia about heart trouble as men do. It's much harder to imagine a woman in her thirties clutching her chest and collapsing to the floor with a heart attack.

At our age, our bodies provide us with hormonal protection against heart attacks, protection that men don't have. At the same time, we are putting ourselves in stressful type A situations far more often than we did in the past, pressuring ourselves enough so that our heart attack rate is heading upward despite our bodies' best efforts.

The truth seems to be that heart attacks aren't, in fact, peculiar to the male body. They result instead in part from the once exclusively male role of leadership and responsibility. We are becoming leaders both at home and at work, and it's taking its toll on our bodies.

Not only that, but in the future, after menopause, our natural protection wanes. So if we develop bad heart habits today, we may be punished tomorrow when we're older. Menopause can virtually turn us into heart risks over the weekend. So heart disease ranks as one of our major worries, and we need to understand it.

Atherosclerotic coronary artery disease, which results in heart attack, is rare in women in their thirties. It results in fewer than 64 deaths per 100,000 women of our age in the United States, but remains a major fear for our future. What we do today may decide whether we have a heart attack or can prevent one.

What occurs in atherosclerosis is a gradual narrowing of the blood vessels that supply blood to the heart. When the blood flow through the coronary arteries decreases below a certain level, we feel a sharp twinge known as angina. Further blood flow reduction produces irreversible damage to the heart muscle, infarction, or a heart attack.

With aging, changes occur in the walls of the arteries.

There is a slow, continuous increase in the thickness of the inner lining. Even in a nondiseased coronary artery there will be an increase in smooth muscle cells and fats, particularly cholesterol esters, over the years. Thickening of the arterial wall results in a gradual increase in the rigidity of the blood vessel. Older blood vessels are more susceptible to "wear and tear" than they were when younger and may develop outpouchings or aneurysms more easily.

The changes of aging are very distinct and separate from those of atherosclerosis. The atherosclerosis of aging causes a patchy abnormality of the blood vessels. The earliest lesion appears as a fatty streak or accumulation of fat-filled muscle cells along blood vessel walls. This fatty streak by itself causes little impedance to the blood flow and no symptoms. The streaks are universal in the United States, occurring in everyone, sometimes as early as age fifteen. With increasing age they appear to involve more of the blood vessels, but the overt effects don't seem much worse.

On to step two: as atherosclerosis develops, fibrous plaques appear. These are a combination of muscle cells that have migrated to the area and additional fats and fibrous tissue. While fatty streaks are ubiquitous, plaques are not. Generally, they appear in men sooner than in women, and in the aorta before the coronary arteries. Their cause is unknown. The generally accepted theory for their origin is the reaction-to-injury hypothesis.

According to this hypothesis, the cells that line the arteries react to stress or injury, losing their ability to adequately cover the underlying tissue. The tissue is then exposed to various components of the blood from which it is normally shielded. At that point a variety of blood factors, including platelets and fats, are deposited on or in the underlying tissue. This stimulates smooth muscle cells at the site, leading to proliferation of the cells. There is narrowing of the vessel, more turbulent flow, and perhaps more injury to the remaining lining cells, bringing about a spiraling process that results in the atherosclerotic plaque. In the end, heart attack or stroke may result.

Now that we have reviewed the background of this dangerous cycle, the natural question is, What can we women in our thirties do to prevent it? Obviously, we can't alter our age or genetic background; we'll just have to accept these irreversible risk factors. We can, however, pay attention to a number of factors that have been found frequently in people who develop atherosclerosis. They include cigarette smoking, high blood pressure, and high cholesterol levels. Although obesity is also a risk factor, its influence may be due to its relationship with high blood pressure, high blood sugar, or high blood cholesterol. Our path seems clear, then. We should stop smoking; high blood pressure, if it exists, should be treated; our diet should be low in saturated fats.

The exact relationship of diet to coronary artery disease remains a controversial area. Studies show that no population with a diet low in saturated fats and cholesterol has much coronary artery disease.[4] However, tribes such as the Masai in Africa have diets loaded with saturated fats and cholesterol, but they are also virtually free of coronary artery disease. This may be due to their genetics or to their extraordinary activity level. There has never been a definitive prospective study of the effect of diet on coronary artery disease in the general population. Still, it seems prudent to lower cholesterol and decrease the amount of saturated fats in our diet to less than 10 percent of total calories.

Total avoidance of cholesterol and saturated fat will *not* result in a plummeting of blood cholesterol levels. This is due to the fact that we can synthesize cholesterol in our bodies. If we eat less, we make more; if we eat more, we make less. Cholesterol is both necessary and desirable, as it plays an important structural role in cells and is the backbone component of certain hormones. Recent evidence shows that not only is the total cholesterol level important but so is the ratio of different types of cholesterol. One type, called high-density cholesterol or high-density lipoprotein, has been shown to be protective in terms of heart attack. That is, more high-density lipoprotein is better. Exercise increases this HDL.

The biggest cholesterol offenders, of course, are eggs, with one egg having 250 to 300 mg of cholesterol, largely contained in the yolk; butter, which contains 80 to 85 mg per ounce; certain types of shellfish, such as lobster and shrimp; and various organ meats, such as liver and brain. An interesting study in animals has shown that primates fed a typical American diet with added cholesterol and fat developed scores of aortic and coronary atherosclerotic lesions.[5] When a cholesterol-free diet was then fed, many of these lesions proved reversible. Of course, extrapolation to humans is difficult, but it's interesting nonetheless.

Thus far, we can't do anything to dissolve atherosclerotic plaques once they've formed; our understanding is still in its infancy. Our best approach is to avoid allowing them to form in the first place. It is important to assume responsibility for yourself and to try as best you can to maintain good habits regarding diet, body weight, smoking and exercise.

One way to possibly cut down your chances of heart problems is to stay fit. Exercise makes the heart strong so that it pumps more efficiently, improves the way you use oxygen from your blood, and makes you feel better. Long brisk walks are worthwhile, and jogging is even better. But to be truly beneficial, your exercise has to be both regular and challenging. You have to work out three times a week at least and work hard enough at each session to increase your pulse rate for 15 minutes or more. If you haven't exercised in a long time or if there is any history of heart trouble in your family, check with your doctor before undertaking a heart conditioning program.

Women in the thirties are blessed, by and large, with strong hearts that have a lot more time ahead of them before showing any serious problems. The natural protection we have at this age against heart problems is one of the nicest aspects of young womanhood. If we avoid falling into bad patterns now, we should be in good cardiovascular shape later.

HYSTERECTOMY

Only mastectomy commands as great a level of anxiety for women as hysterectomy. Like a breast removal, this surgery involves the loss of more than just a body part! It means the incontrovertible loss of the ability to have children. It is seen by many women as a clear line between youth and age, between being fully feminine and simply going through the motions.

It is also a controversial medical practice. It should be fairly uncommon, and it isn't. The unnecessary ubiquity of the operation has vastly increased the fear it carries.

Some women become afraid of going to the doctor because they fear something is wrong with them that might lead to a hysterectomy. A surprising number of us ignore female problems rather than face the chance—however remote—that we may lose our reproductive capacity. This is particularly true of those of us who wait longer to have children. It's unnerving to think that you may have waited all these years to use your uterus and now may lose it before you have a chance to use it. It bothers me—a little; it doesn't prey on my mind because I know hysterectomy in a healthy individual with normal menstrual function is extremely unusual at our age. But even with all my medical knowledge, the thought of being stripped of my ability to have children—even though I haven't even made up my mind whether I want to have a family—shakes me. It's the loss of something essential, something that belongs to me as other parts of my body don't. It defines my womanhood as a hand or eye doesn't.

When someone our age does have a hysterectomy, she is often stricken with a feeling of being totally unfeminine. All the articles about how we remain the same sexually and don't age differently after hysterectomy won't change this gut reaction: *"I'm less of a woman now. I'm dried up, out of the game."*

This happens particularly when the woman is younger. Often she feels her youthful years have been cut short, that she's old before her time. I've seen vast self-pity in women our age who have needed a hysterectomy. So much of this reaction is unfortunate. The loss of an organ requires a serious mental adjustment, and the resolution of our feelings about this crucial loss is even harder. This is made more difficult because many of us still hold vestiges of traditional ideas, in which our self-esteem and femininity are tied to our reproductive function. Consciously, we may know that we are still feminine after a hysterectomy but our subconscious cries out in fear.

Still, the loss of something hidden like the womb or uterus or ovaries doesn't affect us as much as a mastectomy does. Loss of a breast feels as if it must be obvious to the outside world. Even with prosthetics or breast reconstruction, we may feel the knowledge of our cancer—and our loss—precedes us almost everywhere we go. With hysterectomy, we can be diagnosed in the hospital, operated on, and out again before most of our associates know that anything has happened. It can remain our secret, if we wish, and for many of us that's a saving grace.

What irks me most of all about hysterectomy is that all this unhappiness and anguish is many times unnecessary. Doctors perform too many hysterectomies for inadequate indications, from my perspective as a non-gynecologist. But from the gynecologists' perspective, a uterus that is removed will never get cancer or cause another problem. The operation is relatively safe. So hysterectomies are performed.

The only indications for hysterectomy in women our age are fibroid tumors, cancer, or persistent bleeding. If there's a very large fibroid that cannot be cut free of the uterus, the entire uterus may have to be removed. Severe trauma to a pregnant uterus may be a cause for hysterectomy, but this is not common among women in their thirties—or later, for that matter. Endometriosis—the spread of uterine cells to other parts of the body—may result in the removal of both ovaries, and that's devastating too. I've had patients in their late twenties and thirties whose ovaries were removed because of endometriosis, and who were quite shaken because of their sudden sterility. They still have their uterus, but they can't conceive; it's maddening for them. But remember, all this is fortunately uncommon.

As a healthy thirty-year-old woman, you need not worry about hysterectomy. However, if you're having abnormal or very painful periods, heavy bleeding or clotting, you should be checked to catch endometriosis or a fibroid tumor early, and nip it in the bud.

ARTHRITIS

Contrary to popular belief, arthritis is not exclusively a disease of the elderly; it is a fact of life for a quarter of a million children, and many of us as well. The most serious form of the disease, rheumatoid arthritis, often begins almost imperceptibly in our twenties or thirties. This tissue-destroying crippler attacks both the joints and the connective fibers, wearing them down through unpredictable flareups throughout life. Rheumatoid arthritis can also be accompanied by diseases of the heart, lungs, blood vessels, and spleen. In addition to pain, sufferers often experience weakness, fatigue, loss of appetite and weight.

Rheumatoid arthritis seems to develop in women who have an inherited vulnerability to the disease. Its origins are unclear, though we do know that whatever agent exploits this genetic tendency—most likely an infectious agent like a virus—it begins by disrupting our immune systems. The damage in arthritis stems from a misguided response by immune cells. They attack joint tissue as though there were an infection, causing inflammation, destruction, and pain.

What is it that causes this reaction of the body against itself? The principal suspect is some sort of virus that scientists think lurks somewhere in the body, like a spy behind enemy lines, for long periods. Then, for unknown reasons, researchers speculate, the virus emerges, setting off alarms in the immune system. Somehow, though, this virus lures the immune system's defense forces into attacking the body they're supposed to protect. Having set this nefarious scheme in motion, the virus slips away, leaving the immune cells to do its dirty work. That is why the root cause of arthritis is so hard to pin down.

Research evidence suggests that the suspect may be the Epstein Barr virus, which causes infectious mononucleosis. By age thirty, most of us have developed antibodies to the Epstein Barr virus in our systems. This is the result of early infections, even if they caused no noticeable symptoms. Arthritis sufferers may not be able to generate a strong response against the virus, allowing small amounts to float about from time to time, wreaking havoc.

Synovitis is the name of the underlying problem in arthritis. A cycle is established in which the inflammation of the joint membrane releases enzymes that very slowly damage the surrounding joint structures. The damage increases the inflammation, which in turn increases the damage, and so on. Treatment can reduce this inflammation and stops further damage. Painkillers can increase comfort but do not really address what's going on in the joint. In fact, the presence of pain helps protect the joints by discouraging too much use. So, in rheumatoid arthritis, pain should be treated only by reducing the inflammation that causes the pain. Pain relievers alone should be avoided.

Women with rheumatoid arthritis frequently notice problems in parts of their bodies other than their joints. Usually, these are general complaints such as muscle aches, fatigue, morning stiffness, and sometimes a low fever. Morning stiffness, one of the commonest complaints of rheumatoid arthritis sufferers, arises from a situation termed the "gel phenomenon." When an arthritis sufferer rests or even just sits motionless for a few minutes, her body "gels," stiffening and becoming difficult to move. Once the body gets loosened up, the gelling effect eases and motion becomes easier and less painful. Arthritic women often have problems with fluid accumulation, particularly around the ankles.

And the disease can also generate unusual features due to joint inflammation. A lump called a Baker's cyst can form behind the knees. It may feel like a tumor, but the cyst is just a small sac full of fluid. It can however extend down to the back of the calf and cause pain.

Rheumatoid arthritis is still a major medical mystery. Antibiotics are ineffective against noninfectious forms of arthritis, so doctors still rely heavily on simple aspirin as the mainstay or backbone of therapy, because it is safe and reduces inflammation and pain, as well as a variety of antiinflammatory prescription drugs.

One of the oldest treatments for rheumatoid arthritis, and still among the most reliable and astonishing, is gold. Powdered and mixed with chemical ingredients, gold injected over a period of several months seems to work strongly against the early stages of the disease. Although symptoms may remit, the course of the disease is not halted by gold, merely controlled.

To deal with some drawbacks of gold injections, the SmithKline Corporation has developed a new oral gold medication compound, Ridaura. In clinical trials at 150 centers in the United States and in Britain, it was found to be effective in preliminary testing, with less severe side effects than injections.

Nobody really knows why gold works so well against rheumatoid arthritis. In some mysterious way it corrects the immunological imbalance and prevents the release of the enzymes that feed the destructive cycle. Other promising techniques for treating the disease include:

Arthroscopic knee surgery. Until now, knee surgery for arthritis was a messy, problem-laden procedure. Cutting open the joint and removing inflammed tissue was serious enough, but the ensuing complications—hidden tissue that brought residual pain, physical therapy requirements to restore the joint, unending stiffness—raised the price beyond what many were willing to pay. Now, the arthroscope, an optical viewer about the size of a drinking straw, has improved the operation. The doctor can view the inside of the joint through the scope and insert her surgical instruments with it, as well. The procedure requires just a few stitches and has a much greater chance for complete success than the old method.

Blood-filtering. Using elaborate equipment similar to kidney dialysis machines, many doctors are treating rheumatoid and lupus patients by cleansing their blood of presumably harmful immune complexes and lymphocytes. The process, called plasmapheresis, removes, filters, and then returns the blood through tubes inserted into the veins. However, plasmapheresis technology is still fairly primitive and quite risky.

Radiation. Radiation has shown the ability, at low doses over a relatively long period of time, to reduce swelling, stiffness, pain and tenderness for many arthritis sufferers. Why does it work? Apparently because the radiation suppresses the activity of the immune cells that play a major part in exacerbating arthritis. However, this treatment is still experimental and unavailable for most of us.

The proper balance between rest and exercise in rheumatoid arthritis is often hard to strike. On the one hand, rest reduces inflammation, which is good. However, rest allows joints to stiffen and muscles to weaken.

With too much rest, tendons lose some strength and bones soften. Obviously, this is bad. Moderation should be your goal. Follow your body's signals. If it hurts too much, don't do it. If an activity doesn't set off physical alarms, go ahead. As a general rule, if your exercise-induced pain lasts for more than two hours after exercising, you have done too much. Next time, cut down.

Is there anything pleasant with respect to arthritis? Yes, one delightful coincidence: sex can actually help the pain of arthritis. The excitement of sex, it appears, stimulates our bodies to produce cortisone, adrenaline, and other chemicals that help to ease pain naturally. So get out there and ease your pain.

LUPUS

Arthritis may also accompany a rare disorder called systemic lupus erythematosus or SLE, or lupus. SLE is a disease predominantly of women, occuring ten times more frequently in women than in men, and striking more women in their twenties or thirties than at any other age. Lupus is a multi-system immune complex disease, which in fancy language means that the body turns against itself, injuring multiple organs—not only the joints, but also the kidneys, heart, lungs, skin, liver, and the nervous system. The cause of this devastating disease is unknown, but as with rheumatoid arthritis, doctors suspect that a viral infection in a genetically vulnerable person is at fault.

Women with lupus may suffer from a variety of problems, including pain and stiffness of the joints, fever, fatigue, chest pain or shortness of breath, muscle aches, and emotional or mental changes. A characteristic facial rash in a butterfly pattern over the nose and cheeks occurs in almost half of the affected women.

The course of this disease is variable, with some women having spontaneous remissions and others not responding to even the strongest medication. There is no cure for SLE but the outlook for women with lupus erythematosus has improved dramatically in recent years. Until the past decade, survival time for lupus victims was frequently measured in months. But a new survey of 609 lupus patients treated at the University of Southern California Medical Center finds that 80 percent are still alive ten years after the disease was diagnosed. Other studies are less optimistic, though.

Credit for this belongs to both the medications used to treat the lupus—steroids and antimalarial drugs— and the positive attitudes of the patients themselves, says Dr. Edmund L. Dubois, director of USC's lupus clinic and a coauthor of the survey. The outlook for lupus sufferers should continue to improve.

VARIETIES OF ARTHRITIS

Some of us suffer from a milder (but more common) type of arthritis called osteoarthritis. This degenerative joint disease is the result of aging, after years of ordinary wear and tear on our joints. Other forms of arthritis include ankylosing spondylitis, a chronic inflammation of the spine that usually begins in the teens or early twenties, generally in men, traumatic arthritis, infectious arthritis (as may occur with gonorrhea), and gout, an intensely painful inflammation of the joints, with a special preference for the large joint of the big toe. Psoriasis may be accompanied by arthritis as well.

Extreme stress on joints has been implicated as a cause in osteoarthritis. The problem is most likely to develop in joints that have been injured in accidents or sports, or subjected to the stresses of excess weight or strenuous jobs.

The bony knobs that form around the end joints of the fingers in osteoarthritis are called Heberden's nodes after the British doctor who first described them. Similar knobs can sometimes be found in the middle joints of the fingers. Usually, these enlargements occur gradually over a period of years and are hardly noticed. Most cases involve all of the fingers more or less equally.

Osteoarthritis of the spine does not cause symptoms unless there is pressure on one of the nerves or irritation of some of the other structures of the back. If someone tells you that you have arthritis in your spine, do not assume that the pain you feel is necessarily related to that arthritis. Most women with X rays showing arthritis of the spine do not have any pain at all.

Osteoarthritis of the weight-bearing joints, particularly the hip and knee, develops slowly and often involves both sides of the body. Pain in the joint may remain fairly constant or may wax and wane over a period of years. In severe cases walking may be difficult or even impossible. Fluid may accumulate in the affected joint, giving it a swollen appearance, or a knee may wobble a bit when weight is placed on it. In the knee, the osteoarthritis will usually affect the inner half of the joint more than the outer half; this may result in the leg becoming bowed or splayed and may cause difficulty in walking.

Another subset of arthritis, bursitis, is often dismissed as "just getting old." It is true that more older women than younger women have bursitis and osteoarthritis, and they do have something to do with the way that our bodies age. But they do not necessarily need to happen either now or later. These problems are sometimes due to abuse of a joint, as in prepatellar bursitis from scrubbing floors on your knees. Occasionally, however, they are due to disuse. In our society, as you get older you are expected to be less active. And then you acquire health problems that accrue to inactive people of all ages. The relationship between joint problems and age is real, but there is also an association between joint problems and inactivity, particularly for the shoulder joints, which may become "frozen" with disuse.

Injection of a joint affected by bursitis with corticosteroids is often helpful, and sometimes removal of some fluid from a joint may help. Injections should not be frequently repeated, though, because the injection itself may damage the cartilage and the bone.

We need to be active. If our muscles are trim and in good tone, our heart and lungs conditioned, our body weight normal and constant at that level, and if we have a regular exercise program, we will have far fewer health problems, and we may not age as rapidly. These measures will keep calcium in our bones, our bursae free and well lubricated, our tendons firm and strong, and our joint cartilage well nourished.

Having spent some time, now, confronting the realities of major body worries, I recommend that you get out immediately and reaffirm your youth, health and life. Play a few sets of tennis. Take yourself out for a fancy lunch. Buy yourself something special. Life may be surrounded by trouble, but it's awfully rich for us right now, and we should dwell on that fact rather than on any potential miseries nature may hold in store.

Conclusion

WE HAVE MOVED through dozens of topics in this book, and we have examined many different aspects of our bodies and our feelings during the decade of our thirties. One concept emerged in every subject—change.

Change is the constant. It comes to all of us. Our thirties are the time when most of us confront the reality of change for the first time as adults. So many parts of our bodies and so many of our sensations have changed from earlier times that it is almost as though we have become different people. Now, the knee-jerk response in our culture is, "How terrible!" Isn't it a shame to see the bloom of early youth fade? Isn't it awful to realize that the parts of our bodies aren't as instantaneously active and impervious as they once were? Isn't change sad?

But I respond, "How marvelous!" In our thirties we are quite remarkable. Our bodies are strong and our minds are flexible. We have gained experience, maybe wisdom too, and have lost very little physically. It's wonderful. We can confront our problems. Our options are varied. We can take greater pleasure in every sensation our bodies offer us, because we know now what we like and what gives us satisfaction. The thirties are a very rich time of life.

If you finish this book with merely the sense of change—the feeling of being poised at the edge of a long, slow slide toward old age—you've only picked up half the message. We all change, each one of us a little differently. The end. Big deal.

What *is* a big deal is how we respond to inevitable changes we see and feel. Change is not a sentence; it's an opportunity. Every time we change we become different, brand-new people able to take on life from fresh perspectives and with new abilities. The process of change stimulates us away from complacency, away from shallow physical myopia, and toward a richer, fuller awareness of ourselves and of our lives, wants, needs, capabilities, and limitations.

That's what this book has been about. I, as a doctor, can tell you all about bones and muscles and organs. I can quote statistics and studies, case histories, and learned opinions. I can quantify change and report my findings to you. But the important part, the response to the information, comes from you.

I revel in the knowledge of change. I anticipate the possibilities it brings with gusto. I'm grown up, vibrant, responsible for myself, in the prime of my life. I can finally start trying to achieve my potential, and I can't wait to begin.

I hope that your changes will bring great promise to you in your thirties. It's a splendid time of life; go out and run with it.

Notes

OUR PSYCHE

1. W. Dorfman, *Psychosomatics* 19 (1978): 702ff.
2. R. Ehrlich, *The Healthy Hypochondriac* (Philadelphia: W. B. Saunders, 1980.)

OUR SHAPE

1. S. Abraham, *American Journal of Clinical Nutrition* 33 (1980): 364ff.
2. *Metropolitan Life Statistical Bulletin,* 1959.
3. G. Bray, *Annals of Internal Medicine* 77 (1972): 779ff.
4. J. Hirsch, *Clinical Endocrinology and Metabolism* 5 (1976): 299ff.
5. S. Hashim, *Clinical Endocrinology and Metabolism* 5 (1976): 503ff.
6. J. Mayer, *Annals of the New York Academy of Sciences* 131 (1965): 502ff.

7. J. Flier, *New England Journal of Medicine* 304 (1981): 539ff.
8. C. Sims, *Recent Progress in Hormone Research* 29 (1973): 459ff.
9. S. Griboff, *Current Therapeutic Research* 17 (1975): 535ff.
10. *Medical Letter,* 10 August 1979.
11. G. Gwinup, *Archives of Internal Medicine* 135 (1975): 676ff.
12. D. Carr, *New England Journal of Medicine* 305 (1981): 560ff.

OUR SUPERFICIAL SELVES

1. L. Wilson, *American Journal of Ophthalmology* 17 (1971): 1298ff.
2. Ibid.
3. "Scientific Skin Care," *Family Circle,* 1 August 1981.
4. Ibid.
5. Quoted by Julie Hatfield, *Boston Globe,* 3 July 1981.
6. G. L. Grove, *Journal of Investigative Dermatology* 75 (October 1980).

OUR SEXUALITY

1. J. Kaufman, *Wall Street Journal,* 19 May 1981.
2. K. J. Isselbacher et al., eds., *Harrison's Principles of Internal Medicine,* 9th ed. (New York: McGraw-Hill Book Co., 1981).
3. L. Westrom, *Lancet* 2 (1976): 221ff.
4. W. Faulkner, *Journal of the American Medical Association* 235 (1976): 1851ff.
5. Isselbacher, *Harrison's Principles of Internal Medicine.*
6. V. Beral, *Lancet* 2 (1977): 727ff.
7. M. Beffey, *British Medical Journal* 2 (1969): 659ff.

8. *New England Journal of Medicine* 288 (1973): 871ff.

9. *Physicians' Desk Reference for Nonprescription Drugs,* 35th ed. (New York: Litton Educational Publishing, 1981).

10. *Journal of the Royal College of General Practitioners* 13 (1967): 267ff.

11. I. Fisch, *Journal of the American Medical Association* 237 (1977): 2499ff.

12. *Lancet* 1 (1973): 1399ff.

13. M. Vessey, *Journal of Obstetrics and Gynecology* 80 (1973): 562ff.

NUTRITION AND MEDICATION FOR OUR BEST HEALTH

1. K. J. Isselbacher et al., eds., *Harrison's Principles of Internal Medicine,* 9th ed. (New York: McGraw-Hill Book Co., 1981).

2. *Journal of the American Medical Association* 244 (1980): 1077ff.

3. Ibid.

4. *New England Journal of Medicine* 304 (1980): 1367ff.

5. H. J. Roberts, *New England Journal of Medicine* 304 (1981): 423ff.

6. Ibid.

7. R. Davis, *New England Journal of Medicine* 305 (1981): 168ff.

8. M. Sporn, *Federation Proceedings* 38 (1979): 2528ff.

9. T. Mauzer, *Science* 186 (1974): 1198ff.

10. *Cancer* 43 (1979): 193ff.

11. *Medical Letter,* 22 February 1980.

12. *Clinical Geriatrics* (Philadelphia: W. B. Saunders, 1980).

13. *Journal of the American Medical Association* 244 (1980): 1077ff.

14. Isselbacher, *Harrison's Principles of Internal Medicine.*
15. D. Ulmer, *New England Journal of Medicine* 297 (1977): 318ff.
16. R. Hoover, *New England Journal of Medicine* 302 (1980): 573ff.
17. *Medical Letter,* 24 July 1981.
18. S. Chung, *Nature* 283 (1980): 243ff.

OVERCOMING OUR MINOR COMPLAINTS

1. R. Rubin, *Journal of the American Medical Association* 244 (1980): 561ff.
2. G. T. Johnson and S. E. Goldfinger, eds., *Harvard Medical School Health Letter Book* (Cambridge, Mass.: Harvard University Press, 1981), p. 136.
3. *New England Journal of Medicine,* 9 April 1981.
4. J. Morrison, *Southern Medical Journal* 73 (1980): 999ff.
5. K. J. Isselbacher et al., eds., *Harrison's Principles of Internal Medicine,* 9th ed. (New York: McGraw-Hill Book Co., 1981).
6. L. Chapman, *Archives of Neurology* 3 (1960): 223ff.

CHANGING OUR HABITS

1. J. Tager, *American Journal of Epidemiology* 110 (1979): 15ff.
2. J. White, *New England Journal of Medicine* 302 (1980): 720ff.
3. K. J. Isselbacher et al., eds., *Harrison's Principles of Internal Medicine,* 9th ed. (New York: McGraw-Hill Book Co., 1981).
4. G. Nahas, *Journal of the American Medical Association* 242 (1979): 2775ff.
5. G. G. Nahas and W. D. Paton, eds., *Marijuana:*

Biological Effects (Elmsford, N.Y.: Pergamon Press, 1979).

6. I. Elliot, *Journal of the American Medical Association* 243 (1980): 15ff.
7. T. Gordon, *Annals of Internal Medicine* 87 (1977): 393ff.
8. *Science* 88 (1981): 288ff.
9. *Proceedings of the Canadian Addictions Foundation Conference,* 1981.
10. Z. Creiss, *New England Journal of Medicine* 304 (1981): 539ff.

CONFRONTING OUR MAJOR WORRIES

1. K. J. Isselbacher et al., eds., *Harrison's Principles of Internal Medicine,* 9th ed. (New York: McGraw-Hill Book Co., 1981).
2. Ibid.
3. *Woman's Day,* 24 April 1981.
4. C. Glueck, *American Journal of Clinical Nutrition* 31 (1978): 727ff.
5. Isselbacher, *Harrison's Principles of Internal Medicine.*

Index

FOR TODAY'S WOMAN!